LIMITED EDITION OF 750 COPIES

HISTORY OF TIPTON

IN STAFFORDSHIRE

BY

FREDERICK WM. HACKWOOD
FELLOW OF THE ROYAL HISTORICAL SOCIETY

AUTHOR OF
"SOME RECORDS OF STAFFORDSHIRE"
"HANDSWORTH: OLD & NEW"

RE-PRINTED FROM THE "DUDLEY HERALD"
OF
November 22nd, 1890 – August 22nd, 1891

EDITED BY ALAN A. VERNON

Brewin Books

First published in a Limited Edition
and printed at the
'Herald' Steam Printing Works, Wolverhampton Street,
Dudley. 1891.

This edition of 750 numbered copies published by
Brewin Books Ltd., Studley, Warwickshire B80 7LG, 2001

British Library Cataloguing in Publication Data
A catalogue record for this book is available from
The British Library

ISBN 1 85858 195 8

Made and Printed in Great Britain by
Warwick Printing Company Ltd.
Theatre Street, Warwick CV34 4DR

Dedicated to the people of Tipton who help
to keep alive its history and its traditions.

Published in a limited edition
of 750 copies

No: 224

FREDERICK WILLIAM HACKWOOD

F. W. Hackwood was born to Enoch and Sarah Hackwood on the 18th April 1851 at 69 High Street East, Wednesbury. His father, Enoch was a tailor, the family had settled in Wednesbury in the middle of the 18th century, the Hackwoods originally came from Stoke- on-Trent.

In 1868 he was admitted to St. Peter's Teachers Training College, Saltley and in 1871 he was appointed headmaster of St. Bartholomew's Church Schools at Wednesbury. In 1878 he was Headmaster of Dudley Road Board School, Birmingham and in 1888 he became Headmaster of Soho Road Board School, also in Birmingham where he stayed until 1916 when he retired.

In 1874 he married Sarah Phoebe Simkin and they had two children, a son, Harold and a daughter, Louisa. He lived with his family at Comberford Lodge, Bridge Street, Wednesbury, until a subterranean fire at a neighbouring colliery forced them to leave the house and move to Handsworth. During the course of his life Frederick Hackwood wrote 28 books about Staffordshire and the Black Country, a 'History of Tipton' being one of them, and was published in 1891. Apart from writing on local history, he wrote books on a variety of other subjects including Natural History, Education, Church Lessons, Biography, Marriage, Sport and Food.

In addition to being a teacher and an author, he was also a magistrate, a town councillor, a footballer, and the founder of several clubs and societies and was involved in creating open spaces like parks, allotments and the re-afforestation of reclaimed colliery waste areas.

The last years of his life were spent at 2 Veronica Road, Balham near to his son, where he died on the 4th December 1926 aged 75 years.

PREFACE

Owing to the exigencies of periodical publication by weekly instalments many errors have inevitably crept into this compilation; in fact they are known to exist in many parts of the work. The author regrets them, and trusts some future writer on the same subject will detect and correct them with due care. It has entailed some amount of labour to prepare sixty chapters on a subject so unpromising.

F. W. H.

Wednesbury,

St. Bartholomew's Day, 1891.

ACKNOWLEDGEMENTS

I wish to thank the following for their help and assistance in republishing this volume. Firstly, to Alan Brewin, in agreeing to my suggestion to make this book available once more to a wider public. Keith Hodgkins for his help, advice and for writing the foreword to this book. The Tipton Civic Society. The Local History Archive Section at Smethwick Library. Finally the people of Tipton who are proud to be part of that historic town.

BOOKS BY F. W. HACKWOOD.

Notes of Lessons on Moral Subjects.	1883
Darlaston.	1887
History of Tipton, in Staffordshire	1891
A History of West Bromwich.	1895
Some Records of Smethwick.	1896
Sedgley Researches.	1898
Handsworth Old and New.	1908
Annals of Willenhall.	1908
Oldbury and Round About.	1915
The Story of the Black Country.	1892
Chronicles of Cannock Chase.	1903
Staffordshire Curosities and Antiquities.	1905
Staffordshire Stories.	1906
The Birmingham Midlands.	1906
Staffordshire Worthies.	1911
Staffordshire Sketches.	1916
Staffordshire Customs, Superstitions & Folklore.	1924
Staffordshire Glimpes.	1925
Staffordshire Miscellany. [posthumously]	1927
Through the Midlands.	1905
Westward of the Wash.	1906
Story of the Shire.	1921
Olden Warwickshire.	1971
Notes of Lessons on Kindness to Animals.	1892
The Practical Method of Class Management.	1896
Natural History Reference Notes.	1897
Notes of Lessons on the Church Service.	1897
New Object Lessons. [Animal Life]	1898
Chatty Object Lessons in Nature Knowledge.	1900
Old English Sports.	1907
The Good Old Times.	1910
Inns, Ales and Drinking Customs, of Old England	1909
Good Cheer, The Romance of Food and Feasting.	1911
William Hone, His Life and Times.	1912
Life of Lord Kitchener.	1913
Dragons and Dragon Slayers.	1923
The Bridal Book. The Lore, History and Philosphy of Love, Courtship and Marriage.	1923
The Wednesbury Papers.	1884
Wednesbury Workshops.	1889
Olden Wednesbury.	1899
Religious Wednesbury.	1900
Odd Chapters in the History of Wednesbury.	1920
Wednesbury Notes & Queries 3 Vols.	1902
Wednesbury Ancient & Modern.	1902
Pocket Guide to Wednesbury.	1908
Christ Lore.	

FOREWORD

Tipton is an ancient parish recorded in the Domesday Book as Tibintone, 'having land for five ploughs'. In common with most of the smaller settlements which were later to be encompassed within the Black Country, Tipton led an uneventful life in medieval times. The Civil War battle of Tipton Green, in which parliamentarian troops intercepted a royalist column on its way to defend Dudley Castle was not decisive enough to put Tipton into the history books, but in 1712 an event which marked an opening chapter of the industrial revolution conferred immortality on the town.

In that year the engineer Thomas Newcomen erected the world's first successful steam engine to pump water from the 'Coneygree coalworks'. Curiously, Hackwood does not mention this ground breaking event possibly because the engine had become known as the Dudley Castle engine due to its proximity across the open countryside to that local landmark. Only more recent research has proved that the location was within Tipton parish.

In addition to the coal measures which were described as 'inexhaustable' in the early 19th century, iron ore and limestone were found in abundance, thus providing all the necessary raw materials for the establishment of an extensive iron industry.

The arrival of the Birmingham canal in 1770 opened up Tipton and the emerging Black Country to the rest of England and the world beyond. Such was the growth of the canal system in Tipton that it became known as the 'Venice of the Midlands' with over 13 miles of waterway within the parish. Hackwood overstated the length variously as 20 and 30 miles, but it is certain that within its modest area of 2167 acres, Tipton possessed a greater density of navigable waterway than any other inland town on the canal system.

With the three vital ingredients of minerals, steam power and efficient transport all established, a massive industrial expansion took place throughout most of the 19th century with an associated seven-fold increase in population.

In addition to the making of iron, Tipton became especially well known for its heavy engineering trades which included the production of castings, forgings, structural ironwork, steam engines, boilers, chains and anchors. Technical innovation and achievement were prolific. In 1825 the Horseley Ironworks built the world's first iron steamship and in 1829 Telford's Galton Bridge in Smethwick. The following decade saw the invention of the 'wet puddling' process by the Tipton ironmaster Joseph Hall, which revolutionised iron production. In 1843 the Gospel Oak Ironworks made the cast iron columns for the Albert Dock in Liverpool which survive today as part of Britain's largest listed building complex. The world's biggest anchor was produced in 1866 for Brunel's steamship the Great Eastern by the firm of H.P. Parkes. It is no wonder therefore that Tipton was described by Hackwood as 'palpitating with the beat and throb of a thousand engines. It is a town whose contribution to the industralised world should never be forgotten.

Keith Hodgkins Tipton Civic Society.

INTRODUCTION

This year marks the 150th Anniversary of the birth of Frederick Hackwood on the 18th April, 1851. Amongst the many books he wrote about the towns of the Black Country was, a 'History of Tipton in Staffordshire' first published in 1891.

To capture some of the character of Tipton in Hackwood's era we can do no better than to read the author's own words from an article contributed by him to the 1907 Tipton and District Illustrated Annual.

'To the visitor Tipton is not an inviting spot; it is certainly bewildering, if not exactly depressing. It labours under the disadvantage of being a widely-scattered region. To all intents and purposes it consists of four separate and distinct townships: Tipton proper, Great Bridge, Dudley Port, and Princes End; all of them being on the outer border of the parish; and enclosing as in a ring the remainder of the area.

'There is no concentration, nor are the interests of the various manufacturing centres always identical; one part using its railway communications, another rejoicing in its canal facilities, and yet another relying on its tramway services.

'It is related that a baffled and despairing stranger was once enquiring his way about this region of unexplored territory, intersected by its impassable barriers of railway embankments and unbridged canals; this slum'and of squalid cottages in derelict alleys, and tumble-down houses in un-named streets, most of them with sunken doorways, and their upper- storey windows on a level with the roadway; this land of cracked bridges, oblique walls and leaning chimney stacks; and that when he asked a native how the people got from one specified spot to another, he was met by the laconic but expressive answer, "Anyhow".

'And yet many of the place-names of the parish conjure up visions of a once pleasant landscape, whose pristine surface was varied by a village green that extended its borders into breezy heathlands; by undulations of hill and dale, by fruitful gardens and smiling pasture lands intersected by purling streams—the imagination easily recalls all these in the names Tipton Green, and Horseley Heath, in Ocker Hill, and Tividale, in Summerhill, and Bloomfield; in the Lea Brook, and the pastoral Sheepwash that of yore could be seen by the wayfarer plodding his lonesome way across the old "Greet" Bridge. All these rural spots of reminiscence have vanished long ago:

'In Tipton, Vulcan is everywhere supreme; and from the thousands of hearths that constitute his altars, never cease to arise columns of incense. To the Tiptonian, therefore, a smoke laden sky is always regarded as the outward visible sign of the town's prosperity'.

To the present day resident of Tipton it is difficult to imagine what the the town was like a hundred years ago, progress has swept away the slum'and houses and many of the older manufacturing trades have been replaced with modern houses and smaller service industries. Tipton has a past to be proud of and a future to look forward to.

Alan A. Vernon
A & B Books

July 2001.

CONTENTS

CHAPTER.		PAGE.
I.	Nomenclature	1
II.	Domesday Status of Tipton	3
III.	Condition of Tipton at the Conquest (1066)	5
IV.	Territorial History, from 1151 to 1279	8
V.	The Wyrley Family	9
VI.	A Family Dispupte at Tipton, in 1278	12
VII.	Land Values: Wastes, Forests, and the Right of Assart (1279)	14
VIII.	A Vivary in Tipton: Tipton lands alienated in Mortmain: Hugh le Despenser, the Royal Favourite, claims lands in Tipton (1293–1317)...	17
IX.	How Tipton was taxed for the Crusades (1288–1291) ...	21
X.	How Tipton was taxed for the Scotch Wars of Edward III, in 1327 and 1332	23
XI.	Some Manorial History, from 1306 to 1472: The Wyrley Coat-of-Arms	26
XII.	The Manor (1509–1562): Charity Lands in Tipton (1535– 1551): John Dudley, Duke of Northumberland... ...	28
XIII.	Tipton Chancery Suits in Elizabeth's Reign (1558–1603): Tipton Families of Position. and Names of Note during the Sixteenth Century	31
XIV.	The Descent of the Manor of Tipton	34
XV.	Extent of the Manor, and Recent Landowners in Tipton ...	37
XVI.	The Manorial Court and Tenures: The Manor Farm: The Tenants in Capite	41
XVII.	The Heronville Interest in Tipton: The Whorwood Family; the Dudleys of Tipton	45
XVIII.	Livery of Seisin: The Dudley Family of Tipton (Younger Branches)...	51
XIX.	Tipton during the Great Civil War	54
XX.	Ecclesiastical History: The Church Goods of Tipton in 1552	58
XXI.	The Advowson of Tipton	62
XXII.	The Beneficed Clergy of Tipton, &c, &c....	65
XXIII.	The Fabric of the Parish Church: Its Dedication and the Wake	69
XXIV.	Some Parochial Advertisements: The Church Plate: The Church Bells	72
XXV.	Tipton Parish Registers	76
XXVI	Tipton Church Act, 1794	81
XXVII.	Tipton Benefactions: Lost Charities: Sheldon's Doles: Woodhall's School Endowments	88
XXVIII.	Charity Lands: Trustees under the Act, and the Close of the Trust: Old Churchwardens, &c....	93
XXIX.	St John's Church: The Origin of the Tipton Surname of "Whitehouse": St Paul's Church...	97

CHAPTER.		PAGE.
XXX.	St Mark's Church, Ocker Hill; St Matthew's Church, and Tividale Church	103
XXXI.	History of Nonconformity from Puritan Times: Presbyterians, Independents, and Baptists, in Tipton ...	108
XXXII.	The History of Wesleyanism: Park Lane Chapel: Great Bridge Chapel: Dudley Port Chapel	111
XXXIII.	Tipton Wesleyanism, continued: Gospel Oak Chapel: Ocker Hill Chapel: Bloomfield Chapel Missions: and Local Wesleyan Bibliography	121
XXXIV.	The Offshoots of Wesleyanism: The History of Dissent in Tipton concluded	126
XXXV.	Progress of Education and the Provision of Schools in Tipton	
XXXVI.	Local Administration of Justice...	130
XXXVII.	Poor Law Administration	134
XXXVIII.	Progress of Local Government: Parish Vestry: Highway Surveyors: Board of Health	137
XXXIX.	Parliamentary and County Representation: Contribution to National Defence	139
XL.	The Postal History of Tipton	146
XLI.	Local Topography: Place Names: Old Mansions: Roads and Maps	149
XLII.	Intercommunication with Tipton: Canals, Railways, Tramways, &c	151
XLIII.	(*a*) James Keir's Connection with Tipton: His Chemical "Factory"...	157
	(b) Mineral Resources of Tipton	163
XLIV.	The Gradual Development of the Tipton Iron Trade ...	164
XLV.	Barrows and Son, Bloomfield Ironworks	168
XLVI.	John Bagnall and Sons, the great Ironmasters, of Tipton, Wednesbury, and West Bromwich	173
XLVII.	Philip Williams and Sons, of Wednesbury Oak Ironworks ...	175
XLVIII.	William Millington and Co, of Summer Hill Ironworks ...	179
XLIX.	The Horseley Works	181
L.	Ocker Hill Pumping Station, and the Birmingham Canal Navigations...	182
LI.	The Tipton District of the Mines Drainage Area	186
LII.	The Chain and Anchor Trades	184
LIII.	Roberts and Co, of the Tipton Green Furnaces and Colliery	
LIV.	Various makers of Iron, and other Ironworkers	190
LV.	A Tiptonian Description of the Burning of Dudley Castle in	193
	1750	195
LVI.	Reminiscences of Tipton Half a Century Ago	198
LVII.	Tipton Bibliography...	200
LVIII.	Habits, Sports, and Pastimes	204
LIX.	The Tipton Slasher, Champion Prize-Fighter of England ...	206
LX.	One of the "Slasher's" Fights: Tipton *v.* West Bromwich ...	211
	Lloyd's Proving House.	219
	Index	221

HISTORY OF TIPTON

BY

FREDERICK WM. HACKWOOD, F.R.H.S.

CHAPTER I.–NOMENCLATURE.

For many years past a "History of Wednesbury" has been in print, and more recently a "History of Darlaston" appeared from the pen of the present writer. It is, therefore, not surprising that some attempt should now be made to produce a "History of Tipton," thus to complete, in some degree, the records of the trinity of populous parishes which at the present time go to make up that great industrial centre known as the Parliamentary borough of Wednesbury. Till recently (1885) this borough of Wednesbury was the largest constituency in the three kingdoms represented by only one member—that was when West Bromwich was also an integral portion of Wednesbury borough. While the name of Wednesbury is perfectly and absolutely unique, never having been reproduced in nomenclature even as the designation of a London street or as that of a settlement in some far-off colony, it has been seen that the name of Darlaston appears twice even in the one county of Stafford. Similarly is Tipton to be found in duplicate as a place name. Not only is there a Tipton in Staffordshire (which is to form the subject of these pages), but there is a district in Devonshire also known as Tipton—a place near Ottary St. Mary, as beautiful and as charming, from a merely residential point of view, as the subject of these researches is uninviting, so considered. But at one time even our Tipton was not without its own natural beauties, as the lingering evidences on its brighter borderland still reveal to the closely observant eye. Indeed, within living memory Tipton has even been considered "a pretty place." Alas, that man's eager search for the wealth hidden below its surface, should so have transformed the prospect of its landscape in these later days!

Now to consider the etymology of the name "Tipton." Kemble, in his "Saxons in England" (appendix to vol. I.), has traced nineteen of the Saxon (or rather Angle) settlements in Staffordshire, identifying them as original Marks from existing names of places, Thus—

Almington (near Market Drayton)	indicates the	settlement of	Ælmingas
Billington (near Stafford)	,,	,,	Billingas
Bobbington (near Stourbridge)	,,	,,	Bobbingas
Chillington (near Brewood)	,,	,,	Cyllingas
Edingale (near Tamworth)	,,	,,	Edingas
Essington (near Bloxwich)	,,	,,	Essingas
Ettingshall (near Bilston)	,,	,,	Ettingas
Hollington (near Cheadle)	,,	,,	Holingas
Horninglow (Burton-on-Trent)	,,	,,	Horningas
Marchington (near Uttoxeter)	,,	,,	Myrcingas
Packington (near Tamworth)	,,	,,	Pæccingas
Pattingham (near Wolverhamgton)	,,	,,	Pætingas
Stallington (Stone)	,,	,,	Steallingas
Tibbington, or Tipton	,,	,,	Tibbingas
Tillington (Stafford)	,,	,,	Tilingas
Werrington (near Longton)	,,	,,	Werringas
Whittington (near Lichfield)	,,	,,	Wittingas
Winnington (near Market Drayton)	,,	,,	Winingas
Withington (near Uttoxeter)	,,	,,	Withingas

It will be observed that in all these modern names there is one common syllable, "ing." This suffix, "ing," denotes (in the plural, as it is here) "a family," or "a tribe"; so that "Tibbington" signifies literally "the town of the 'Tibbings.'" The corruption in the pronunciation of the old name "Tibbington" to the modern form "Tipton" is easy to understand. By that common tendency to the contraction of words by a quick utterance, we have the elision of the syllable``ing"and the sharp labial "p" substituted for its flat "b."

Once more then, Tipton in full was formerly Tibbington, that is, the ton, town, or settlement of the tribe or clan, or descendants of the Saxon leader and warrior, Tib. The reader will be interested to note as this history proceeds, the various and manifold forms of spelling in which the name Tibbington appears.

After this settlement of a Saxon community in the sixth century we have no record of Tipton till we come to Norman times, when the Conqueror ordered the great Domesday Survey of 1085-6.

CHAPTER II.—DOMESDAY STATUS OF TIPTON.

Although the "Domesday Book " gives us the first written record in the history of Tipton, we are not without data upon which to estimate its actual condition and relative position as compared with other places in its immediate vicinity during the Saxon period. No doubt Wednesbury, with its castle erected in A D. 916, had become a centre of political and commercial life, equal in importance to Tamworth and Warwick, in the midland kingdom known as Mercia The Rev. J. F. Bright, the eminent historian, says "In conjunction with his sister, the Lady of the Mercians Eadward the Elder attempted to secure himself from further molestation by the erection of numerous stone castles. These castles [as erected by Ethelfleda at Wednesbury, Tamworth, Warwick, Stafford, &c.], which seem to have been built on a new and better plan than any erected before (that is, than the mere stockaded and moated forts of the earlier Saxons), became also in many instances the origin from which towns sprang, for laws were passed creating them into markets, and forbidding bargains to be made without the walls. Some sort of monopoly of trade was thus secured for fortified posts."

The "Domesday Book" merely informs us that in Tibintone five carucates of land were held of the Bishop of Lichfield by one William. A carucate means a "carved" land, that is, a piece of arable land as large as could be tilled by one plough in one year; a variable quantity according to the stubbornness of the soil in various parts of the country, but often equivalent to a hide of 120 acres. Probably "carucate" was a Norman term for the hide, cassatus or mausa. Of course this quantity would be altogether exclusive of meadow land, woodland, waste, &c.

But a better conception of the aspect of Tipton during the Saxon period, may be gathered from a glance at the Teutonic system which then prevailed. We have seen that the parish was settled by the tribe of the warrior or leader Tib. It thus became a village community, sometimes called a Mark (literally a boundary mark). As a Mark, the parish would be divided into three parts, in which every free man had an equal interest. There was first the village itself, then the arable mark (cultivated land) then the common pasture, and beyond that the waste. Every free-man had a share in the arable land, and in the common pasture, but he was bound to sow the same crops as his neighbour. The common fields were divided into three strips by broad greasy mounds; one was sown with autumn crops, one with spring crops, and one left fallow. The grass mark was similarly partitioned; but frequently all enclosures were removed at the close of hay harvest, and the cattle grazed in common. Now the extent of the arable mark in Tipton we have seen to be about 500 acres of the common lands no vestige now remains, except perhaps, in the name Tipton "Green"; while the outlying waste will be mentioned in a succeeding chapter.

The village community became a township (afterwards called a vill, which sometimes was equivalent to a parish), and the hundred was a collection of such townships. If a township was established on the land of a Saxon lord—that is, when feudalism developed itself in the later portion of this period—such a township formed a manor. But the Saxon had a natural dislike to town life. And so Tipton, in accordance with the true Saxon spirit of its early founders, failed to attain an urban character to that very latest period, when its mineral wealth and valuable resources attracted to it a large industrial population about the close of the last century. Its straggling shape, too, and widespread area, no doubt contributed largely to its long retention of that non-urban character, notwithstanding its close proximity to the dominating influence of Dudley Castle. For, as Shaw puts it in his "History of Staffordshire" (1799), "Tipton is an extensive tract of flat country, bounded on the south by the lofty Rowley Hills, on the south-west by the limestone rock on which the magnificent ruins of Dudley Castle rear their lofty towers; yet it appears not, though so nearly situated, ever to have been subject to the lords of that great barony." So while Dudley, in due course, crystallised into an important town and a borough, Tipton, on the other side of the same hill, remained a mere district. But the growth and development of Dudley were slow, and took centuries to strive at full fruition. We cannot find from "Domesday Book" that Dudley, in common with all other ancient boroughs, had any organised municipal life; for the burgesses of that time were of different ranks, and were actually the property of different lords—as in Dudley they were of William Fitz Ansculf —and had not yet dared to act as a body. But gradually the *folk mote* and the *firma burgi* gave the town a status. The burgesses held their tenements by a tenure of free *socage*; that is, service at the plough. The word *socage* is derived from *soke*, a plough; and free socage, freely interpreted, means that the people of Dudley held their lands and dwellings in freedom so long as they rendered as much agricultural service a year to their lord, William Fitz Ansculf. But, in course of time, a change came over the condition of townsmen, for certain dues, called fee farm rent, were collected by civic officers, who gradually assumed charge of the town's internal affairs. These dues were not payable to the lord, but were certain fixed rents of the old public lands and royal domains. And so, under the earlier Plantagenets town government became purely democratic. But after the reign of Henry III. a retrograde movement was made towards oligarchy. The wealthier classes gradually assumed sway, extorting money on various pretexts, and impoverishing the less wealthy, and eventually dispossessing these poorer citizens of their privileges. Then came the close corporation, usurping the place of the old democracy, and controlling the town from the later fifteenth century, to the legislative enactment of 1835; of which democratic Birmingham soon took advantage to become a living municipality—and Birmingham itself was once part of the great barony of Fitz Ansculf, Lord of Dudley.

CHAPTER III.—CONDITION OF TIPTON AT THE CONQUEST (1066).

In the Saxon period Tipton had lain midway between the two castles of Dudley and of Wednesbury. At the Norman Conquest there were but 30 castles in the whole of England, and those that existed were placed, as already stated, more for the protection of market towns than as the centres and strongholds of baronial influence. The open hall of the Saxon thane frequently erected with more material of timber than of stone, was the home of even-handed justice and open-handed hospitality. Not so the Norman castles subsequently erected. These heavy massive structures seemed to frown over the whole of the wide territory they commanded. And as the Normans and their immediate successors seemed to possess a positive passion for architecture (both military and ecclesiastical) in due course of time it came to pass that in some single counties more than 30 castles were to be found; in Staffordshire no fewer than 12 were built. But some of the Saxon positions were not re-fortified after they had fallen into decay, or had suffered demolition in the stormy years of resistance to the Norman invaders. So Wednesbury Castle passed away, while the Saxon fortifications of Dudo, on the dominating eminence of Dudley hill, grew into one of those repressive strongholds—entirely different in character to the patriarchal hall of the Saxon noble— which so alarmed the English, but in which the Normans reflected as much their architectural genius as their military prowess.

When Dudley passed from the Saxon Earl Edwin to the Norman Baron Fitz Ansculf, Tipton was included in no part of the domain. The Domesday Book informs us that with the manor of Dudley were Woodlands two miles in extent. The Rev. Luke Booker, in his "History of Dudley" (1825) opines that the figures convey no real notion of the size of these woods, which he states extended from Pensnett Chase on the west, to Gornal on the north, and Tipton on the north-east. It is also certain that in the estates restored by Edward VI (1546) to John Dudley, Duke of Northumberland (the great protector, who was afterwards attainted and executed) was included Willingsworth, on the far side of Tipton. Willingsworth Hall stood within half a mile of Wednesbury Church (in which are the monumental tombs of the Parkes' family, of Willingsworth), and there was born a progenitor of the present Lord Dudley, namely, the son of William, second Baron Ward by his marriage with Anne Parkes in 1672. On the other hand the mediæval possessions of Wednesbury Manor would seem to have extended beyond this outlying portion of Sedgley parish (Willingsworth) and to have reached over into Tipton parish, if we are to attach any significance to the place-name, "Wednesbury Oak." The explanation of this matter is that these additions and alterations of boundaries are of much later date than that of which we are treating.

How meagre was the population of Tipton at the Conquest may be judged, first, by the fact that so much of it was waste (*vasta*) or unoccupied; and, secondly, by comparison with the important manor of Dudley, which had not 20 occupiers (of land) of all grades to be enumerated in Domesday Book. But it is interesting to observe that in this primitive census Dudley possessed a "smith," a prototype of the town's sturdy ironworkers in these later manufacturing days of its industrial development. But in the years of Saxon revolts and insurrections Stafford town and castle would seem to have been the only places of importance in the county and its vicinity. In the year 1069 the Conqueror, marching from the north into Staffordshire, which was in a state of insurrection then, found nothing but anarchy, the people, armed and unarmed split into factions, impiety rampant, while discipline, civil or religious, was entirely set at nought

From the Domesday Book, then, we have learn that the "tenant in fee," or in possession of Tipton, was one "Willelmus," or William. But it has been said that the land was held by him of William the Conqueror, who had a double claim to the lordship thereof, first, he held it in the right of his crown; and, secondly, in his right as earl by escheat of the Saxon thanes, dispossessed at the Norman Conquest. Indeed, very many valueless plough-lands were in the king's hands. We further learn from the same source that in the time of King Edward the Confessor Tibbington had been held by the Bishop of Lichfield. There were also certain adjacent episcopal forests, nominally attached to the see of Lichfield by the Domesday Book, but which did not lie in any of the parishes of Offlow Hundred. But undoubtedly the greatest forest lord in Staffordshire at this date (1087) was the Bishop of Chester, after this date it is curious to observe that as the royal forests increased in dimensions the bishop's woods as steadily, but as certainly, diminished in size, even to contracting the Hundred of Offlow itself. Even in the Year 1224 we find (according to the Tenure Poll of

Offlow) that the extent of the manor of Longdon and the town of Lichfield, both held by Alexander, Bishop of Chester of the King in Barony, was 24 hides, or 2,880 acres, "of which one-seventh was in Tybinton and Hintes." Yet another writer (Erdeswick), as we shall see, places these lands in the domains of the Bishop of Lichfield. The fact is Domesday Book is not explicit as to the *tenant in capite* of Tipton—that is, the superior lord of the place, whether the King himself or his immediate tenant. It does clearly state that it was in the fief of the Bishop of Lichfield during Edward Confessor's time, and we have noted the extent of the fief of *Episcopi de Cestre* (Bishop of Chester). Could there be any confusion of this Latin name with that of *Ecclesia Sancti Ceddœ*,—that is Lichfield Cathedral of St. Chad?

Tipton, indubitably, was never comprehended within the limits of the royal forest, for the boundary of Cannock Forest just excluded it, running, as it did along the highway from Wolverhampton to Wednesbury Bridge. It may be safely hazarded that it was materially to the disadvantage of Tipton that its "waste" was never included within the royal forest and that the place was in consequence so thoroughly neglected that its civic development was retarded century after century, even to the verge of stagnation. There can be no doubt that the immense forests created by the Conqueror and his immediate successors were notwithstanding the harshness and severity of the Forest Laws by which they were regulated and governed) a boon and an administrative gain to the locality affected thereby. For the aim of these Norman and early Plantagenet kings is again and again made clear to the student of history; it was to use the same staff of officials who maintained the forests and administered the Forest Laws as an efficient body of police as well. Or to put it in a more popular form, it would seem that in those days these royal officers were first of all gamekeepers, but were afterwards invested with the full powers of a modern police-constable as well.

Tipton, then, was in this forlorn and neglected position; on the one side it was out off from the organised administration of a royal forest domain, and on the other it was not thought worth while to include it in the great and powerful barony of Dudley.

Rowley Regis, at the Conquest, remained in the king's demesne till the 20th year of his reign.

West Bromwich was probably reckoned in with one or other of Fitz Ansculf's manor. Its acreage was 5,719, while Tipton contained 2,697 acres only. Fitz Ansculf would certainly not miss this territory of Tipton, for, being a great favourite of William the Conqueror, he had been presented with no less than 90 manors.

CHAPTER IV.—TERRITORIAL HISTORY FROM 1151 TO 1279.

The balance of testimony leads to the conclusion that in the year 1087 Tipton was included in the domains of the Bishop of Lichfield. We learn from Shaw that "in 1151 Pope Eugenius III. confirmed, with the rest of the Bishop's estate, *Tibintone cum appendicüs suis*." The reader will smile, no doubt, to contemplate the fact that a Pope of Rome ever had pretensions to the disposal of the soil of Tipton.

Shaw further states that Tipton was mentioned (in the Tenure Poll of the Hundred) as being among the *same*(?) bishop's lands in the time of Henry III.; and he then proceeds to quote another county historian, Sampson Erdeswick, who wrote in the 16th century—

"Tame, passing from Oldbury northwest for two miles or more, receiveth a little brook at Tibbington, *vulgo* Tipton, which comes from Sedgley. At the Conquest one William held Tibbington of the Bishop; not long after one William, the son of Warren, was lord thereof, in right of his wife, Lucia Savage, who had by her Sir Jeffery Fitzwarren, Knt., who had issue John Fitzwarren; but afterwards in Henry the Second's time, Robert Wirley, *alias* Wyrely, was lord thereof, in whose posterity it continued to this day",—that is, in 1538, when Erdeswick wrote. Shaw quotes this without comment, although the Fitzwarrens evidently held possession long after Henry the Second's time, namely, in the reign of Edward I. There is probably something wrong about the period here fixed by Erdeswick. The Plea Rolls, giving intelligible accounts of the pleadings in the various courts (and especially interesting to the local historian are those in which it was litigation respecting manorial rights), have been fully published since Shaw's time: and from them we learn something more respecting Tipton and its territorial history.

Edward I., sometimes styled the English Justinian took a personal interest in the efficient administration of justice, and his frequent presence in Court is testified on the rolls, not only of the Curia Regis, but on those of the Common Pleas, and of the Itinerant Judges. Therefore, the correctness of the Court records in and after his reign can rarely be impugned. The charter establishing the Court of Common Pleas at Westminster was granted by John and amended by Henry III, and directed that assizes of novel disseisin and of mordancestor should not be taken out of their shires. This was afterwards modified, and so suits which the Justices Itinerant could not determine on the spot, from such causes as defect of jury, non-appearance of one party (as will be noted was a default in a Tipton case about to be quoted), &c., were adjourned to another time and place on the same circuit. Staffordshire pleas are, from this cause, found in the Assize Rolls of no less than fourteen other counties.

The Plea Roll for Staffordshire, Trinity Term, 7, Edward I. (1279) says -

"Alice, the widow of William Fitz Geoffrey, sued William de Hondesacre [near Armitage] for a *third of two messuages and three carucates of land [*i.e.* about 300 acres of carved or ploughed land, 30 acres of meadow, 100 acres of wood, 200 acres of pasturage and 100s. of rent in Tybeton (Tipton). And she sued Avice de Hondesacre for a third of a messuage and a carucate of land, 20 acres of meadow, 40 acres of wood, 100 acres of pasturage, and 20s. rent in the same vill [village, parish], which she claimed as her dower. The defendants did not appear, and the sheriff is ordered to take the dower claimed into the King's hands, and to re-summon them for Michaelmas."

At the following Michaelmas Assize the record runs—"Alice, the widow of William, son of Geoffrey Fitz Warine, sued Henry de Hereville, Stephen de Pret and Letitia his wife, William de Oxele and Alice his wife, Robert de Blome and Isolda his wife, and Alienora, the daughter of Geoffrey de Warine, for a third of two messuages and two (*sic*) carucates of land, &c., in Tybeton (Tipton) as her dower. Henry and Alienora did not appear, and Stephen and Letitia state they only hold 8s. and 6d rent, and Robert and Isolda the same. And they were ready to render one-third of the above rents as dower, and they say the said Henry had deforced [wrongfully withheld] them of their reasonable purparties of the residue. And the said Alice stated that she had brought a writ of dower in the Curia Regis against William de Handisaker and Alice his wife for the same tenements (*sic*); and the said Henry and all the other co-parceners [holders of equal shares] whilst the plea was pending had brought a writ of mort d'ancestor against the said William and Alice, by which assize they had acknowledged themselves to hold the tenements in question, and Stephen and the others admitted this. It is,therefore, considered that Alice should recover dower as claimed. And as Henry and Alienora did not appear, and had previously made default, and the dower claimed from them had been taken into the King's hands, Alice is to have seisin of it by their default."

CHAPTER V.—THE WYRLEY FAMILY.

In the previous chapter it will be observed that considerable doubt exists as to the exact period when the family of Wyrley came into the possession of Tipton. The line of division between their possession of the manor, and that of their predecessors, the Fitz Warrens, is so vague that we

*One-third for life is the dower portion of a widow.

are driven to the conclusion that it is clouded under an intermarriage of the two families—probably a Wyrley married the heiress of the House of Fitz Warren about this period. Anyway it is certain that very few landed families have retained so enduring an association with a particular portion of the soil as the Wyrleys have with Tipton; the present lord of the manor being Mr. Wyrley Birch a descendant of this ancient and honourable family. It will be further observed that in the earlier of these two tenures the manor of Tipton seems always to have been an adjunct to the manor of Hints—a village just beyond Littlehay, and near to Tamworth. These possessions may, indeed, have extended beyond Tamworth as far as Edingale, the boundaries of the hundred of Offlow North having been somewhat vague and undefined during the Norman period. But the possessions of the Wyrley family, though perhaps quite as extensive, were more compact, and seemed to have embraced much of the and intervening between these two extreme points (Tipton on the south-west, and Hints on the north-east), comprising, as they did, Handsworth, Hamstead, Perry Barr, and Oscott.

When England was sub-divided by the Conqueror amongst his favoured vassals, they had to render him military service in return. This was the Feudal system. According to the size of the estate to the extent of this service was duly proportioned. In the infeoffment it was accordingly specified the exact number of knights the estate was to furnish to the king's service. Most frequently these lands were sub-let by the vassal-in-chief, by various and curious tenures. So the barony of a crown vassal was said to be composed of so many knights' fees—a knight's fee being supposed to be as much land as would suffice to maintain the knight and his retainers, men and horses, and equip them ready for the field. It was, therefore, essential that the crown should know from time to time, for monetary and for judicial purposes, national as well as local, the exact position of all its vassals and sub-vasals. So Inquisitions, or Enquiries, were made from time to time, up and down the country, before sworn juries, at which the barons made their returns on oath. These returns are amongst the earliest of our national records, and as their authenticity is absolute, they are invaluable. To the two chief documents of this class we are indebted for some further early records of Tipton. The first is the "Liber Niger," or "Black Book" of the Exchequer; this is a record of the time of Henry II., and merely repeats that the Domesday Survey included Hintes and Tibinton amongst the manors in the Barony of the Bishop of Coventry [and Lichfield]. The second is the "Testa de Nevill," a document compiled in the reign of Edward II., but upon evidence mostly taken during the previous two reigns. From this we learn, that in the reign of

Henry III., Galfrid fitz Warine held one-fourth of a knight's fee in Tipton under the aforesaid bishop. The exact extent of this holding cannot be given, for, as we have seen, a knight's fee was a most indefinite quantity of land according to its fertility or its barreness; being anything between one and five hundred acres of cultivable land. In Staffordshire a fee averaged as much as 3,000 acres, but this included wood and waste as well. A third and similar document, known as "Kirby's Quest," of the reign of Edward I., also states that one Hugh de Meignall held half a knight's fee of the bishop in Hints and Tibinton. Now, this Hugh de Meignall, according to Dugdale in his "History of Warwickshire" (under head of Babington), married Philippa, sister and co-heir of Geoffrey Savage, who died without issue in 32 Henry II. (1186). Reference to the last chapter will bring to memory that a Lucia Savage had married William, son of that original Warren, who seems to have been the first recorded holder of Tipton manor.

A pedigree of the Wyrley family, "of Handsworth," will be found in the Salt Society's "Staffordshire Collections." vol. iii., pt. 2, p. 153. This is the one sworn to in the year 1583 before Robert Glover, Somerset Herald; for in former times it was customary for an inquiry, called a "Herald's Visitation," to be made in order to register pedigrees and to declare who were lawfully entitled to bear arms. While the Wyrleys passed the ordeal satisfactorily a neighbouring landowner, William How, *aliaes* Hoo, of Bradley, was "disclaimed." The next Herald's Visitation of Staffordshire was made in 1614, followed by another in 1663-4, held before Sir William Dugdale Norroy King of Arms. On April 11th, 1663 Dugdale, dined with his friend, Sir John Wyrley, at Hampstead. In the spring of the following year (1664) sitting at Lichfield for the business of the hundred of Offlow, Dulgdale disclaimed one Edward Nitingale, of Tipton, who had adopted arms he was not entitled to bear. The claims, however, of Wyrley, of Hamstead Barr, and Oscott were duly allowed, and the pedigree then established is printed in the "Staffordshire Collections," vol v., pt. 2, p. 333, from which we note that an important marriage into the family of Sheldon, of Rowley Regis, was made during the reign of Henry VII. This family tree is signed by Sir John Wyrley, who was knighted by Charles I. at Whitehall in 1641.

At the same Visitation of 1663, Josiah Freeman, of Wednesbury, was disclaimed, not being entitled to bear the arms he had adopted—like Edward Nitingale, of Tipton William Hopkins, of Oakeswell Hall, Wednesbury, aged 27, had his arms recorded, although he could produce no proof of them. William Smallwood, of the Delves, near Wednesbury, was also disclaimed John Hoo, of Bradley, aged 58, had his arms recorded and his crest (granted in 1614) confirmed.

CHAPTER Vl.—A FAMILY DISPUTE AT TIPTON IN 1278.

Since the Conquest considerable progress had been made by all social grades. The socmen had developed into the yeomanry class, while the thanes had become the gentry. But above the latter class came the aristocracy, distinguished by two great privileges, to which allusion has already been made in passing. The first privilege, devised in the 11th century, was the possession of a surname, as in Fitz Warren, *fitz* being the Norman form of *filius filü*, signifying "son of." A surname itself was originally a nickname (an eke name), so that the first Warren was probably so called from the office he held of "warding" the king's "warren," or preserved hunting grounds. But we note also another method of distinction in the territorial title *de* or "of," showing the possession of the specified land under some covenanted tenure, as "William of Hansacre, or "William de Hondesacre." The second privilege was that of bearing arms, to which reference has been made; such armorial bearings or coats of arms at first only used in warfare or the tournament, were adopted by the nobility as family badges in the 13th century.

So much in explanation of what has already been alluded to; the matter of the Wyrley arms will again be referred to further on. And now in explanation of what is to follow. It must be noted that profusion rather than refinement characterised the tables at this period, and in the households generally of the Anglo-Norman gentry it was quantity before quality. Utensils of all kinds were very primitive in make, wooden trenchers to eat meat from, and lethern jacks to drink from, were in common use among the gentry and their guests: earthenware dishes and metal plates were only to be met with in baronial halls. Bearing in mind the state of things, we may the more readily grasp some of the details of the following case, contained in a similar law report to that quoted at the close of Chapter IV.

At the Hillary Sittings next following those quoted we find the same plaintiff Alice Fitzwarine suing the afore-mentioned William of "Hondesacre" [Hansacre] and one "Richard le Wodeward of Berdon for assaulting her at Tibbenton [Tipton] and taking her goods and chattels to the value of £10." The defendants did not appear, but by Easter term the sheriff had attached the said William to answer the complaint of the said Alice, who claimed £40 as damages for the insult. The complainant stated that on Thursday of the Feast of St. Simon and Jude, 6 Ed. l [28th Oct. 1278] he had taken a horse from her worth 20s and an ox worth one mark [13s. 4d.] and had driven away and killed and eaten two of her pigs, and had taken other goods belonging to her to his house at Hondesacre, viz., 3 brass pots worth 20s. and other utensils specified."

The defendant put in an appearance this time on compulsion, but denied the trespass and appealed to a jury. The sheriff was ordered to summons a jury for the following Quindene of Michaelmas, but in the roll of the Michaelmas Assizes no record of the suit is to be found. This is probably because the defendant had died in the meantime. Anyway during the next three or four years various suits are recorded in which "Ala widow of William de Handesacre" sues for dower, and in which mention is made of "William, son of William de Handesacre," a ward under age, part of whose land is in the custody of Roger the Bishop of Coventry and Lichfield.

About a dozen years after the same case seems to have entered on a new phase, for we find in 1293 at the Epiphany sitting that "Ala, formerly wife of William de Handesacre, and Thomas le Harpour of Handsacre, were attached to answer the plea of William de Waleton and Alice his wife, that they had come with others unknown, on the morn of All Saints, 6, Edward I, to the said Alice and had carried away her goods and chattels to the value of £20." It will be observed that this statement of the act of trespass does not agree with the first statement, the value of the goods removed is not given the same, and the date is now fixed as November 2nd, of the year 1278. Furthermore, "Alice widow" of William Fitzwarine seems to have remarried, her husband now being William de Walton. " The defendants," as before,' "denied the trespass." The jury stated that William of Hansacre, Ala, his wife, this Thomas, and other servants of William's household unknown had come on the date named to the house of William Fitzwarine, in Tipton [Tibeton], immediately after the said Fitzwarine's death, William of Hansacre claiming to be his nearest heir for the tenements in Tipton. They had stayed there some time till William of Hansacre was called away to London on business, but Ala, his wife, stayed eight days longer in Tipton, and when she went away took goods to the value of £4 12s, 10d. from the house in Tipton to her house at Hansacre. Further, that William, on his return from London, went to the house in Tipton and asked for drink, and Alice offered him drink in a certain *cipho de mazere*, but William threw away the beer and handed the *ciphum* to a certain esquire whose name is unknown, and in this way he carried away the *ciphum*. And the jury being asked what chattels did remain to Ala after the death of her husband, William of Hansacre, they stated that she had obtained a *pelium*, a *lotorium*, a *ciphum de mazere*, and a brass pot and a dish from the executors of the said William and they estimated the damages of William and Alice at 20s. William de Walton and his wife Alice afterwards withdrew their original plea." In the goods and chattels thus specified (under their bastard Norman-Latin names) the modern reader will discover nothing more valuable than washing basins, drinking vessels, and such household stuff as in those Mediæval times was considered valuable enough to become "heirable" property.

CHAPTER VII.—LAND VALUES: WASTES, FORESTS, AND THE RIGHT OF ASSART (1279)

Food for reflection may readily be found by any thoughtful reader of the last chapter. The most casual reader must have been struck by the comparative values of commodities in the thirteenth century, and in the present time. It was astonishing, no doubt, for Tipton readers to discover that within the history of recorded times, lands in the parish—where now every inch, both on the surface and below it, is of very considerable commercial value—were once deemed of value so inconsiderable as to have remained unappropriated, for such in effect is the meaning of the Domesday description *vasta*, or waste. Within two centuries of that great national survey, we begin to note the growing value of lands in the frequent mention of "rents," and the more frequent cases of litigation over their eagerly contested possession. Then leaving the consideration of "real" property, we are more forcibly struck with the extraordinary values attached to "personal" property. On the one hand we have found a horse valued at 20s. and an ox at 13s 4d.—perhaps one-thirtieth of their present value, if the money standard were to be taken at its present value. But it is not. The money standard is here deceptive, for money in actual coins used as a medium of exchange was scarce. Arable land could be rented at 6d. an acre and meadow land at 1s. per acre per annum. Wages even at harvest time were 1d. per day, and at other periods of the year a halfpenny—literally a silver penny cut in half, for copper coinage was not then current. But the most striking incident in this chapter of Tipton's history was the value attached to that drinking vessel yclept *cipho de mazere*; the name *mazer* signifying a spot or scar, and the full term meaning a broad stand-up cup or drinking bowl, so called because made of wood having a spotted or speckled grain. Possibly it was mounted with gold or silver. Now this piece of "real property," which to the modern reader appears such a very ordinary article of household stuff, is considered of so great value in the 13th century that a gentleman of position, a knight, gallant, valorous, courteous, and honourable—as no doubt William of Hansacre was, for he came attended by his squire, and was of such a position in society as to be called to London on business a most costly, rare, and dangerous expedition in those times – made a special journey to Tipton to surreptitiously, if not forcibly, appropriate it, and did not deign to carry it away to his mansion near Armitage.

To proceed: Once more reverting to the Assizes taken at Stafford on Saturday after the Feast of St, Matthew 7, Ed. I.—that is after 21st September, 1279 – we find the following record:—

"An assize, &c., of William, son of Geoffrey de Tybyton, uncle of Henry de Herevile [Heronville] and brother of Lucy, wife of Stephen de Prewes, and brother of Alice, wife of William de Oxele, and brother of Isabella, wife of Robert le Blomere, and brother of Alienora, daughter of Geoffrey son of William, was seized, &c., as of fee of a messuage, a carucate of land, and 50s. of rent in Tybiton [Tipton] when he died, and which tenements and rent are held by Amice de Hondesacre and William her son. The jury find in favour of Henry Lucy, Alice, and the other co-heirs, and they state that William de Hondesacre had held the said tenements after the death of William, son of Geoffrey. Henry and the other co-heirs are, therefore, to recover damages which were taxed by the recognitors of the assize at 57s."

To the same "William, son of Geoffrey," allusion is made by the county historian Shaw, who says—

"If an old deed I find that John Prior, of Parva Malverne, grants to John Coleshull, clerk, the manor of Tybinton. Test. Martin, Abbot of Hales, John de Heronvile, John Rushall, Ralph de Bushopesburi, &c. Likewise, William, son of Geoffrey Fitzwarine, lord of Tybinton grants to John Coleshull. Test. John de Heronvile, &c."

The John de Heronville here mentioned as a witness attesting both deeds, was lord of the manor of Wednesbury,

Again Shaw mentions "William, son of Geoffrey," in another deed he quotes as follows, and which contains reference to a place in Wednesbury, on the confines of Tipton, namely, Finchespath, the site of an ancient fishery and a water mill, with most important water rights on the Tame at Wednesbury—

"William, son of Milo de Finchepath, grants to Henry de Herovile all his right in the assert which he held of William, son of Geffry, lord of Tybinton, near the tenement which Henry Attolle held of the waste of Tybinton. Test. Robert de Blower, Robert de Cambwell, William de Walleshull," &c. With regard to the waste of Tipton, it may be again observed that this parish lay outside the limits of Cannock Forest, the boundaries of which ran along the king's highway through Bilston to Wednesbury Bridge, and that probably this intervening "waste", lay between that royal woodland and the Chase of Pensnett. which then approached as near it as the Castle Hill. Another "waste" lay near Walsall at the "Pleck," as this name signifies in its literal sense. On the other hand, the word "forest," as applied mediævally, does not necessarily denote a large wood but merely an extensive tract of uncultivated land, kept in a virgin condition for beaste of the forest (boar, wolf, &c.), beaste of the chase (buck, fox, martin &c.), and beasts and fowl of warren (hare, rabbit, pheasant, and partridge). The boundaries of such "forest" were fixed by record and proscription, and it was regulated by special laws and special officers. It often included manors belonging to private lords but their rights were much restricted, as they could not change their land from pasture to arable, nor cut down their woods, nor make enclosures (such as would stop access to larger game), nor do anything likely to interfere with forest rights. Now Tipton was never afforested, as we have seen. The phrase, "his right in the assert," would seem to imply that he possessed a right to clear the timber and underwood on the land —for the word "assart" usually signifies an offence in old Forest Law, namely, that of grubbing up by the roots those trees or bushes that are large enough to afford covert for beasts of the chase. Several centuries later, that is in the reign of Elizabeth, another document (to which allusion will be made) relating to certain lands in Tipton and Wednesbury, which supported the chantry priest of the Guild of St. Mary at Wednesbury Church, expressly reserves to "our brother" (that is, to Edward VI,, who first made the grant, February 6th, 1551), his heirs and successors, "all large trees and woods of, in, and upon the premisses growing and being." This reservation probably because Tipton had been too much "wasted." So that the term "waste," in the course of two centuries, had now come to bear a meaning much nearer its present signification than when translated from "vasta," at the Domesday survey.

Once again, quoting from Shaw, we note more familiar names in the attestation, "Blower," no doubt being a clerical error for "Blomer," or "Blome," and after which family perhaps "Bloomfield" was called—"And by another deed Alice, late wife of William de Oxeley, and daughter of Geffry Witzwarine, Knt. lord of Tybinton, in her pure widowhood, grants to Sir John de Herovile all her rights in a meadow situated between the churchyard of Tibinton and the Blakeley, rendering, &c, in the hall of Tibinton *Test.* William de Walton, Robert de Blower, William Walleshall, *cleric*, &c,"

Besides mention of "the Blakeley," we have, perhaps the earliest allusion to Tibbington Hall, a mansion long since demolished, which formerly stood somewhere near the site of the Tibbington Foundry, at Princes End. In ancient days it was fortified by the usual moat, or ditch from which the Moat Colliery is named and near which the present Mr. Alfred Hickman, the great Staffordshire ironmaster, was born.

CHAPTER VIII—A VIVARY IN TIPTON: TIPTON LANDS ALIENATED IN MORTMAIN: HUGH LE DESPENSER, THE ROYAL FAVOURITE, CLAIMS LANDS IN TIPTON (1293-1317).

This chapter will show in some measure how the history of Tipton has interlaced itself with the history of England; and this, as the heading shows, with regard not only to the mediæval extravagances of the aristocracy, but also with regard to legislative developments, brought about by the intricacies of the clerical mind, and various legal proceedings arising out of the favoritism of a foolish monarch. Minor local causes tried in the law courts are also recorded in this chapter to preserve the chronological order of the narrative as much as possible.

'The Staffordshire Assize Roll, 21 Ed. I. [7 January, 1293] shows, amongst other things, that John de Heronville, of Wednesbury, was a man of considerable importance in the county. He was one of four knights summoned to elect a jury as soon as the assizes commenced; he had a suit relating to rights to common lands in Darlaston (see "History of Darlaston," p.44), and the following entry exhibits him exercising certain feudal rights over lands in Tipton:—

"An assize &c, if John de Heronvile had unjustly disseised William, son of Robert and Adam de Walton and Alice, his wife, of the third part of a messuage and of a vivary in Tybinton. John stated he claimed nothing but the custody of the tenement, by reason of the minority of one Henry de Heronvile, who was not named in the writ, and the suit was dismissed."

It is difficult to say whether this "vivary" was anything more than a pond or a warren for keeping strange creatures, although it must be borne in mind that in these olden times the wealthier nobility had a weakness for keeping all sorts of foreign wild beasts caged up. The lions at the Tower of London were a survival of this habit handed down through a long line of English monarchs since the time of Henry I., who first made a perfect menagerie at Woodstock, near Oxford, where he caged lions, leopards, lynxes, camels, porcupines and the like. When his successor, Henry II, made the same site into Fair Rosamond's Bower, the royal estate was extended by acquiring the neighbouring manor of Stonesfield in exchange for the manor of Wednesbury, which thus ceased to be a royal possession. It was in this way Wednesbury manor passed to one Ralph Boterel (whose manor of Stonesfield was not nearly so valuable the one he thus obtained in exchange), and through him to his descendant John or Henry de Heronville, who now is found wealthy enough to possess a vivary of his own in Tipton (1293).

At the same assizes was tried an important suit between the Bishop of

Lichfield and the King. The former produced a charter from Henry III, granting him and his successors many rights over certain manors in the county (Lichfield, Rugeley, Cannock, Brewood, &c.), including free warren, and rights to hold in some of them markets and fairs. He also produced a charter from Richard I., granting to the Bishops of Lichfield the right to hold a Sunday market at Eccleshall: the Bishop also claimed a weekly market and yearly fair at Lichfield, and view of frankpledge, and he stated that Longdon, Fisherwick, Horton, Handacre, Hammerwich, Harborne and many other places, including Typinton (Tipton), appear yearly at the said view of frankpledge

It may be explained that *Frankpledge* dated from Saxon times, and was a surety given by the lord of the manor, to the government of the country, for the peace of his district, and the good behaviour of his tenants, servants, and retainers. The lord held his courts periodically for the trial of offences committed within his jurisdiction, as he was responsible to the crown for their prevention or punishment. Hence his court was denominated the "view of frankpledge"—that is, "the peace pledge," or assurance given on oath for the preservation of the king's peace.

The next year the Plea Rolls of 22 Bd. I. (1294) inform us that the Prior of Sandwell sued Nicholas Comitassone of Grete for a mill and half an acre of land in West Bromwich and Tipton as the property of his Priory. No appearance was put in, and evidently a verdict was given in favour of the Prior. It would appear that two years later, at Trinity term 24 Ed. I., a jury declared that there was no collusion between these two parties, and that the mill had been given, time out of memory, to a predecessor of the Prior by a William Fitz Guy, lord of Bromwich; while the half-acre of land had been given by Geoffrey Fitz Warine, lord of Stybinton (Tipton) in the reign of Henry III. to the then Prior of Sandwell, who held it in right of his Church before the statute of Mortmain. The possession of this bit of land, and the more important property the mill, both in Tipton, will well illustrate a great legal principle which cropped up at at this period.

Lands in the possession of monasteries, like Sandwell, were said to be alienated in Mortmain (*in mortuam manum*, or in dead hands) because the members of a corporate body (as chapters and monasteries) are dead persons in law. And as corporate bodies never die, the lord lost all his feudal profits; for at the time of changing hands at the death of one and the succession of another, feudal fines totalled up considerably towards a landowner's income. But beyond this the national power was weakened, because a diminution of military tenants naturally followed the acquisition of lands by the church. So at last the crown had to interfere, and the Statute de Religiosis (1279) forbad religious houses to alienate lands in Mortmain. The clergy evaded the law; for discovering that the Act only extended to *gifts and conveyances* of the land, they set up a fictitious title to it, with the consent of the donor, who, of course.allowed judgment to be given against him. This was the origin of *Common Recoveries*, which are still in use, and it gave rise to a second act bearing on the matter, the Second Statute of Mortmain (1285), which enacted that such cases should be sent to a jury, and if fraud was discovered the land should be forfeited. Hence this trial over Tipton lands and mill in 1294, a few years after the passing of the Act. In fact, Tipton thus affords us an object lesson in the legal procedure for restraining alienation in mortmain, and the integrity of the clergy in evading such legal restraints from acquiring land for the Church. Those monkish lawyers were afterwards clever enough to distinguish between the *possession* of land and the *use* of it. Hence the introduction of *uses* and *trusts*, the foundation of modern conveyancing. Evidently the Prior of Sandwell was as accomplished in legal lore as any of his ecclesiastical brethren, if we are to judge by the verdict he gained at Stafford.

The Plea Rolls of Easter 30 Ed. I. (1302) record the suit of Christina, widow of John son of Walter de Mere, of Dudley, against Robert le Blomer for one-third of a watermill, four acres of land, and four acres of meadow in Tipton, as her dower. As Robert had not appeared at the previous term (Hillary Sittings) the dower claimed had been taken into the king's lands for Christina, who now claimed it by his default. But Robert now came forward and stated that he was ready to prove he had never been summoned, and offered to wage his law. He was, therefore, ordered to appear with his compurgators at the Octaves of St. John. In this case we note not only feudal customs, but even some legal procedure handed down from the Saxon period. For instance compurgators were persons, generally neighbours, who came forward to swear on oath on behalf of a defendant the effect of the said oath being estimated by their worth or rank and not by their knowledge of the matter in dispute. At the same sittings Christina recovered a third of six acres in Tipton by default of Thomas de Horsley, and another third of six acres in the same vill by default of Adam de Telle.

The Banco Roll, 5 Edward II. (1312), shows:—

Roger Baset, of Bromwich, gives half a mark for license of concord with Richard Paynel, and Alice his wife, in a plea of warranty of charter respecting tenements in Wednesbury.

And at Easter, 6 Edward II., the Banco Roll states—

Richard Paynel, senior, and Alice his wife, were summoned by John Hillary, clerk, to carry out a covenant made between them respecting two messuages, three acres of meadow, and half a carucate of land in

Wodensbury and Tybington (Tipton). A concord was made, and they had a chirograph (of a fine).

Although we are already acquainted with the nature of the Plea Rolls (see Chapter IV.), we have here the new term "Banco Roll" to explain. In and immediately after the time of Henry III., in addition to the local Manorial Courts, and the County Courts held by the Sheriff, there were the Coram Rege Court, which (as its name implies) followed the king's person; the Court de Banco whose *bench* was fixed at Westminster; and there were also the proceedings of the Justices Itinerant, and the Justices assigned specially to take Assizes annually, all leaving us Rolls of record to this day. In the matter of their nomenclature it may be said that under the general heading "Plea Rolls" we include the first two, while the latter may be found described as Assize Rolls.

In the records extracted from the Banco Roll regarding these West Bromwich and Tipton lands, we have two strange phrases, namely, "license of concord," and "chirograph of a fine." These will be best understood by quoting Mr. Cecil T. Davis, author of "The Brasses of Worcestershire," &c. He says:—

"FINE OF LANDS..—A fine is sometimes said to be a feoffment of record, though it might, with more accuracy, be called an acknowledgment of a feoffment on record. They were thus levied:—

1st—The party to whom the land is to be conveyed commences a suit at law against the other, generally an action of covenant.

2nd.—Next come the licence of concord (*licentia concordandi*), for as soon as the action is brought, the defendant, knowing himself to be in the wrong, is supposed to make overtures of peace and accommodation to the plaintiff; who, accepting them (but having upon suing out the writ given pledges to prosecute his suit, which is endangered if he now deserts it without licence), applies, therefore, to the Court for leave to make the matter up, which is readily granted.

3rd.—Now comes the Concord or agreement itself after leave obtained from the Court; this is usually an acknowledgement from the deforciants (or those who keep the other out of possession) that the lands in question are the right of the complainant. This acknowledgment must be made openly either in the Court of Common Pleas, or elsewhere as directed.

By these acts all the essential parts of a fine are completed.

4th—Comes next the note of the Fine, which is only an abstract of the writ of covenant, and the Concord naming the parties, the parcels of land, &c, which must be enrolled with the chirographer.

5th.—The "Foot of the Fine," or conclusion of it—this concludes the whole matter. Of these there would be Indentures engrossed at the

Chirographer's office, and delivered to the cognizor and cognizee.

Thus the Fine is completely levied at Common Law."

This detailed explanation will enable the reader to understand the legal processes referred to in the Banco Roll. When we are informed that Paynel and Hillary, the two parties to the suit over the Tipton and Wednesbury lands, had a "chirograph of a fine," it simply means that the document in No. 5 above was divided between them, cut irregularly; as indentures always are, and hence their name. The deed would be engrossed *contrariwise*, and cut zig-zag through the word "Chirograph" itself; by this means the indented edge of the parchment would be at the top of each party's moiety of it, and they could not afterwards break from their mutual recorded agreement, as no other document produced could possibly fit in exactly with the other irregularly cut half, its own complement. The duplicated document began thus:—

——— CHIROGRAPH ———

This is the Final Agreement made in the Court,. &c

The Plea Rolls for Hillary term, 10 Edward II. (1317) of the counties of Stafford, Worcester, Salop, &c., have an important case recorded, in which the royal favourite, Hugh le Despenser, senior, is the plaintiff and in which a local estate is involved. Among the lands affected were half the manor of Wolverhampton and certain lands in Tipton, &c. Every school boy knows the history of the two Despensers, father and son, who were the favourites of King Edward II; Tipton school boys will be interested to know that the elder favourite, into whose hands many estates seemed so luckily to fall, was in this way connected with the soil of their native parish. This tyrant was executed at Bristol (1326) nine years after the trial respecting those lands in Tipton and elsewhere.

NOTE.—By 3 and 4, Will. IV., c. 74, the old cumbrous machinery of barring entails by Common Recoveries was abolished. A simple deed enrolled in Chancery Court is now sufficient.

CHAPTER IX.—How Tipton was Taxed for the Crusades (1288-1291).

Pope Nicholas IV., to whose predecessors in the See of Rome the first-fruits and the tenths of all Ecclesiastical benefices had for a long time been paid, granted the tenths, in 1288, to Edward I for six years towards defraying the expenses of a Crusade. That these might be collected to their full value the King caused a Roll to be drawn up, which was completed in the year 1291, under the direction of the Bishops of Winchester and Lincoln. Amongst others, there is a capital copy of *Taxatio Ecclesiastica P. Nicholai IV.* in the Chapter Library, Lichfield. This Roll has been frequently used as a basis for very many taxings since 1291. The *Valor Ecclesiasticus* held good, and all taxes from the benefices, to our own Kings as well as to the Popes, were regulated by it until 27, Henry VIII. Then, with the commencement of the Reformation, first-fruits and tenths ceased to be forwarded to Rome, and were transferred to the Crown—in 1703 the receipts were appropriated for the augmentation of smaller livings, and are known now as Queen Anne's Bounty.

Now to see how this taxation, which originated with the Crusades affected our local history. We find Tipton and Sedgley (which latter was attached to Dudley Priory) included under the head of the Deanery of Lapley and Trysull, while Wednesbury was in the Deanery of Tamworth and Tutbury. Thus it is recorded:—

TAXATIO ECCLESIASTICUS P. NICHOLAI.
Decanatus de Thomwurth and Tuttebur.

	Taxatio.			Decima.	
	£	s.	d.	s.	d.
Ecclia de Wodnesbury	5	13	4	11	4
Decanatus de Lappeley and Tresel.					
Ecclia de Tybynton	4	0	0	8	0
Ecclia de Seggesley, app. Priori and Conv. de Duddley	8	0	0	16	0

Another return, known as the *Nonarum Inquisitiones*, may be included almost as a military roll dealing with knight's fees. It consists in the finding upon oath by parishioners of the value of the ninth lamb, fleece, and sheep, and in cities and boroughs of the ninth of such goods and chattels as in 14, Edw. III. (1341) were levied towards the expenditure of the Scotch and French Wars. This ninth of all articles assessed and sold was to be levied according to the aforementioned taxation of Pope Nicholas in 1291-2. We have just seen the valuation of Tipton church benefice at that time, and probably this allusion to "Ecclia de Tybynton" is the earliest we shall find referring to a church in Tipton (1291). The word "Ecclia" is a contraction of "Ecclesia," signifying a church; as in contradistinction "capella" signifies merely a chapel (of ease ?). For these wars, however of 1341, one ninth was to be reckoned worth as much as one tenth of the tytheable commodities of the taxation of 1291. Therefore, before this military tax was made in Tipton certain parishioners appeared at the Inquisition and gave information on oath to the Commissioners as to the true value of their corn, wool, lambs, &c., but if one-ninth was found less than the original tax in 1291, the Commissioners had power to disregard it, and levy the true value of one-ninth; hence the name of the records—*Nona Rolls*.

CHAPTER X —HOW TIPTON WAS TAXED FOR THE SCOTCH WARS OF EDWARD III. IN 1327 AND 1332.

Edward III. came to the throne of England in 1327 while he was but in his sixteenth year. The Scots determined to take advantage of the young king's minority, and invaded England (under Randolph and Douglas), breaking a truce agreed upon in 1323. The young king's first Parliament promptly granted him a subsidy to carry on the war. The grant was set forth to be "a twentieth part of all movable goods for the defence of the kingdom against the Scots." The collectors for county Stafford were John de Acton and Richard de Hampton. They were directed to summon the best and most loyal men of each village (there were but few large towns, boroughs, and cities in those days) from whom they were to elect four or six or more, to make the assessment. These were duly sworn to make full inquiry into the goods possessed by every man of the vill (or parish) on Michaelmas Day, 1 Ed. III., in the house and out of the house, and to tax the same according to their full value. Certain goods were to be excepted as not liable to the taxation, namely—(1) Armour; (2) mounture (horses used for riding), (3) jewels and robes of knights, gentlemen, and their wives; (4) their plate of silver or pewter; (5) "des viens de meseaux" (probably tools and implements for agriculture and trade); and (6) the goods of those whose moveable property did not amount to 10s. The Commissioners made no distinction between freemen and others, and the villein tenants of each manor were taxed equally with the freeholders; and this no doubt gave good cause for the discontent which showed itself soon after—as in the insurrections of the following reign. While in these days we should grumble at some of the exemptions—as the jewels and plate of the upper classes—still we must bear in mind that in those days the landowners provided the military strength of the nation. So that if the nobles and landed gentry possessed privileges, they also had great duties to perform. It is easy to see that armour and cavalry horses should naturally be exempted from a military tax, being part of the necessary equipments for war.

The record of this taxation is still preserved to us and is known as the Subsidy Roll of 1327. In it the hundreds are named, but vills are grouped together irrespective of any manorial or ecclesiastical connection. For instance Tipton is included with Norton and Wirley. The amounts for Tipton alone are thus stated—

TIBYNTON.	s.	d.
De Petro atte hurst	v	vj
Rob'to de Kyngesleye	iiij	
Joh'e atte noke	v	
Rog'o de Hemehu	ij	vj
Joh'e atte telle	v	iij
Thoma de Blakeleye	iij	
Joh'e filio Reginaldi		xviij
Ph'o de Horseleye		xiij ob.

The *summa* or total for the three vils is given as "lv s. iiij d. ob pb."—that is, 55 shillings and fourpence halfpenny of the public currency; while for Tipton alone the above items cast to 27 shillings and tenpence halfpenny—"ob." being a contraction of "obolus," or halfpenny.

Other contractions in the foregoing list may be explained and extended; for instance, Joh'e is contracted from Johanne or John, Ph'o may stand for Philip, Thoma of course is Thomas, Rog'o is Roger, Rob'to is Robert, and Petro is Peter. The connective "atte" signifies "dwelling at," while "de" sometimes means "of," and in rare cases it is almost a territorial title but not often. In the first name here it means "From," as "From Peter dwelling at the Wood" who pays the largest amount, namely 5s. 6d. John dwells at the Oak (probably Wednesbury Oak, or Gospel Oak) the same quaint form being used by Piers Plowman—

> For sum tyme I served
> Simme atte Noke.

The "leye " termination of three of the place-names signifies a lea, a pasture, or a clearing in a wood, and two of these names, Horsley and Blakeley, are familiar to the reader.

For the same subsidy Wednesbury produced 27s. 1d. and West Bromwich and Darlaston together 45s. 9½d. In the West Bromwich list we note the names of Roger de Ruggiacre (now Ridgacre) and Roger Golde (probably of Gold's Hill); Thomas atte Hoo was undoubtedly tenant near Hoo Marsh, Wednesbury, but included in Sedgley manor.

This first Scotch war being unsuccessful, another had to be undertaken in 1332, as Baliol had been crowned at Scone that year, and the English arms had lost their prestige in the north. To provide the necessary sinews of war another subsidy had to be forthcoming, and the record of its collection is also left to us for examination and investigation.

The Second Subsidy Roll of Staffordshire, which is extant, is the fullest and most complete, and contains fully the taxation of boroughs like Stafford and Newcastle [Burgum Novi Castri], Lichfield and Tamworth and of the vills [parishes other than boroughs or cities] like Typton, Wednesbury, &c. It is for the subsidy of 1332-3, and was granted by Parliament to Edward III. for the expenses of the renewed Scotch war, and consisted of a tenth of all goods held on Michaelmas Day, 6 Ed. III., in cities, boroughs, and ancient demesnes of the king, and of a fifteenth of the same in counties. Wednesbury and Walsall being of ancient demesne paid one-tenth [decima], while Tipton, West Bromwich, Darlaston, and Bentley [Derlaston et Bentleye] paid one fifteenth [quintadecima].

The instructions for levying the aid, given in the Patent Roll of 7 Ed. III., were:—The chief taxers were to call before them from every city, borough or vill the most loyal men, from whom they were to elect four or six of each vill, by whom the taxing could be best accomplished. These were sworn on the Holy Evangelists to give a full and true account of all the goods of each inhabitant, both in their houses and out of their houses, and to fairly tax them according to their true value, saving the things excepted. And the chief taxers were to go from vill to vill, and from hundred to hundred to see that the sub-taxers had fully taxed and presented the goods of the commonalty saving (as before) armour, saddle horses [*mounture*] jewels and robes of knights and gentlemen and their wives, and vessels of gold and brass (including the hanaper of silver, or mazre, from which they drank); and in cities and boroughs one robe for each man and woman was to be excepted, also a bed for each, &c., goods outside boroughs, cities, and the king's demesnes valued under 10s were not to be taxed, and inside if they did not exceed 6s. in gross value.

TYBINTON.

	s.	d.	
De Rob'to de Rynggeley..................	iiij	ix	
Rog'o de Hemhull............................	iij	iiij	ob. qu.
Thoma Atteblakeleyge....................	iiij		
Mattho Attehurst	vj	vj	ob. qu.
Joh'ne Paynel	iiij	viij	
Joh'ne Attenoke	iij		
Ric'o Attehurst	v	iij	
Joh'ne Reynald	ij		
Ph'o de Horseley..............................		xvj	ob.

These amounts are totalled with those of Barre et Alerwych [Great Barr and Aldridge] and Bromwych [West Bromwich], the "summa" for all these vills being vij li. vij s. x d.

CHAPTER XI.—SOME MANORIAL HISTORY FROM 1306 TO 1472: THE WYRLEY COAT-OF-ARMS.

The *Originalia* are another class of public records being the estreats transmitted from the Court of Chancery to the Exchequer Office of all grants of the Crown inrolled on the Patent and other Rolls, whereon any rent is reserved, any salary payable, or any service performed. These rolls commence early in the reign of Henry III, and in the time of Edward III, the following entry relating to Tipton may be found:—

"It is ordered to John de Swynnerton, escheator for the king in the county of Stafford, that having received security from John, son and heir of John de Heronville, defendant, for the relief to himself and of the said John, son of John, concerning the Manor of Wednesbury, which he hold from the king *in capite* by the service (payment) of 20 and 1 shillings yearly to have full possession, and concerning the fifth part of the Manor of Tipton and its belongings in Tipton, which he holds from another, he should not allow another to enter [into possession]."

In translating the foregoing document it is quite possible that some minor errors may have crept in, as the original Latin is written in a much contracted form. But it will be noted that while Wednesbury Manor is held directly of the king (as a tenant in capite), Tipton is held of "another" lord superior, other than the king.

In several inquisitions *post-mortem*, given at length in the "History of Wednesbury," mention is made of lands in Tipton. In an inquiry taken upon the death of Henry Heronville, lord of the manor of Wednesbury, in 1306, it is sworn that he held lands near Tybynton, of Matilda Burnell, at 4s. per annum. In a similar inquiry taken in 1355, on the death of John Heronville, also a *tenant in capite* for the same manor, it is stated that he held a fifth part of the Manor of Tipton, with its appurtenances, of Nicholas Burnell, who held it *in capite* by military service. Again, in 1406, Henry Heronville is said to have held land in Tipton, including 20 acres of wood (xx acras bosci), of Hugh Burnell. One of the witnesses was William Sponne, from whom perhaps we have derived the name "Spon Lane," just as "Harvill's Hawthorn" is named from the Heronvilles. In 1420 William Leventhorpe, by right of his wife Johanna (heiress of the Heronvilles), is lord of Wednesbury and tenant of a third part of 40 acres of land in Tipton. Lastly, in 1472, on the death of Sir Henry Beaumont, Knt. lord of Wednesbury, and who was buried in Wednesbury Church, a *post-mortem* again shows that lands were held in Tipton as before

Another deed is quoted by Shaw as follows.—

"Roger de Wyrleye [of Hampstead] grants to Henry de Wyrleye, parson, of Sekindon [in Warwickshire]; Thomas de Defford, chaplain; and William de Smythes, chaplain, and their heirs, &c, his manor of Tybynton, with the appurtenances. *Test*, John de Heronvile, John Wilkys, Richard de Darlaston, &c. Dated at Tybynton, 39 Edward III [1366]."

The same writer quotes the following document of the year 1422:—

"Roger de Wirley, of Honnesworth, Esq., grants to Richard Warde and Thomas Penford, *capell.* all his manors of Tybynton and Aston in Colefield, &c., with the reversion of the lands, &c, which Alice Haggeley then held for life by consent of Cornelius Wirley his father in Hondesworth and Tybynton. *Test*, John Hemhull de Tybynton, Thomas Swynfen, John Ruggeley, Cornelius Wirley de Wamer, &c., dated at Tybynton, 1 Hen. VI. Seal of arms, a chevron engrailed between 3 bugle horns, impailing a bend between a rose and fleur-de-lis."

This allusion to the Wyrley coat of arms needs further expansion, which may fittingly be made here.

At the Herald's Visitation of Staffordshire in 1663-4, before referred to, Sir John Wyrley, of Hampstead who had been knighted in 1641 by Charles I., and who was lord of the manor of Tipton, recorded his arms as follows:—

Argent, 3 bugle-horns sable, stringed vert.

Crest, In a ducal coronet or, two wings endorsed argent.

Motto, "A plesance."

But, says straw, "the Wyrleys have not kept constant to any one coat of arms, for some of them have borne—

(1) Argent, 3 horns sable, tipped and chained or."

"I think," says Shaw, writing in 1799, "in this coat should be a chevron engrailed sable, for so it is in Handsworth Church. Another hath borne—

(2) Sable, two lions passant crowned or, and holding in each fore-paw a fleur-de-lis.

This was given them by a friend of theirs, in whose memory they bear it. Another hath borne—

(3) Argent, a chevron gules between 3 horns rampant vert.

These three coats they have severally borne as their paternal coats. They quarter—

(1) Argent, a bend between a rose and a fleur-de-liz, gules [for Aldersey] and

(2) Sable, a fesse between 3 swans [sheldrakes] argent [for Sheldon].

And I have a deed made by Roger Wyrley concerning land at Witton 33 Edward III. (1360) and the seal is—

Six fleur-de-lis, and the crest a wing; which these Wyrleys now use; and because I have seen this coat in the windows of Handsworth Church—

Gules, 6 fleur-de-lis argent, 2, 2, and 2,

I think this may be the ancient coat of Wyrley."—Vol II., p.110

It would appear that the "friend" who gave a coat-of-arms to the Wyrleys was Thomas, son of Sir John Heronville, Knight, 31 or 41 Ed. III, who, by a deed dated at West Bromwich, grants to Roger de Wyrley a coat of arms, which he had by descent after the death of his brother John.

In Handsworth Old Church lie many mortal remains of the Wyrley family and the living, a very valuable rectory, was formerly in the patronage of Wyrley Birch, Esq. The gross annual value is £1,502, and is now held by the present rector, Dr Randall.

(Here it may be mentioned that the Sedgley Parish Registers inform us that a Mrs Ann Wyrley, sister of Sir John Wyrley, of Hampstead, died at Mr. Thomas Jevons, the Hall, and was buried at Sedgley, 17 August, 1675.)

Hints and Hansacre have been frequently mentioned in the earlier portion of this history as intimately associated with Tipton. It would appear that Hansacre remained a part of the Bishop's manor of Longdon; while Hints seems to have gone to the family (previously mentioned) of Meignill, Menill, or Meilnil who were connected by marriage to another family, also previously mentioned—Savage or le Sauvage.

The moat exhaustive account of the "Barons of Dudey" yet published will be found in part 2 of vol. ix of the "Salt Collections." It is written by Mr. Sydney Grazebrook. A few quotations bear upon our history at this period. An inquest taken in the year 1401 showed that the Castle of Dudley had been held by Isabella, wife of John de Sutton II, who had remarried a Sir Richard Dudley, and who had lived to a very advanced age. Among the possessions of the barony enumerated are the manors of Sedgley, Himley, Swinford, &c., and certain lands in Tybington (p 58). A similar inquest in 1406 repeats this (p 63). These are all the extracts referring to Tipton. But a perusal of Mr. Grazebrook's account of the barony will disclose the fact that in nearly every great incident in England's glorious history some baron of Dudley will be found playing a most important part; either on the field of battle, or attending the funeral of his sovereign, or even directing the destinies of the whole kingdom.

CHAPTER XII.—THE MANOR (1509-1562): CHANTRY LANDS IN TIPTON (1535-1551): JOHN DUDLEY, DUKE OF NORTHUMBERLAND.

Two other quotations relating to the whole manor of Tipton may be given from Shaw before alluding to certain detached lands in Tipton which provided a revenue for ecclesiastical purposes in other parishes. The first document is of the year 1509, and runs thus:—

"John Wirley, Esq, grants to John Harpur, Esq.., Cornelius Harpur (rector of Walton), John Hoo (of Bradley), his manor of Tybynton, co Stafford, together with the reversion of all the lands and tenements which Clara Wirley, late wife of Cornelius Wirley, his son and heir apparent, for life, &c. Dated anno 24, Henry VII."

The other statement refers to the year 1562, thus:—

"William Wirley, Esq., died February 24, 4 Elizabeth, seised of Handsworth manor called Wirley's Hall, two water-mills, pool, moor, fishery in the Tame, four cottages, 300 acres of land, 40 acres of meadow, 500 of pasture, 40 of wood, 100 of heath, a moiety of the manors of Perry Barr, Hampstead and Oscote, four water-mills called blade-mills, &c, &c, and likewise the manor of Tibington or Tipton."

A blade-mill was a place for grinding (and making) blades, particularly those of a military character—and a most valuable possession in those times.

Allusion was made in the previous chapter to the greatness of the barons of Dudley. From an early period they had taken more than an ordinary share in the government of the kingdom; and between the year 1440 and the reign of Henry VIII had been uninterruptedly summoned to Parliament. At this later period, John de Sutton was (as Dugdale expresses it) "jostled" out of castle and lands by John, duke of Northumberland. This John, duke of Northumberland, was a remarkable man. He was said to have been the son of one Edmund Dudley and claimed to be of a younger branch of the family of the barons of Dudley. The latter portion of this claim is extremely doubtful; it is almost certain that he was of humble origin, and. it is equally well-known to readers of history that his power and influence in England were paramount during a great part of Edward VI.'s reign, his greatness only crumbling away with the overthrow of his daughter-in-law, Lady Jane Grey. Anyway his unscrupulousness was only equalled by his overbearing ambition. John de Sutton, lord of Dudley having become entangled in the usurers' bonds, John Dudley (then Viscount Lisle and Earl of Warwick but afterwards Duke of Northumberland) thirsting for Dudley Castle, the chief seat of the family, made those money merchants his instruments to turn the poor lord out of his paternal property. At least this is the tradition handed down by Dugdale. But the date of the acquisition of these honours is certainly not correct, For instance, the Patent Rolls of 1539 show that at the dissolution of the monasteries, King Henry VIII, made a grant of the advowson of Wednesbury, among other places, to "Sir John Dudley, knight "This is the same individual who was created Viscount Lisle in 1543. Besides "Sir John" was in possession of Dudley Castle, and had been granted the dissolved priory of Dudley, about the same time that he acquired Wednesbury—three or four years before he became a viscount.

The document relating to the Wednesbury grant of 1539 was translated in the "Wednesbury Parish Magazine," of January, 1890. The translator however, expresses an opinion that Colonel Bagnall was unacquainted with the existence of the said document when in his "History of Wednesbury" he says the "manor" of Wednesbury came into the possession of the Comberford family in 1502, and was purchased from them by one Gilpin, and afterwards sold by this person to John Shelton, of Birmingham. It will be noted, however, that Mr. Bagnall on p. 25, distinctly alludes to its contents, for he there states that the "rectory" of Wednesbury was held by Sir John Dudley in military tenure. The other places conveyed to Sir John in the same deed were Horneburne (Harborne), Smythwyke (Smethwick), Rowley, West Bromwich, &c.

Again the Patent Roll of 1564 contains a grant of certain lands in Tipton which were in the first instance granted, 4 Edward VI, towards the support of a Chantry Priest at the Alter of St. Mary, Wednesbury (see chapter vii for an allusion to this same document of 1551). Probably this side altar in the parish church of St. Bartholomew was situated in the south transept. The guild priest thus endowed at a period as near the advent of the looming Reformation was of a very unenduring kind; for the guild of St. Mary's, Wednesbury, passed finally and completely away when its endowments were by this Patent Roll of 1564 conveyed to two laymen therein mentioned for the sum of £1,050 4s. 8d. The five closes or crofts of pasture in Tipton had been in the occupation of George and Richard Hopkis; and another close in Wednesbury and Tipton in the tenure of one William Dudley. George and Richard Hopkyns (*sic*) paid 31s. 8d, and Dudley paid 16s., which was for the sustenance of "our ladies guilde prest." This document also has been given in full in the same *Wednesbury Parish Magazine* of April, 1890. Describing these Chantry lands in Tipton, the document says "there are no woods growing upon the premises other than bushes and small trees in hedgerows necessary to be reserved for fencing the same." The first chantry priest endowed with these lands was one Richard Janens (clerk), *alias* Janyns, *alias* Jennens, a member of the celebrated Jennens family, of litigious fame, who were connected with Wednesbury for generations. The tombstone of Richard Jennyns and Isabel his wife, dated 1520, was found in the flooring of Wednesbury old church during the recent alterations (1890). A book galled "The Jennen's Estates," published at Sheffield in 1879, gives a history of this great case; and it is curious to observe that the female name "Joyse," which is mentioned in the aforesaid Patent Roll of 1564, seems to be very commonly used throughout the family history. On p. 68 of the same work, an extract from a letter dated "16 May, 1800" is to the effect that the writer's "great grandfather, by my mother's side, was John Jennens, proprietor of Wednesbury Hall, which he sold, as will appear from the writings now in the hands of Lord Viscount Dudley and Ward, the present possessor."

Before leaving this matter it may be first necessary to explain that a Chantry was a chapel founded with the express purpose of ensuring the constant chanting of masses, either for the good estate of the living, or for the repose of the souls of the faithfully departed. And secondly, it must be mentioned that the Dudley estates (forfeited to the crown by the attainder of the Duke of Northumberland) were restored to Edward Lord Dudley, the son of the John de Sutton (known as the Lord Quondam), who had been robbed of them by the "great" Northumberland.

But Tipton lands at this period also assisted in maintaining another guild priest at Walsall According to the Church Valuation (of 1535) part of the lands supporting a Chantry priest at Walsall were situated in "Typpynton." And not a little of the present financial prosperity of Walsall Grammar School may be attributed to the richness of the mines under the said piece of land in Tipton. When the Chantries were suppressed with other "superstitions" at the Reformation, the public conscience had to be appeased by applying the revenues of these religious foundations to something which commanded itself as admirably as "the education of youth in vertue and godliness"; so Queen Mary, in the first year of her reign (1554) and on the execution of John Dudley, Duke of Northumberland (1553), who was lord of the manor of Walsall, granted letters patent for establishing a grammar school in Walsall, devoting the revenues of these chantry guilds, &c., to the purpose. In 1797 an Act of Parliament was obtained for powers to sell certain mines under these lands for the benefit of the said school; and the coal under the land at Tipton was sold in 1800 by the governors of the school for a term of 42 years at £505 per acre, producing altogether the sum of £12,243 1s. 10½d.

CHAPTER XIII.—TIPTON CHANCERY SUITS IN ELIZABETH'S REIGN (1558-1603): TIPTON FAMILIES OF POSITION, AND NAMES OF NOTE DURING THE SIXTEENTH CENTURY.

Certain lands in Tipton, consisting of some 20 acres of pasture, and forming part of a disputed claim in the Court of Common Pleas, had been bequeathed by the will of one Richard Fraunces in the last year of Elizabeth's reign (see "History of Darlaston," p 50). But more important cases connected with Tipton at this period were tried in the Court of Chancery.

Among the chancery proceedings in the reign of Elizabeth, relating to Staffordshire, were the following, thus recorded:—

PLAINTIFF.	DEFENDANT.	OBJECT OF SUIT.	PREMISES
John Bardell	Isabel Jennings and Agnes Heath.	Claim by deed of gift.	Land in Wednesbury, Tebbington, *alias* Tipton, and Breerley, in county of Stafford.
Thomas Cockayne, infant by Elizabeth Cockayne, widow, his guardian.	Goodeth Wirley, widow of John Wirley, deceased.	Bill for injunction and to establish title by lease.	Lands in Tibbington, *alias* Tipton; the inheritance of John Wirley, deceased, and by him demised to plaintiff's father.
John Pershouse.	Thomas Gibbens ans Richard Bradley.	Claim under a settlement.	Land in Tybington, *alias* Tipton, late of the estate of John Pershouse, deceased, and settled by him *temp.* Henry VIII. to divers uses.
Hugh Nightingale.	Richard Tole.	To protect plaintiff's title by purchase.	Land in Tybbington, *alias* Typton, purchased by plaintiff of Edward Nightin-gale.
Thomas Smith.	George Lee.	To set aside a leaase.	A tenement and ground at Typton, held of Andrew Wallys, in consideration of £10, money lent.
Erasmus Wollseley, Esq., A. 1579.	Humphrey Wynot, *alais* Wynce.	Claim as heir.	A messuage and lands in Tipton, *alias* Tibbington, some time the estate of John Wollseley, Esq, the plaintiff's grandfather, and afterwards of Anthony Wollseley, Esq., the plaintiff's father.

There was a certain William Cockayne, who was defendant in another Chancery suit by William Comberford (23 Elizabeth), to recover rent due under lease of certain land, "parcel of the manor of Wednesborough, or Wednesbury, granted by Thomas Cumberford, Esq, the plaintiff's late father, and Dorothy, his wife, to Thomas Comberford, and which afterwards vested in the defendant," Cookayne.

William Comberford was plaintiff in four other Chancery suits: (1) Against Richard and Thomas Sheldon, in a claim by purchase of the Manor of Wednesbury, formerly the estate of John Beaumont, Esq., and purchased by said plaintiff of his descendants, (2) against Elizabeth Nicholas and others, in a famous suit to ascertain the right of tenants to dig coal for their own use in the manor and lordship of Wednesbury; (3) against William and Thomas Jennings, for deeds to support a title of purchase of a messuage called New Hall Place and lands in Wednesbury, sold by the defendant

William to the plaintiff; and (4) against Richard Jennings and Isabel, his wife, in a claim by lease of a messuage and land in Wednesbury demised to plaintiff by John Jennings, the owner of the inheritance.

With regard to the surname Nightingale, we have already observed that it belonged to a family of some importance in Tipton; while the defendant Tole may have belonged to a family which gave us the placename Toll End, although this locality may have derived its name from the toll-gate which in later times was situated there.

Other Tipton families, who held some position during the second half of the sixteenth century, may be traced by the probate of their wills, &c.

Amongst the wills and administrations registered in the Consistory Court of the Bishop at Lichfield are the following:—

A.D. 1559, William Hallum, of Horsley.
1557, Nicholas Johnson, of Horsley.
1558, Henry Johnson, of Horsley (an administration)
1559, Henry Johnson, of Horsley.
1543, Henry Kay, of Horsley (an administration).

The name of the Wyrley family has been mentioned very many times previously in this history, but its recurrence has been chiefly through the fact of the prolonged lordship,which this family held over the manor of Tipton. There was one member of the family at this period, however, whose claim for notice stands much higher than that gained by mere territorial possessions. This was one William Wyrley, who was amanuensis to the county historian, Samson Erdeswick, about 1590. He was a son of Augustus Wyrley of Leicestershire, and a grandson of William Wyrley of Handsworth. His *MS. Church Notes*, probably written during his connection with Erdeswick, gave much valuable and reliable information. He is mentioned by Shaw (vol. II, p. 111) and in Wood's *Athenœ Oxoniensis* (vol. I, p. 363).

No doubt towns and localities have often given their names to individuals born in them: the surnames of Darlaston and Wedgebury are perhaps instances of such an origin. In the same way Tipton may have given her name to some of her sons. If so, a native of Tipton some three centuries ago occupied a very prominent position "Master John Tipton" was the first Englishman to become consul anywhere, and he was Consul at Algiers, first appointed by the newly-formed Turkey Company about the year 1580, and in 1585 officially named Consul of.the English nation by Mr Harebone, our ambassador at the Sublime Porte. However, it is only right to add that if this man did derive his name from the place of his origin it is more than probable he came from a stock native to the Tipton near Ottary St. Mary, rather than to an inland village such as Tipton in Staffordshire. Besides, his adventures savour very strongly of Devonshire—the pride of naval England in Elizabeth's glorious days!

CHAPTER XIV.—THE DESCENT OF THE MANOR OF TIPTON.

Here, perhaps, the whole history of the tenure of the manor of Tipton may be profitably reviewed, from the time of its earliest possessors to the present day. There is no need to go exhaustively over the earlier portion of that history, beyond quoting from a topographical survey made in the year 1730, entitled *Magna Britannia et Hibernia*, and which contains the following quaint entry in Vol V., pp 47 and 48:—

"Tibbington, or Tipton, which at the Conquest was held by one William of the Bishop of Litchfield, and not long after by another William who galled himself William Fitz-Warin; but he became Lord of it in Right of his Wife Lucia Savage, and had by her Sir Jeffrey Fitz-Warren, Kt., whose son John inherited it, but this Family possessed it no longer for in the Reign of K Henry II Robert Wirely *alias* Wyrely was Lord thereof, in whose posterity it continu'd to the Beginning of the last century, if it doth not still."

Proceeding once more with the detail of our history we may quote again from Shaw—

"In the account we have given of the Wyrley family under their ancient seat at Hamstead, are several of their grants of this manor (of Tipton), it being likewise mentioned in the inquisitions there introduced; in addition to which are the following particulars—

John Wirley, Esq. died March 24, 3 Henry VIII. (1512), and William Wirley, son of Cornelius the son of the aforesaid John, was his heir, (*œt.* 12) seised of one messuage, 135 acres of land, &c, 30s. 10d. in Tibington, held of John Wolseley, Esq, by fealty, and 8s. rent. And by another inquisition it appears that William Wirley, Esq., died February 24, 4 Elizabeth (1562) and Thomas Wirley was his son end heir (*œt.* 42) seised, *inter alia* of the manor of Tibington *alias* Tipton, one messuage, two cottages, 200 acres of land, 100 of meadow, 500 of pasture, 60 of wood, and 100 of heath, &c, and 40s. rent, held of the lord Paget, as of his barony or manor of Longdon, by unknown services, and valued at £20."

In this extract from Shaw we first note that Lord Paget is now found in possession of the free barony of Longdon, of which Tipton, together with some 30 other manors and townships, formed a part. Hitherto the barony had been held by the bishops of Lichfield, even from the time of the Saxons. It would appear that in 1546 the bishop had surrendered the manors of Longdon and Hayward, with all their appurtenances (including the manor of Tipton) to King Henry VIII. for an annuity of £183; and in the same year his Majesty granted them to William, Lord Paget. This nobleman, so high a favourite of that dread monarch as to be appointed an executor to his royal will, and a member of the Council to his successor, Edward VI., was a most talented man of but mean origin, his father having been a man of humble circumstances in Wednesbury, and who went to London, secured a post as serjeant-at-mace to the City Council, and managed to educate his son so excellently well as to fit him to shine prominently as one of the very ablest statesmen in three different reigns. This Paget is the ancestor of the family of the present Marquis of Anglesey, who still hold the barony of Longdon, and by whom the manor of Tipton is still "let" to the present mesne lords, the Wyrley Birch family.

The reader will observe in the same extract that beyond 100 acres of meadow land, there is an area of no less than 500 acres devoted to pasture. In this, Tipton but followed the prevailing current of commerce and custom in those days, when feudal power was every day decreasing and the power of wealth increasing. Tenants and labourers were no longer needed by landowners to make a retinue of retainers; and it paid.better to feed sheep than to plough the land. To this day the "woolsack" remains an emblem of those Tudor times, when the trade in wool was the most lucrative in all commercial England.

The next link in the chain of the succession of the manor is also taken from Shaw, who says:—

"Likewise John Wirley, Esq, died February 10, 39 Elizabeth (1597) and Humphry was his son and heir (*œt* 21), seised of this manor, &c., and held as before."

Another family, into which that of Wyrley ultimately merged, may have its history traced from this period.

Thomas Birch, Esq., of Birchfield, in the parish of Handsworth, Co. Stafford, and of Birch Green and Aston, Co. Warwick, was living at Birchfield, 7 Elizabeth (1565), and was buried at Aston, 1613. His son and heir, Thomas Birch, Esq., of Harborne, was father of George Birch, of Harborne Hall, born 1616, whose son George Birch married Mary, daughter of Thomas Foster, and dying 1721, left issue, among whom were,

(1) Sir Thomas Birch, his heir

(2) John Birch, rector of Handsworth (died without issue)

This Sir Thomas Birch, Knt, the eldest son, born 1690, was a Judge of the Common Pleas. He died in 1757, and left, with other issue, an eldest son, George, through whose marriage with an heiress of the house of Wyrley, we now find Tipton in the possession of the Birch family. This George Birch, of Hamstead Hall and Handsworth, was born in 1739 and married Anne, third daughter of Thomas Lane, Esq, of Bentley Hall and a grand-daughter of John Lane by Mary his wife, who was the eldest daughter of Humphrey Wyrley, Esq., and a co-heir with her sister,

Sybill (married to Rev Peter Birch D.D., a Prebendary of Westminster). By her (who died February, 1806) George Birch left at his decease in February, 1807, besides three daughters,

Wyrley Birch, of Wretham Hall, Norfolk, born 1781 and died 24th December, 1866, was succeeded by his grandson Wyrley Birch, whose son, Wyrley Edwin Birch, was born 12th November, 1867, and who is the present lord of the manor of Tipton.

The family residence is Wretham Hall, near Thetford.
Arms: Azure, three fleur-de-lis, and a canton argent
Crest: A 'fleur-de-lis, argent, entwined by a serpent proper.
Motto: Prudentia simplicitate.

The family of Birch, of Armitage Staffordshire, as well as this Birch family of Hamstead, are also descended from Birch, of Birch, Lancashire.

It may by added that in 1728 Humphrey Wyrley Birch, son of the Rev. Dr. Birch, of Hamstead, petitioned Parliament that he might bear and use the surname and arms of the Wyrleys, a petition agreed to by private Act.

Two other facts in the history of these families may be given here: one will show the patriotism of the Birches and the other will perhaps disclose the political leanings of the Wyrleys. (1) In 1588 John Birch contributed £25 to the Spanish Armada Defence Fund. (2) During the period of the Commonwealth, when the Puritans became dominant parish registers were frequently neglected or very irregularly kept, and at West Bromwich Church several marriage entries may be found signed by Sir John Wyrley of Hamstead, by the Mayor of Walsall (1655), and by Henry Stone, the Parliamentary leader of that ancient borough.

The Wyrley arms were formerly to be found in the windows of West Bromwich Old Church.

CHAPTER XV.—EXTENT OF THE MANOR, AND RECENT LANDOWNERS IN TIPTON.

Although Tipton parish never contained but one manor, it does not necessarily follow that the area of that lordship was always equal to that of the ecclesiastical (and civil) parish. The manor, dating from Saxon times would doubtless include all that is now known as the parish of Tipton, excepting always those parts we have described as unoccupied "wastes". The parish, as an ecclesiastical and civil area of administration, would be formed at a later period, in fact, when a sufficient population had crystallised on some portion of the manor to justify the erection of a church fabric and to call for the ministrations of a parish priest. At that period, perhaps, the boundaries of the lordship and those of the parish would be co-terminous. From that time forward, if indeed not from some anterior period, the dimensions of the manor would have a tendency to contract while those of the parish (once settled definitely) would remain constant. In addition to the gradual absorption—by occupation —of the said wastes, there would always be a process of multiplication of land-holders going on. A few freeholders would grow into existence by sheer appropriation of waste-land, and sometimes by a daring encroachment upon the manorial domain. This latter method of acquiring land in a cheap and easy form is not altogether unknown in Tipton, or throughout England, to the present day. Then there would be the more sure but gradual creation of freeholders by the enfranchisement of the lord's copyholders.

The large amount of waste or unoccupied lands in Tipton we have already noted in the opening chapters of this history. The sparseness of the population may be further inferred from the fact that in the sub-infeudation of the great barony of Longdon, Tipton manor was included with other manors (Hintes and Hansacre) in the same grant. And yet the word "manor" is derived from the Latin *manere*, "to remain," because it became the usual residence of the holder, who occupied it, or as much of it as was necessary to support him and his own immediate family, while he granted or leased the remainder to tenants for stipulated rents or services—and it was thus that were originated "copyhold" estates, that is, those held by the "copy" of the roll of the court of the manor. Now as to the extent of the manor of Tipton. First we find Shaw, writing in 1798, says:— "From an old survey of the lordship of Tipton, belonging to Humphry Wyrley, Esq., 1690, it then contained as follows:—

	A.	R.	P.
The Moat Farm (with an old moated house, where the lords of the manor antiently lived perhaps) which contained	112	1	22
This is situated eastward of the church, and near the road to Wolverhampton			
And next beyond it, Mr. Jeaven's farm containing	125	0	29
South-west of the church is Samuel White's farm	62	3	33
And adjoining to it John Goodridge's farm	43	2	7
At the extremity, north-east Richard Fullward's farm	24	0	29
Tipton Green, north-west	18	2	29
And other lands	12	2	24
And from an elegant plan and terrier surveyed and drawn by James Sheriff, of Birmingham, 1789, for the present lord of the manor, George Birch, Esq. The above farms are seven in number.			
Tipton Green, cottages, &c	32	1	27
Roads and waste land	79	2	0
The mine under Tipton Green, &c, purchased by Mr. Richmond Aston	14	2	20
Total belonging to the lord of the manor	509	0	20

The whole parish and manor contains 2,160 acres, the circumference of which is 9 miles and 220 yards." To attempt to identify these farms, after the lapse of two centuries, would be a task somewhat too risky for anyone, however intimately acquainted with the parish he may be. Place-names and field-names not unfrequently change: and this is particularly the case where a parish, like Tipton, has long since abandoned every claim to be considered a pastoral and agricultural district, as it then was 200 years ago. In fact, no parish in the kingdom, perhaps, has undergone such an absolute change in this period as Tipton has. Not only has its landscape been defaced superficially but its surface has actually suffered vertically as well—mining operations, as conducted in the Black Country, always giving to a place the pleasing variety of gently undulating scenery; depressions locally known as "swags" or "crownings-in" always alternating with clunch-heaps and spoil banks in endless succession.

Bearing this in mind, and the further disadvantage of the parochial area being cut up by numberless canals, and Intersected by several railway lines, an endeavour shall be made to locate some of these old farms, however unsuccessful the attempt may be.

The "Moat Farm," of course, is readily identified with the site of the "Moat Colliery." It will be observed that Shaw says "perhaps" the lords of the manor dwelt there in ancient times; there is, indeed, a grave doubt on the point. The "road to Wolverhampton" was the ancient road from Ocker Hill running round by the site of the present Ocker Hill Church, as it did before the New Road was cut towards Gospel Oak through the glebe lands, including Lower Wood.

The "farm next beyond" probably occupied the site of what is now known as Lea Brook and The Coppice; the present "Doe Bank Cottage," now an inn, was perhaps the homestead. It is an old house, but seems to have been altered from time to time. Almost within living memory The Coppice was what its name literally indicates, and Lea Brook was then a clear purling stream. The acreage of this farm pretty well coincides with the size of a mining area, a 99 years' lease of which is just expiring, and which during a goodly portion of that time has been connected with the Haines family, as in the firm of Haines and Underhill, and in other partnerships. In the said lease are various out-of-date covenants, not the least antiquated of which was a provision that the surface should not be sown too frequently with flax—presumably that the soil should not be impoverished by a succession of such exhausting crops. One part of this area is still known as "Flax Leasur" and the name with its surrounding associations, carries the mind back to those olden times when Tipton, like the rest of "merrie England," was chiefly agricultural in its industrial pursuits; when flax was very extensively grown; when a spinning-wheel was to be found in every cottage and a weaver in every town; and when a marriageable girl was literally as well as nominally "a spinster," preparing her household linen with her own fingers. Those were the days when linen—not calico—was really used for household stuff; stored up in great oak chests and capacious presses, bed-linen that on winter nights needed the application of that good old-fashioned utensil, the warming-pan—now seldom seen in our households because the warmer texture of calico sheeting has made it obsolete, although housewives in Tipton, or Dudley, or Wednesbury would never at that time have considered their houses furnished without one.

"White's Farm" was perhaps what has since been known as Tibbington Farm; and "Goodridge's Farm" may perhaps have been what is called Comball's Farm —an area held by the Dudley family in succession to the Jeavons' Family.

Coming to the portion of the table made out in 1789, we note that by this period "cottages" had begun to locate themselves round Tipton Green—that part of the parish which claims still to be the centre of the township, although the outlying portions at the present day are equally urban in their character, and perhaps quite as densely populated.

The Mr Richmond Aston, mentioned in the last item as a Tipton landowner, died at Bescot Hall, having purchased the Bescot estate about 1794 for £4,000. He commenced some extensive alterations at the Hall which, on his death, were completed by his widow; but the estate soon after passed into the hands of Mr. James Russell, of Wednesbury.

The total area of the manorial estate, it will be noted, comprised at that period about 500 acres: an area that has since considerably shrunk, from the various causes just enumerated.

The acreage of Tipton at the date of the Tithe Commutation Award (about 1849-50) was given as 2,095 acres distributed as follows:—

	Acres.
Arable	590
Meadow	490
Canals	112
Roads and spoil-bank	903
	2095

A list of the principal landowners in Tipton in 1849 is given as follows:—

Aston and Rowley (repres of Richmond Aston	20	0	4
Bagnall and Sons	12	3	21
Barrows and Hall	7	2	7
Bate and Robins	6	1	11
Wryley Birch (lord of the manor)	310	0	11
Birmingham Canal Company	114	0	24
L and N.-W. Railway Company	21	3	2
Roberts and Everhardt (late Foley and Whitby, lords of Wednesbury manor)	81	2	11
Collis and Wills	9	0	2
Edward Dixon	26	0	38
Dixon, Amphlett, and Bedford	308	0	0
Thomas W. Fletcher (of Lawneswood)	35	1	7
Frederick Giles	43	0	3
Hopkins and Son	18	3	21
Jonathan Howl	46	2	20
William Jones	40	0	35
Lichfield Dean and Chapter	24	2	27
Thomas Morris	50	0	7
George Parker	23	2	17

Price's Exors.	5	1	10
J. J. Russell and J. Best (bought by Solly later)	25	3	25
Sydney Sussex College Cambridge	6	0	1
South Stafford Railway Company	33	0	0
Sir Horace St Paul	195	0	0
Tipton Moat Colliery Company	18	0	0
Lord Ward (now Earl of Dudley)	174	0	0
J. and E. Walker (now Grazebrook and Aston)	59	1	10
James Whitehouse	35	0	0
Philip Williams and Sons	31	0	0
Sites of churches and churchyards	6	3	6

The remainder of the parish was held by small owners.

CHAPTER XVI.—THE MANORIAL COURT AND TENURES: THE MANOR FARM: THE TENANTS IN CAPITE.

An old directory for the year 1831 says of Tipton that "Officers for the internal regulation of the parish are annually appointed at the Court Leet of the lord of the manor." It is said that this court was towards the last held at the Scott Arms Hotel, Great Barr and that the last inhabitant to be annually elected constable was Mr. Whitehouse, father of Mr. William Whitehouse, Star Hotel, Bloomfield. These courts have lapsed many years.

No copyholders now remaining in Tipton, of course there is no Court Leet held; nor is there any freeholders' Court Baron.

At the present time the agent to the Lord of the Manor holds some semblance of the ancient manorial court, about every two years, at the Black Cook Inn, Owen Street, but no officers are appointed, no surrenders are made, nor any manorial custom observed. It would appear that there are some 20 or 30 occupiers of small tenements on the waste lands of the ancient manor, who pay a small and quite nominal acknowledgement of a few shillings per year for their "encroachments", but these holdings are strictly regarded as yearly tenancies by the Lord of the Manor, who receives such rents as absolute owner, and not under any manorial custom. In fact the tenure of these "cottagers" in Tipton would seem to be a pure tenancy at will, and, therefore, possibly possess a less degree of fixity than the tenure of the "base copyholders," under Lord Dudley on the neighbouring manor of Sedgley, which is a tenure terminable at certain fixed periods without right of descent to heirs and successors.

The Lord of the Manor still holds about 300 acres in the parish, of which only five acres remain in his own hands; this is the "Ash Lesur" or old

"Wake Ground," for which his Tipton representatives (Messrs Powell and Brown) collect the rents. The remainder is let on lease, chiefly for mining purposes; and one of the terms of the covenant always sets forth that the Lord of the Manor, not knowing the custom of his ancestors, removes all responsibility for damage done to the surface by such operations, from his own shoulders to those of the lessee of the mines and minerals.

The parish stocks, which the Lord of the Manor was compelled to provide, stood till some 70 years ago in Church Lane, opposite St Martin's Church.

The Pound or Pinfold, now in ruins and long since obsolete—Tipton having nothing left in the shape of pasture – stands at the junction of the roads at Toll End, where the traveller from Tipton turns to the right hand for Birmingham and the south, or to the left hand for Wolverhampton and the north.

The Moat House has been claimed as the manor house of Tipton. The moat now runs round but three sides and is fed by a spring on the old roadside. The fourth side, spanned by a bridge, formerly ran between the house and the outbuildings, of which the original barn is the most interesting feature, being timber-framed, and consisting of six bays, divided by strongly framed wooden principals, with massive tie and collar beams and roof timbers. The present house dates only from the last century. The only feature in it worth remarking is the structure of the fireplaces, all the flues being clustered into one central chimney stack, and the kitchen hearth possessing an ingle nook.

That this is the site of a manor or dower house is quite probable, and the fact of its enclosure by a moat would carry its existence back to the fifteenth-century at least. But, as we have seen, the lords of the manor of Tipton have nearly always been non-resident. He was, however, an occasional visitor, as we have also noted; and if his estate had been very extensive, during his absence he would have been represented by a Steward or Seneschal, who would hold the manorial courts on behalf of his lord. In fact, his duties would be more legal than economic in their character.

Let us glance at the whole system of estate management, as practised from the 13th to 15th centuries.

If the lord of Tipton manor resided at Hansacre or at Hamstead, at that place would be situated his chief home farm, or domain land. Tipton itself would have been Bailiff farmed. The Bailiff would be a practical farmer, responsible for the detailed working of the manor, seeing that every labourer paid his proper service. Then the next official was the Provost (*prepositus*), a foreman elected and presented by the township or manor as the best approver among the villans, and who was responsible for them. Another foreman, called the Hayward (*messor*) superintended the work and saw that each man's supply of seed was duly forthcoming.

The Home Farm in Tipton was no doubt the Moat Farm. On this farm the villans of the manor would have to work so many days each week, according to the season of the year, and would discharge certain occasional duties as well. In return they would each have a small holding to cultivate on their own account on the other days. These villans' virgates are sometimes called "servile lands" because of this obligation, and if a freeman ever acquired one of these tenures he had to discharge his obligations on the domain lands—generally by payment of money. The villan was not paid wages for his work on the domain land, but had his meals on the working days, and his holding, aforesaid, of about 30 acres (*virgata*) was stocked with a yoke of oxen and six sheep when he first entered on his tenancy. (Horses cost too much to keep, especially in winter).

The value of a manor depended entirely upon the number of villans, or labourers, upon it. After a war or a plague, or if villans deserted an estate, its value declined immensely. To retain the labourers and make their progeny liable to the same services was the chief aim of the lord of the manor. Therefore villans were hindered in putting their children to school, or getting them ordained, or apprenticed to freemen in any town. Then the villans were made responsible as a whole for the work to be done on the domain farm, and by this stress of communal obligation, the others had to make good the deficiency of any one of their numbers.

As time went on these villans' obligations had to be commuted for cash, and gradually villans purchased their own freedom. The Bailiff and his Hayward at Tipton would find it less trouble to collect the payments than to superintend the man's work throughout the year, and there was decidedly less difficulty about the quality of the coin than about the diligence of the service—for much fraud was practised by "customary servants neglecting their work." For although, in these pre-Reformation days, there were no less than "eight weeks for holy days and other hindrances "allowed in each year, the labourer on "custom work" often defrauded his lord, not only in time service, but more frequently by scantiness of measurement in his labour – as, for instance, narrowing the ridge of his plough work. In fact, it was found more profitable at last to hire labourers for wages, and to allow villans to buy themselves off from their obligation by paying a *quit-rent*.

There were no root crops and no artificial grasses and the field system was a fallow every other year, or every third year. The villans had always to provide the seed. When their own wants were satisfied, and the supplies had been sent in for the lord and his household, a very small proportion of the produce was available for sale. Trade was almost an unknown quantity. There was a scarcity of the circulating medium (a silver coinage) and roads were bad, even for the transport of produce between two such near points as Tipton and Handsworth—a highway little better than a quagmire in the wet season, and whose tediously circuitous route lay all round West Bromwich old church. The annual fairs or wakes were then the only opportunities for general trading.

Such was the condition of agricultural Tipton in the 13th century. At the present time it is interesting to note that the Moat Farm is, after an interval of a mining era, reverting to agriculture, under the management of Mr. Cliff, who occupies the Moat House and is farming some of the fields adjacent thereto.

* * * * * *

The confusion previously noted (Chapter III.) as arising from the Bishop of Lichfield, and sometimes the Bishop of Chester, being indifferently named at various times as *tenants in capite* of Tipton, is no doubt due to the fact that the see of Lichfield was moved in 1075 to Chester, by Peter, the first Norman bishop; and was removed in 1102 to Coventry.

In Chapter XIV. it was recorded that the Wyrleys held Tipton under the Pagets by "unknown services"; and just previous to the acquisition by the last-named family (in 1546) of the free barony of Longdon, in which Tipton manor is included, the Wyrley family had, in 1512, held this manor under John Wolseley, Esq, "by fealty"—that is, by the mere oath of fealty, he held it in the freest manner.

* * * * * *

CORRECTIONS AND ADDITIONS TO CHAPTER XVI.

The reservation clause as to mines applies only to the cottage properties, or encroachments, sold by the lord of the manor, and not to the portions of the estate leased as collieries. In all cases it is usual for colliery proprietors, and those working mines, to assume responsibility for damage done to the surface by such working; and the owner of the estate, or lessor, is never accountable.

When the lord of the manor of Tipton sells to cottagers, some such clause as this is generally inserted in the deed (as when Wyrley Birch, of Wretham Hall, Norfolk, Esquire, lord of the manor of Tipton, was living in 1860):—

"Whereas the said Wyrley Birch is seized of, or well entitled to, the manor of Tipton aforesaid, in fee simple, and his wife is excluded from dower thereout by Ante-Nuptial Settlement, and he hath agreed [with the purchaser] for the sale to him of all such estate and interest as he, the said Wyrley Birch. has as lord of the said manor and otherwise, of and in the piece of land hereinafter described." * * * * "The said Wyrley Birch, by way of conveyance only and not of warranty and covenanty," conveys all the piece of land, &c, "which said piece of land was heretofore part of the waste, or reputed waste, of the said manor of Tipton, and was some years since enclosed, and has since been treated and considered as the freehold inheritance of the lord of the said manor" * * * "together with all ways &c ," * * * "save and except any mines or minerals under the said land and hereditaments which may have been granted or sold to any person or persons by the said Wyrley Birch, or any of his ancestors or other persons under whom the said Wyrley Birch claims title."

And as this reservation does not reserve any power to work the minerals, the purchaser can recover damages for any injury done to the surface or erections thereon.

Sometimes the Court Leet for Tipton was held at Lichfield, and amongst others the Town Crier was always in attendance there.

The remnants of the parish stocks—to which a whipping-post was attached—were in existence even 30 years ago.

CHAPTER XVII.—The Heronville Interest in Tipton: The Whorwood Family: the Dudleys of Tipton

The interest which the Heronvilles of Wednesbury acquired in the Manor of Tipton arose, in the first instance, from a marriage of Alienora, a sister and co-heir of William Fitzwarren, with Sir John de Heronville, Knt, who died in 1315, when his son Henry de Heronville, was 50 years of age. In the family dispute which afterwards arose respecting the dower of Alice, widow of William Fitzwarren, the orthography of the proper names of the disputants may lead to confusion, unless we note that Isabella is equivalent to Isolda, de Blome to le Blomere, Lucy to Letitia, and de Pret to de Prewes. (See also "Magna Britannia," vol. v., p. 25.)

* * * * * *

Other ancient families have from time to time had considerable interest in Tipton.

The Whorwood family were the possessors of the Sandwell property after the dissolution of the monasteries, and before it passed into the hands of the present possessors, the family of Lord Dartmouth. Had this daring act of robbery and spoilation (the suppression of the religious houses) been committed by a political party or a religious sect, who can say what might not have happened in the shape of rebellion, civil wars, or religious strife? But, being the act of one man – a haughty, overbearing, and absolute monarch – nothing so dreadful followed the arbitrary closing of these religious establishments. In the case of Sandwell Priory the consciences of both giver and receiver may have been eased by the high clerical position of the primary recipient; for Henry VIII gave it to Cardinal Wolsey. It was soon after granted to Whorwood, of Compton and Stourton Castle; Robert Whorwood came to reside on the estate, and built a chapel to West Bromwich Church (now used as a vestry), and the vaults under which formed the family mortuary.

In 1526 Sandwell Monastery had held considerable lands at Tybenton, Dudley, Wednesbury, &c., and a watermill in West Bromwich. This mill, mentioned in Chap. viii., stood in Sheepwash Lane, on the parish boundaries, it was a wire and nail-rod mill about a century ago. In 1590 died Robert Whorwood, Esq., seised of the Manor of Sandwell, with its appurtenances, late a part of the possessions of the monastery, including the mill aforesaid, and the lands in Tipton, Barr, Handsworth, &c., held in capite by knight's service and the hundredth part of a knight's fee. His son, William Whorewood, was knighted and died 1614, seised of the same lands and the Fryer's Park, containing 400 acres of land, in West Bromwich.

The will of William Whorwood, of Tipton, who died July, 1614, is at Somerset House. In this he mentions his sons William and Gerard, and his wife Elizabeth and his daughter Elizabeth. He bequeaths his portion of the rectory of Tipton to his family. He mentions Sir Thomas Whorwood.

Arms of Whorwood:—Argent, a chevron between three stags' heads caboshed, sable.

Among the possessions to which the Whorwood family succeeded was one of more importance to this history than even the considerable landed estate they acquired in Tipton – they became the possessors of the living of Tipton.

Sir William Whorwood (1617) was also "seized in fee of the rectory of West Bromwich and the tithes thereof." A charity left by him to that parish was till the year 1816, distributed annually at Sandwell Hall.

There seems to have been a branch of this family connected more intimately with Tipton. Thus we have It on record—

"21 April, 1612 – Mr. William Whorwood, of Tipton, did seale and deliver to Rychard Jesson, of Brierley, a release and surrender of one closse &c. medowe in Brierly, called Birchin Crofte, and presently after Richard Jesson and his sonne Henry sealed and delivered a lease and an obligacion to John Hawkes, of the same meadow for sixteen years, which were executed upon the said meadows in the presence of William Whorwood, gent Richard Hopkyns stranger, William Fellowe, and me Symon Ryder and Richard Jesson." The place here called "Brierley" is evidently Brereley, a part of Sedgley parish bordering on Tipton.

To quote again from the same quaint old record still preserved (see Appendix to Willetts' "History of West Bromwich"), we have amongst many others equally interesting, the following entries:—

"Richard Sheldon, of Wednesbury, died the 9th day of September, 1613.

"Sir William Whorwood, Knight, died the first daia of July, about 6 of the clocke in the morning, Anno Domini 1614, att London, and was buried at West Bromwich.

"William Whorwood, of Tipton, died 4th day of Julye, 1614, about 7 of the clocke at night, and was buried the 5th daia of July at Tipton."

This William "of Tipton" was the second son of the former William, who was succeeded by his eldest son, Sir Thomas.

* * * * * *

Erdeswick, in his survey of this county (1590), says "In Sedgley is a large goodly park of the Lord Dudleys; and in the same lordship is the ancient seat of a gentleman that beareth the surname of Dudley, who (as I take it) descends paternally from the Someries, Lords of Dudley, for he beareth—A chevron between 3 lions heads erased, gold."

On this, Shaw remarks—

"The Dudleys of Tipton had (as shown) a house on the borders of Tipton parish adjoining to Sedgley which was taken down, and the middle part of the present house built of the materials; so that Erdeswick might easily suppose it to be in the same lordship."

And again—

"In an old visitation book of this county it appears that about the time of Edward IV. or Henry VII., Thomas Dudley, of Tybington, married Joan, daughter and co-heir of John Wells, *alias* Clarke of Tybington."

These Dudleys of Tipton were certainly of the same stock as those of Sedgley. They held an important position in the pariah for a long period. During the Civil War they lent money to the Parliament, and one received a commission in the army from Cromwell himself. In 1646 Henry Dudlye was an overseer of the poor of the parish of Tipton—an overseer in those days was a most important official, combining all the authority and performing all the functions of a modem Board of Guardians. Edward Dudley left by will (1652) £100 for the poor of the parishes of Tipton, Sedgley, Bilston, and Wednesbury—20s. to each parish annually.

This Edward Dudley is described as "of the Green House, Tipton, gentleman," He married Isabella Shilton, daughter of Richard Shilton or Sheldon, of Wednesbury Hall; Their son, Thomas Dudley, also described as "gentleman, of Tipton," is so mentioned in the Freeholders Book, or Voting List, for the county, in 1653.

Shaw says that the mansion called the Green House, in Tipton (the remains of which, shaded by a small grove of trees, then existed [in 1800]), formerly belonged to the ancestors of the present Thomas Dudley of Shutt End, Esq., and his brother, the Rev John Dudley, rector of Himley. This mansion was on the borders of Tipton parish adjoining to Sedgley—hence the error that "it was in the same lordship." "It was taken down," continues Shaw, "and the middle part of the present house built of the materials."

Mr Grazebrook has printed the following pedigree of 1583:—

Thomas Dudley, of Tipton =

Cornelius, of Tipton = Ann, dau. of - - Hoo.

Thomas Dudley of Tipton. = Elizabeth, dau of Edward Swinnerton. — Richard.

Edward Dudley of Tipton. = Elizabeth, dau. of Richard Sheldon of Rowley.

Thomas Dudley of Tipton. = Katherine, dau. of Edward, Lord Dudley.

Edward Dudley, of (*sic.*) sone and heir app.

He says, in reference to the foregoing tree—

John Dudley, of Tibinton, otherwise Tipton, married before 14 Hen. VI., 1435, Margery, daughter of —. Turnpenny and Katherine his wife, by whom he was father of a son, Thomas Dudley, of Tipton, on whom, and Joan his wife, and the heirs of their bodies, the lands called Barnfield within Tibbington were settled in 9 Ed. IV, 1469. This Joan was the elder of the two daughters, and co heirs of John Welles, alias Clarke, of Tipton, and by her Thomas Dudley had issue, a daughter Margaret, married to John Phillips of Birmingham, and a son Cornelius, or Cornes Dudley, of Tipton, who died before 29 Hen. VIII., 1537-8. With Edmund Ringley he was petty collector of the subsidy for Tipton in 15 Hen. VIII., 1523 and married (Harl. MS. 6128) Anne Hoo, sister probably of John Hoo, of Bradley, living 16 Hen, VIII. (Vis. Staff 1614) and by her he is stated in the Harl MS. 6128 to have had two sons, Thomas and Richard the former of whom married Elizabeth, daughter of Edward Swinnerton, and had issue Edward.

Probably (among other inaccuracies) a generation was omitted from the pedigree quoted, and it is surmised that Thomas D., who married Elizabeth Swinnerton, was the son of Thomas and Agnes, and the father of Edward.

This Edward (really the eldest of five sons), was of the Green House in the parish of Tipton, gent. On 16 November. 1620, he was summoned to appear at Lambeth to answer before the Commissioners on Causes Ecclesiastical. According to Shaw, and a pedigree compiled by Mr. Beltz, Lancaster Herald for the Rev. Ed. Dudley in 1827, he married "Isabella, dau. of —, Shelton, Esq., of Wednesbury Hall." But, says Mr. Grazebrook "he really married at Wednesbury 23 November 1591. Elizabeth, daughter of Richard Sheldon, of Wednesbury, yeoman, in whose will, dated 1 Dec., 1610, and proved at Lichfield, 25 Nov., 1613, she is referred to as having a son Thomas Dudley."

This Richard Sheldon was buried at Wednesbury, 10 September, 1613, and his wife Isabel 26 May, 1607. Edward Dudley was a man of some importance. He was fined £14 for not taking the order of knighthood at the coronation of Charles I, He lived to an advanced age, and was buried at Tipton, 2 March 1653-4, his wife, Elizabeth, was buried at Wednesbury, 9 October, 1592, having died (apparently) in child-birth, their only child, Thomas, being baptised at Tipton 3 September, 1592. His will is a very lengthy document, and but few extracts can be given here.

(1) He directs his body to be "buryed in the chancell of the parish (church) of Typton."

(2) To his "sonne" Thomas he leaves "one chayre, a musterde milne, a buffet stoole, the bedstead in the soller over the buttry, with the head and feaster thereto belonginge, the iron-bound coffer, the longe forme in the hall house, the undermost table and frame standinge near the parlour doore in the hall house; all which last-mentioned goods and chattells, cheefes, and heirlooms which I had of my mother at her decease."

(3) After legacies to the various members of his family, he leaves to his "brother Henry Dudley and Margarett, his wife, all that tenement wherein now he dwelleth, called Greet Bridge Meadowe."

(4) To Edward, son of the above Henry, he leaves "my bald nagge, and the pack saddle, dashells and gyrths," similar pieces of furniture to those before enumerated, and also "ye second fire shovell and tongs, and my lesser chest."

(5) After more legacies he does "will and appoynt £25 to be bestowed by my Executors uppon the people poor and rich that shall be present at my buriall, gyvinge unto them four pence a-piece," and any remaining undistributed to be given to the poor of the parish on the following sabbath.

(6) "To the minister that shall make my funerall sermon, 15s. 4d."

(7) "I also will and appoint that £140 shall be bestowed in land, and that the rent shall be yearly given to the poor of . . . parishes, viz., Typton, Bilston, Sedgley, and Wednesbury, viz., 40s. a yeare to the poor of Tipton, and 20s. a yeare to the poor of Bilston yearly. All the others 20s. a yeare to Sedgley, and 20s a year to Wednesbury, the one half to bee paid to the churchwardens and overseers of the poor of each of those parises in and upon the 22nd of June and the other half to be paid upon 22nd December.

(8) There are several other clauses and bequests, and "Mr. Thomas Lane, of Bentley, Esq ," is appointed one of the "overseers" of the will.

Through very many more pages (Salt Coll. vol. X) the various members and branches of this wide-spread family are duly traced by Mr Grazebrook. Presently we come to a Thomas Dudley, of Tipton Green, gentleman, whose will was proved May, 1723 Miraim, his daughter, "borne 8th September, 1702," according to the Tipton registers, was married at Wednesbury on 1st July, 1723, to the Rev, Edward Egginton, vicar of Wednesbury. "Their marriage articles (*penes* Col. T. W. Fletcher) are dated 29th June, 1723; the parties being Thomas Egginton of Doverdale, co. Worcester, gent., and Edward Egginton, of Wednesbury, clerk of the first part; Miraim Dudley of the parish of Typton, *alias* Tibbington, spinster of the second part; and John Egginton, of Robaston, co Stafford, gent., Thomas Aston, of Broome, in the said county gent.. John Fellow, of Woodsetton, in the parish of Sedgley, and Edward Dudley, of Tipton, aforesaid, of the third part." "The Rev. Mr. Edward Egginton, vicker of this parish," was buried at Wednesbury 30th December, 1743, and "Miriam Egginton, widow of the late Edward Egginton, clerk, who was 25 years vicar of Wednesbury, was buried there 14th March, 1748-9."

So meanders on this very prolific family through more pages of its exhaustive history. Suffice it to say here, that in its ramifications the introduction of the following family names may be duly noticed as of local interest:—

(1) John Fellow of Woodsetton.
(2) Richard Keelinge, of Sedgley.
(3) John Keelinge, of Summerhill.
(4) Colonel Fletcher, of Lawneswood.
(5) Joseph Amphlett, Esq., of Horseley House, Tipton.

CHAPTER XVIII.—LIVERY OF SEISIN: THE DUDLEY FAMILY, OF TIPTON (YOUNGER BRANCHES).

In the preceding chapter a cursory allusion is made to an old legal custom being observed in Tipton, which custom being of feudal origin is interesting enough to demand fuller notice than was given to it in passing. It was recorded that the lease of certain meadows in Brerely "was executed upon the said meadows in the presence of" certain witnesses. Such custom is known as "feoffment with livery of seisin"—that is a gift of an estate in the land with livery (*i.e.*, delivery of the seisin, or feudal possession.

There were two kinds, viz,, "livery in deed" and "livery in law."

The former was performed by the delivery of branch, or a twig, or a turf of grass, the feoffor (vendor) and feoffee (purchaser) both holding the deed of feoffment and the material object symbolising the land—as the branch, or twig, or hasp, or ring of the gate—and the feoffor saying, "Here I deliver you seisin and possession of this [field or house] named in the deed," &c.; or by words without any ceremony, the feoffor being in the house [or field] and saying "Here I deliver you seisin or possession," &c., and the feoffee then entered [if a house] alone, shut the door, then opened it, and let in the others. All persons having any interest in the land must have been present and joined in the ceremony, or else have been absent altogether, the idea being to give undisputed possession to the feoffee.

"Livery in law" was made in sight of the land, but not on it. The feoffor said, "I give you yonder land enter and take possession." If entry was at once made, it constituted a good feoffment. But if either feoffee or feoffor died before entry the livery was void. The word "give" was always used, a custom observed from the times when "gifts" from feudal lords to their tenants were the conveyances principally employed.

In the Tipton case in point the same forms and symbolism would seem to have been observed for this temporary grant, as for the more permanent conveyance of a freehold.

* * * * * *

Taking up another thread of the narrative of the preceding chapter, we proceed just a little further with the personal history of the Dudley family of Tipton.

Mr. H. Sydney Grazebrook has compiled an "Account of the Younger Branches of the family of Sutton, *alias* Dudley," for the volumes of the Salt Society. To do this he has made copious extracts from the parish registers of Dudley, Tipton, Wednesbury, West Bromwich, Halesowen, Kingswinford, Oldswinford, Sedgley, Rowley &c. Of those taken from Tipton, a few examples will be interesting, and more particularly so will be Mr. Grazebrook's accompanying remarks.

Of the Tipton registers he observes that they "are not well kept, nor are the entries quite consecutive, one reason for which is that the books have been rebound and some leaves misplaced. They purport to commence in 1513, but it is quite certain that the true date should be 1573. It is no doubt the mistake of the early transcriber." The following extracts may prove interesting, from one cause or other:—

1609.—October 19, Rich Parkeshouse and Jane Dudley, *alias* Sutton, married

1613.—April 25, Thomas, son Jefferie Dudley, *alias* Sutton, baptized.

Between 1619-20 and the year 1635-6 occurs a gap in the register. (Till the adoption of the New Style—in this country in 1752—the 25th of March was New Year's Day, hence January, February, and the first 24 days of March have frequently two years appended, as 1619-20).

1647.—Richard Dudley, a child, bapt. in private by Mr. Needham about the beginning of September.

1655.—Sept 11, a son of Rich. and Fras. Dudley, which died unbapt., buried.

1655.—Sep. 19 (*sic.*), a son of Rich, and Fras Dudley, which died unbapt. born.

1656 -7.—Jan 1., Catherine, dau. of Humbell and Mary Dudley, born.

1670-71.—Jan. 22, Fras. ux. Rich. Dudley, of Wednesbury, bur. at Tipton.

1671.—Dec. 31, Edw. s. Humble and Mary Dudley, born 13 Dec, and baptised last day in Dec.

1674.—Feb. 18, William Dudley, of Wednesbury, bur.

1680.—Oct. 25. Rich. Dudley, of Wednesbury, bur.

1691-2.—Jan. 31, John Whitehouse, of Sedgley, and Eliz. Dudley, of Tipton, m. by license from the Court, per Mr. Nickins.

1692.—Aug 22, Will. s., John Dudley, of ye Delves in Wednesbury parish, bur.

1718—Mar 5, Wm, the son of Edward Dudley and Summery, gent., and Anne his wife, bapt.

1771.—Feb. 7, John Persehouse and Sarah Sutton, m. by license.

1773—April 8, a child of John Dudley, from Hocker Hill, bur.

To make his researches more complete, Mr. Grazebrook has added abstracts of Wills and Administrations from the Registries of Worcester and Lichfield. A few selections will suffice here. Those wills that are interesting in this connection are as follows:

Richard Dudley, of Rowley Regis, 1694, a nailer, Bequeaths to his cousin, Ann Whitehouse, wife of Nathaniel Whitehouse, of Tipton, £8

Thomas Dudley, of Rowley Regis, 1703, leaves £5 to the same, and smaller sums to her sons, Nathaniel, Edward, John, James, and Joseph.

William Dudley, of Wednesbury, 1557; witnessed by Thomas Sale, vicar of Wednesbury.

William Dudley, of Wednesbury, nailer, 1674-5; buried at Tipton, 18 Feby., 1674-5.

Humphrey Dudley, of Wednesbury, nailer, 1724, had married an Esther Whitehouse, at West Bromwich, 1st Feby, 1701-2.

Sarah Dudley, of Wednesbury, 1724, whose son Thomas Browne, the sole executor, takes the mother's maiden name.

Richard Dudley, of Wednesbury, gent., 1726.

William Dudley, of Wednesbury, 1733: administration granted to Anne Sawyer, otherwise called Anne Dudley.

The Wednesbury Parish Registers say:— 1732, July 15th, Mary, daughter of William and Anne Dudley, buried. Her (Ann's) husband Dudley had been dead about eight weeks, and the child died while she was gone out to be married to one Sawyer, a stranger just come into the parish]. Surety, Thomas Sawyer, of Wednesbury, gunsmith.

William Dudley, of Tipton, nailer, 1649, gives all to his wife Eleanor Dudley. [She was buried at Tipton, 15 April, 1656.]

Edward Dudley, of Tipton, 1674.

Katherine Dudley, of Tipton, 1676.

William Dudley, of Tipton, 1741: administration to his father, John, a nailer.

Mary Dudley, of Tipton, 1708.

Thomas Dudley of Tipton, 1723.

William Dudley, of Tipton, 1732, administration granted to Martha, relict.

CHAPTER XIX.—TIPTON DURING THE GREAT CIVIL WAR.

Much of the historical importance of Tipton has been absorbed by the closely adjacent town and castle of Dudley. In fact Dudley Castle overshadows Tipton both figuratively and literally. It is seldom, therefore, that any direct historical allusion to Tipton can be discovered, although there can be no doubt that the tread of troops and the clank of armour have been heard again and again within the confines of Tipton, as from time to time opposing forces have passed on their way to or from the frowning fortress which keeps guard over the whole district from that neighbouring hillside.

The few facts affecting Tipton itself during the Great Civil War are soon told.

In the parish were probably two prominent families who took opposite sides in this dissension. Certainly there was Edward Dudley, of the Green House, already mentioned, who lent sums of money from time to time to further the cause of the Parliament. Later he received a captain's commission under Cromwell to raise men in Staffordshire, dated 1st November 1659, at Wallingford House and signed by Fleetwood. (This Edward Dudley, by the way, was the great-great-grandfather of Thomas Dudley, of Shut End, and the Rev. John Dudley, of Himley.) And if any of the Whorwoods remained in the parish of Tipton at this time, they would no doubt have been found on the opposite side, as Thomas Brome Whorwood, of Sandwell, had to pay the large sum of £872 as a penalty for his loyalty to the king, but he was the last of his family to live in this locality.

The war broke out in August, 1642, and Dudley Castle was immediately strengthened and garrisoned on a war footing, Colonel Levison, a large owner of land round Wolverhampton and Wednesfield, being in command. The next stronghold on the opposite side of Tipton was Rushall Hall, near Walsall, but this was held for the Parliament. No doubt Tipton suffered from the many skirmishes and sallies that were made from the castle, and Tipton men were perhaps requisitioned for its garrison; the men finding soldiers pay even better shall the wretched pittance earned at nail making. Men from Wednesbury and Tipton voluntarily joined the king as he marched from Nottingham to Shrewsbury, and we learn that, as recruits, they made good foot-soldiers. Others even went to join the opposite side at the siege of Newark. In Wednesbury Church registers is the following entry which throws a side light upon this local recruiting—"1703.—Martha, the daughter of Edward and Martha Heywood, was baptised by a Presbyterian minister at a Conventicle at the house of William Clare, of Tipton, an old

Oliverian cornet." As this date is 60 years after the commencement of the wars, William Clare, of Tipton, must have been an old man, and evidently he was little damaged by his hard service as an active officer under Oliver Cromwell. And evidently, too, this Tipton worthy was as sturdy in maintaining his independence of religious thought, as he had been in fighting for his political opinions, for Conventicles, or private assemblies for religious worship, had been prohibited in 1661.

Contributions were levied by both sides upon the unhappy people; and the Parliamentarians assigned the weekly payments of Tipton to go towards the support of their nearest stronghold, Rushall Castle. The Royalists may have assigned their weekly tax towards the support of the neighbouring Castle at Dudley; although Wednesbury money was forwarded to the king's garrison at Lichfield, where for the three months of October, November, and December of 1645 the considerable sum of £5 was received from that Constablewick. It is certain that when men were pressed for the king's service in Dudley garrison, the cost of their maintenance and equipment had to be borne by the Hundred; and the Hundred also had to provide forced labour for the making the entrenchments, &c. But whichever way the money went from Tipton, it is very certain the inhabitants did not escape payment, and that they were compelled to aid in the support of Roundheads and Royalists alike.

It is perhaps probable that Queen Henrietta Maria passed through this parish towards the close of the first year's campaigning. She was passing through Wednesbury from Walsall in July 1643 on her way towards King's Norton, and perhaps would hug that side of the country more closely in which the Royalist power was dominant—as it would be under the shadow of Dudley Castle.

In the December of that year Stafford Castle was destroyed, and Aston Hall suffered a severe attack from the men of Birmingham. In February Pattshull Hall was surprised and in March Stourton Castle was captured by Colonel Tinker Fox, of Walsall. He was no "Tinker," however, as his enemies derisively styled him, but merely a saddler's ironmonger.

But to come to a stirring incident much nearer home, and which took place on June 12th, 1644 Dudley Castle was at this time under the command of Lieutenant.Colonel Beumont; and it was decided by the Roundheads that a determined attack should be made upon this place, which was holding out for the Royalist cause with greater firmness than any of the surrounding garrisons. The king, who was at Shrewsbury, learning of this danger to the Castle, despatched Lord Wilmot, the Earl of Northampton and the Earl of Cleveland, with a brigade of horse and 1,000 foot soldiers, to raise the siege. The siege was being conducted by the Earl of Denbigh, Sir Thomas Myddleton, and Colonel Mytton, with a very large force of troops.

The Parlimentarians pitched their camp on the open expanse of West Bromwich Heath, where, according to Reeves' history of that town, traces of the earthworks were to have been seen at the beginning of this century.

Dr Willmore, in his "History of Walsall," says that the best account of this battle is to be found in a letter from a Parliamentarian, dated from Walsall on the day of the engagement (12 June, 1644), (Dr. Burney's collection).

It would appear that the fight commenced about 9 o'clock on that eventful summer morning, the Roundheads advancing in force from the wide waste of Tipton Green, where they had been drawn up. Tipton then was a large parochial area, with but a sparse population—a number of detached small villages, hamlets, or collections of cottages, widely separated from each other by the intervening waste lands. The inclosure of waste lands and commons was stimulated by Parliament in 1785, and no doubt Tipton parish, from what is known of its history, was extensively affected by this movement. In 1794 there were 14 million acres of waste lands in England, and of these three million acres were taken into cultivation by 1801. This process of inclosure had, however, been going steadily forward since Ket's rebellion in 1549. Up to the year 1801 West Bromwich Heath was a reality and not a mere place-name.

On the opposing side, the Royalists were numbered at about 4,000 besides foot. They ambuscaded every hedge-row and every approach to the Castle. But the Roundheads were not to be denied; they charged furiously, and yet steadily and most persistently, and the cavaliers were put to flight, leaving 60 of their number dead upon the field. The earlier portion of the day had been spent in manœuvring, and in taking up their respective positions; and the actual fighting had lasted only from 2 o'clock to 5. Lord Denbigh deported himself most gallantly, openly declaring that he preferred to sacrifice ten lives rather than lose one piece of artillery—cannon were rather precious in those times, and consequently many of our church bells and monumental brasses evidently found their way from the church to the gun-foundry in those rough and ready times. The loss on Denbigh's side was set down at 8 killed and 20 wounded; but these figures recording the respective losses of the two sides have often been reversed by the contending parties. In fact, both the Royalists and the Roundheads claimed the advantage in this somewhat indecisive affray; the preliminary manœuvring for which probably took place upon Tipton soil.

Rushall Hall had mainly been held all the time for the Parliament, while Dudley had always been in the hands of the Royalists. As force of arms had not yet altered these respective positions, it was now attempted to do something by intrigue and treachery. Colonel Sir Thomas Levison employed a yeoman tenant of his from Wednesfield to try to seduce Captain Tuthill to betray Rushall Hall into the hands of the king. A large bribe was held out, and Tuthill pretended to fall into the plot, but when all was ripe he divulged the whole conspiracy. The poor tool of Colonel Lovison was apprehended, and by martial law was executed at Smithfield, London, October 12th, 1644. His name was Francis Pitt.

As things now went steadily but surely against the King's cause, Dudley Castle was quietly surrendered to the Parliament in May, 1646. In this way the resistance to Parliament gradually died out in Staffordshire. And when the cruel war was over, it would seem that the hard fate of Francis Pitt, of Wednesfield, did not similarly overtake the stalwart Captain Edward Dudley, nor the indomitable Cornet Clare (who perhaps served under him), both of whom returned quietly to their Tipton homes in peace.

Another local worthy did not get off quite so comfortably. When Rushall Hall, after a temporary occupation by the Royalists. had fallen once more into the hands of the Parliamentarians, the two most important prisoners taken on that occasion were the commandant, Colonel Lane, of Bentley, and William Hopkins, of Wednesbury. The latter was suffered to return to his home at Oakeswell Hall; and in due time he fully submitted to the will of Parliament. But, of course, he had to pay his fine. When he petitioned for a favourable "composition" for his delinquency to free his estate from sequestration, he had to file a statement of the said estate, which produced him £69 per annum. One item runs—

"That I am seized [in fee to me and
my heirs] of lands in Tipton, yearly
worth before these troubles ... ... 09 00 00."

This item, like the others in other parishes, is verified by a certificate from the Tipton parish authorities, whose names appear thus—

" Lands in Tipton 9 00 00
(Signed) WILLIAM KEELING, Constable.
HENRY DUDLEY, } Overseers for
WILLM. NICKLIN } the poor."

To modern eyes this sum of "9lb." may seem insignificant, but it is not so.

Land values have changed very much since then, as indeed have the relative prices of all other commodities. But even in the statement referred to, it is evident that in the short period of time comprising the duration of the war, values had considerably altered. For this item of real estate in

Tipton has its value returned, with the addition, of an appraiser's note to the effect that the figure quoted is the true yearly "valew before these trobles."

William Hopkins escaped with a fine of £195 10s. 6d., a heavy penalty in those times, even for a man of his means.

And so closes this chapter in Tipton history, which might perhaps have been made much more interesting with a greater amplitude of detail, if the attention of contemporary chroniclers had completely diverted by the greater importance of the events occurring inside the neighbouring castle of Dudley.

CHAPTER XX.—ECCLESIASTICAL HISTORY: THE CHURCH GOODS OF TIPTON IN 1552.

Of the early history of Tipton Church but little is known. Two records have been preserved to us, and these relate to two widely different epochs. The first given in Chapter IX., enlightens us as to the extent to which Pope Nicholas taxed the Church of Tipton in 1288. The next does not occur until the Papal supremacy in England had become a thing of the past; in fact, we are brought by it to the earliest stage in Reformation when the reformers were still actively engaged in their crusade against Romish rites and ceremonies.

So zealous had some of the newly converted reformers become in the burning cause of Protestantism that they had not hesitated to enter the churches, and appropriate valuable plate, costly vestments, and other "papistical" accessories to the Romish services —to their own private use, of course! Such spoliation might perhaps have been looked upon with calmness and even indifference, by the adherents of the new-born faith, if such acts had not savoured so very strongly of sheer robbery. So those in authority were constrained to take some action; they had merely smiled to hear the Romish sacrament of the altar contemptuously styled "Jack-in-the-box", but when it was commonly known that church plate was openly used on neighbouring dinner tables, and that priestly vestments and rich altar-cloths were used as household draperies, the scandal became too great. Commissioners were appointed for every county, and an investigation was accordingly made. We note many "ornaments" then in use, which the reformed Church of England afterwards dispensed with. But this incident was as yet early in the process of the Reformation (1552) and the King's pleasure – or rather that of the reformers who were advising his youthful Majesty, Edward VI.—was not yet known. Anyway the commission did good, by preventing copes being made into bed-covers, and otherwise putting a stop to such wholesale robbery of the churches. The Commissioners left but one chalice in each church, and of the church goods sold by them the proceeds were paid into the government exchequer.

In the "Annals of the Diocese of Lichfield," volume IV, published in 1863 by the Rev. E. J. Edwards, all the inventories of the local churches will be found printed.

Thus were the church goods in 1552 set forth:—

"Typton

"Fyrste, One Challes of Sylver with a paten.
One cope of satten of burges.
v. Vestements, oone of satten of burges and all the other of saye.
iij. amyces
iij. albes,
iij. towells.
iij. alter clothes.
one lampe of maselen.
One crosse of maslen.
tooe candelstyckes of brasse.
ij. cruetts of tynn.
one sensor of brasse.
iij. belles.
one sanctus bell and one berynge bell."

Glossarial explanations of some kind will no doubt be really necessary to enlighten the ordinary reader on the various items of this inventory, although all the strange words in it are not exactly archaic.

"A challes of sylver with a paten" were, of course the chalice or wine-cup, and the paten or plate for the eucharistic bread—both being of silver.

"Satten of burges" is an antiquated way of writing "Bruges satin," a fabric of famous manufacture in those days.

"Saye," "or saie," was a thin but well-made serge of delicate texture.

The two "cruets of tynn" would be the two tin or white metal jars or vessels, containing respectively the wine and the water before their admixture in the sacramental cup.

The "Sanctus bell" is the small bell rung to call the attention of the congregation to the most solemn portions of the service of the mass, as when the priest pronounced the words, "Sanctus, Sanctus, Sanctus Dominus, Deus Sabaoth." If hung outside the church it was sometimes called the *sancte* or *sawnce* bell. A handbell used inside the church for the same purpose was also called the *sacring* bell.

Silver being a much more precious metal in those days, baser metals such as brass and tin, were used to make church plate, and these we find in the Tipton inventory, as well as the alloy *mas-lin* or *latten*, which resembled brass, but was probably harder, and possessed a slightly "grained" appearance.

The "berynge" bell was the large bell used at buryings or funerals—not the "passing bell"—otherwise a "lyche" [or *dead*] bell.

The Commissioners had instructions to sell all "except the metall of greatt bell and sawnce bells." Those allowed to be retained by Tipton Church were therefore the three bells in the tower and the outside sanctus bell.

Of the vestments, which do not seem to have been handed back into the care and custody of the church-wardens, the cope was the outer cloak of the priest used in the processional office; while the amice and the alb were eucharistic vestments, the former a mere neckerchief or square of silk with a cross embroidered on it, and the latter a linen vestment reaching to the feet, such as the attire in which angels are usually represented. Handing back only a plain surplice (probably one of the albs) for the curate to minister in, the richer vestments were duly disposed of by the Commissioners, as enjoined by the King. The one richer altar cloth seems to have been taken away, leaving two linen ones for use; while all three of the towels, or *houseling* napkins (used at the celebration of the Communion) also disappear from the church.

The Commissioners, all three men of note in the county, made their returns in May,.1553. Their memorandum of Tipton, after the inventory just given, is worded as follows:—

"MD. delivered by the Right Honorable Walter Vicounte Hereforde, Lorde Ferers of Chartley, Thomas Fitharbert, Knight, and Edwarde Littleton, Esquier, Comissionars for churche goodes within the counti of Stafford, to Edward Nightingale and William Thorneton, churchwardens there—

on chales of silver with & patent.
ij linen clothes for the holli comunion table.
a surples for the curat to minestre with.
iij belles.
a sanctus bell.

[All] saffeli to be kepte untill the Kinges Majesties pleasure be therein furder knower. In wittenes wherof as well we the sayd Comissionars, as the said Churchewardens to thes presents interchaungeabli have put-to our handes the xiiij of May, Anno Regni Regis, Edwardi Sexti, Septimo."

Indorsed, "*Tipton.*"

This churchwarden is probably the same "Edward Nyghtingalle," who just three years previously (1551) attended the Manorial Court of "Wednesbray to wit" on a Sunday (November 19th) and had surrendered to him, through the hands of Humphrey Comberford, lord of the said manor, a "croft called Sillimor's Hall, near Dymock's Green"; when a fine of 6s 8d. was paid, fealty was sworn, and the said Edward was duly admitted tenant by Richard Catherall, deputy steward (See also "History of Wednesbury," pp 154-157).

The inventory at Wednesbury Church was—

"Fyrste, one challyce of sylver parcell gylte [*i.e*, partly gilt] with a patent.
iij. pere off vestements, one blew an other whyte and the thryd red sylke, with albes therto belongynge.
ij. copes, one blew and the oder red.
viij. alter clothes.
vj. towells.
ij. clothes of sylke for the alter.
one crosse of laten.
ij. candelstykes.
ij. corporas [or *corporale*, cloth for covering consecrated elements] with cases.
iiij. belles and one smale bell."

The first memorandum to this is—

"MD. that Rychard Forsett, survear, solde the ornements of a stypendare prest ther to Richard Hopkyns, the eldur, for the sume of ijs."

Richard Forsett was the surveyor, or clerk, to the local Commissioners; and the chantry priest, as well as Richard Hopkins, have already been alluded to in Chapter XII.

A second memorandum shows the delivery to "Edwarde Golde and Nicollas Hopkins, churchwardens there,

One Chales of Silver with a Patent parcell gilte,
ij. linen Clothes for the Holli Comunion Table,
a Surples for the Curat to minestre with,
iiij. belles and a Sanctus bell in the Stepull,

[all] safeli to be kepte," &c., indorsed "Wedisbury," 14 May, as before.

CHAPTER XXI.—THE ADVOWSON OF TIPTON.

The Liber Regis or King's Book, contains a valuation of all church livings, taken by order of Henry VIII, in 1535. In this the annual value of the bishopric of Lichfield is given as £559 17s. 3d., and amongst the prebends that of Prees and Ruiton, *alias* Pipa Major (? Parva) is set down at £19. It also set forth the "tenths" payable as annual pension to the King as supreme head of the church, and the "first fruits" to be paid every time the benefice comes into new hands. In this return Tipton is put in the Hundred of Seisdon. It is now, and probably always has been, in the Hundred of Offlow South. In Chapter IX. Tipton was shown in the Deanery of Lapley and Trysull; Tipton is now in the rural deanery of Handsworth and archdeaconry of Stafford.

At Lichfield are preserved many manuscripts and documents relating to the church government within the diocese, and, of course, many references (though mere passing allusions they are as a rule) to Tipton may be found. We find records of the decanal visitations for parochial purposes made triennially between 1756 and 1783, and of the prebendal visitations between 1754 and 1773. With the Tipton visitation of 1754 is a form of Public Penance used in church by a woman when confessing the sin of fornication. [The Chapter Act Books for the year 1415 record that a man of Cannock convicted of adultery was punished by the "decree that he go in procession, clad in shirt only, round the church of Cannock on 3 successive days, and that he should bow down and kiss the steps of the said church, receiving a castigation from the priest with a rod," &c.]

The living of Tipton is (or rather was) "a perpetual curacy in the peculiar jurisdiction of the Prebendary of Prees, or Pipa Minor, in the Cathedral Church of Lichfield, endowed with £200 private benefaction, and £400 royal bounty, and in the patronage of the Dean and Chapter of Lichfield."

"Perpetual Curacies" and "peculiar jurisdictions" are now done away with, but "a perpetual curacy" was generally a living where the tithes were impropriate, and no vicarage endowed: and by "peculiar jurisdiction" was signified one that "hath jurisdiction within itself and power to grant administration or probate of wills, &c, exempt from the Ordinary or Bishop." These "peculiars" were once nearly 300 in number, introduced in most part by the Pope, with the sinister object of curtailing the legitimate authority of an English bishop within his own diocese. Legislation has now given authority to the Ecclesiastical Commissioners to frame schemes for the abolition of these peculiars*; in 1858 their powers of probate were transferred to the Court of Probate.

* In a catalogue of Seals in the Department of MSS in the British Museum. vol. I, p. 827, is a list of the Seals of "Peculiars."

As all incumbents of churches entitled to perform marriages, churchings, and baptisms, and to receive the fees for their own use, are now termed vicars (31 and 32 Vic, c 117), this term has applied to the holder of the living of Tipton since 1869. All the great tithes would seem to have been appropriated in early times by the Sandwell Monastery, leaving only the smaller tithes for the priest who officiated in the parish for them (*vicarius*).

Harwood in his "Lichfield" (1806) also says—

"Pipa Minor, *alias* Prees, is denominated from the impropriated parish of Prees, co. Salop. It once possessed the patronage of St. Chad's, in the town of Stafford, and of the curacy of Tipton."

A prebendary is an ecclesiastic who enjoys a prebend, or a share in the estate of a cathedral; and the name of such prebend would doubtless originate from the place or places in which the profit—generally from lands—arose. The fourth Canon Residentiary at Lichfield is Prebend of Prees and Ruiton, or Pipa Minor, and Prees is in Shropshire, while Ruiton or Ryton is in Warwickshire; there is another place called Ruiton in Upper Gornal.

The living has also been erroneously described as belonging to the "Canonry of Tipton"—which never existed, it may be noted, however, that in 1849 some 24 acres of land were held in Tipton by the "Dean and Chapter of Lichfield." All the property, however, of the Prebendaries of Lichfield, is now handed over to the Ecclesiastical Commissioners.

Yet another description of the living of Tipton was "A donative curacy in the gift of the Prebendary of Pipa Minor." A "donative" is a benefice merely given and disposed of by the patron to a man without either presentation to, or institution by, the ordinary, or induction by his (the Bishop's) order.

With regard to the tithes, the owners of which cannot always be discovered, some remarks may be necessary.

When the Tithe Commutation Award was made (1849-50), in the preamble it was recited that heretofore 1½d had been payable for each milch cow, in lieu of one-tenth of the milk, and 2d per acre instead of the tithe of hay. The prices of grain at the time of the award are given—

	s.	d.
Wheat	7	0¼
Barley	3	11½
Oats	2	9

At the time of the award the Canon of the "Canonry of Tipton" (*sic.*), in Lichfield Cathedral for the time being, was the impropriator of the great and small tithes of Tipton, and after that award the amount of the tithe-rent was £287 9s. 7d.

It seems that these tithes have since been allocated to the augmentation of the district livings of St Paul's, Tipton Green, and St. Mark's, Ocker Hill.

It would appear that when the glebe lands of Tipton were sold some years ago by the Ecclesiastical Commissioners, the sum realised thereby was a very handsome one indeed, on account of the rich minerals contained beneath the surface. This capital was at first invested in console, and produced about £500 per annum, but the Rev. Wm. Ker, the holder of the benefice, sought a better investment, and with the consent of the Commissioners a farm of 101 acres in Bromsgrove was purchased. This farm at the present time produces only £250, of which £27 is paid in tithe to the rector of Bromsgrove. A water mill, also in that parish, produces another £64 a year to the benefice of Tipton. Then from a remnant of the original investment in consols there is a further income of £136. The fees produce only about £20 a year now although in the flush times of the iron trade, when Tipton was prosperous, they produced as much as £136: that, too, was about 1874,before the churchyard was closed to burials. So that the present total value of the living is near £450 a year, for a population (1881 census) of 10,567 souls. But this again is still subject to a one-third retiring pension of £145 per annum payable to the late vicar, the Rev. W. Ker, who is now living in well-earned retirement, and at a good ripe old age, at Highgate, London.

At the time the investment of capital was transferred from government stocks to agricultural land, the present Vicarage House at Horsley Heath was also acquired.

The history of the advowson of Tipton is too difficult to be traced clearly and continuously. Of course, the earliest patron was the Monastery at Sandwell hence the reason for denominating the living a vicarage. Had it been a rectory no doubt the history of the advowson would more easily have been traced in its connection with the history of the manor, or the moities of the manor. But the next holders of the advowson, in succession to the religions house aforementioned, seems to have been the Whorwood family who had acquired the estate of the suppressed monastery of Sandwell—see chap. xvii—but perhaps not all the great tithes, as the living is described (1614) as the "rectory of Tipton."

At present the living is in the patronage of the Hyndman Trustees (a Trust formed by the late Miss Hyndman, like the Simeon Trust) who purchased it from S. S. Lloyd, Esq.

For about 20 years the living of Tipton was, and till recently, in sequestration. This arose about 1866 from the financial difficulties of the holder, the Rev. W. Ker. The parish was large, populous, and poor. To relieve the incumbent as much as possible after ten years of the sequestration the Bishop (Selwyn) of the diocese decided in 1876 that the damage done to the Vicarage House by mining operations could not be regarded as dilapidations to be made good at the vicar's cost, under the Dilapidations Act of 1871. It is also said to have been Bishop Selwyn's wish, at this period, to have placed in the benefice a wealthy man of independent means, such as he felt was really needed in so poor a parish. This relief thus extended, however, allowed the Rev. William Ker to retain the living, still under sequestration, for another ten years, till the Christmas of 1886, when he resigned on account of his age. Then came a period of six months in which the living was vacant. Great hesitancy was manifested to accept such a living; the position was a most honourable one, but the responsibilities were even greater. Eventually, in July, 1887, the Rev. Alex. Arthur Cory M.A, was instituted on the presentation of the Trustees, and the nomination of the Bishop. The Rev. Mr. Cory was pretty well innured to the work of a Black Country parish, having for six years laboured in a similar though much smaller parish—All Saints, King's Hill, Wednesbury and Darlaston (See "History of Darlaston," p 108). The new vicar found his official residence in Tipton to be in a deplorable state, the damage from mining operations, together with the process of natural deterioration and general decay, necessitating not ordinary repairs, but actual structural renovation. This arose in some measure from the interpretation put upon the Bishop's order as to the application of the Dilapidations Act to this exceptional case. Any way, a bill of £635 17s 3d. was incurred in making the Vicarage House habitable; towards this there was an allowance of £132, but other charges left the exact sum of £553 17s. 3d. to be paid out of the pockets of the incoming Vicar, Mr. Cory.

CHAPTER XXII.—THE BENEFICED CLERGY OF TIPTON, &C., &C.

It has been said, and on fairly good authority, too, that from the restoration of the Monarchy (1660) till the beginning of the present century, the parish of Tipton never knew a resident incumbent. All those years the benefice was evidently looked upon as merely a piece of preferment to be enjoyed by some fat pluralist, or as part of the rightfull emoluments of some big dignitary in Lichfield Cathedral. No doubt services were taken periodically in the church by some under-paid curate-in-charge—perhaps by one who divided his many duties among several contiguous parishes. But even if this much were done, it is very certain that.the fabric of the church was never repaired, and that year by year, as it fell gradually into further decay and greater dilapidation, the fact of its becoming less weather-tight might have been used for the less frequency of the services held within its tottering walls. And when at the end of last century the extensive mining operations in the parish seemed to offer an excuse for its ruinous condition and when undermining might be in some degree pleaded as a cause for its unsafe condition, a great weight of responsibility was fortuitiously lifted from the shoulders of those who had previously acquiesced in its neglect. The ever increasing population brought about by that same mining industry called loudly for greater spiritual supervision. And so a new church was decided upon and two great facts connected with its erection stand out very prominently. First it was placed in the middle of the parish for the greater convenience of the population—but, strange to say, the population has not since located itself very closely around the shelter of the building. Secondly, it was to be built very cheaply, money being almost as scarce as religious enthusiasm in the parish; and the contractor was carefully bound down to execute the work for such a very small sum that it needed a very large parchment to contain all the conditions it imposed—which deed is still extant and in the hands of the vicar.

And so the old Mother Church at Princes End was forsaken for this new "chapel." Of at least part of the ruins of the old building one sensible man made some use. He utilised the old roof timbers to cover in part of his ironworks; and in connection with this fact a wonderful legend has grown up. No regret is expressed at the grievous spiritual destitution of the parish, occasioned by the long neglect of those who ought to have known their duty better, but a groan is sent up over a few material substances no one had ever before taken care of. In fact, Simony passes unreproached; but "desecration" is held up to our abhorrence. At Charlemont Hall, near Wednesbury, it appears, there lived a family of the name of Price, about the year 1822. Of them, we are gravely told the following legend:—"This family has a sad history. It is said they took off the roof of Tipton Old Church to cover their engine house, and that no good came to them afterwards. Their tombstone on the south side of the [West Bromwich] churchyard testifies to the early deaths of their children. One of the sons returning home intoxicated at night, and being unable to obtain an entrance into the house, lay on the lawn the whole night. He took cold and soon after died. Mr. Price was found dead with his throat cut in one of the bedrooms, and though the facts was hushed up and no inquest held there is little doubt of its correctness."

But to return to the holders of the benefice. The the "independent" who had held it under the Commonwealth was ejected by the Act of Uniformity in 1662. Of him we have a full record in Calamy's *Nonconformists' Memorials*:—

"Tipton. Mr. Richard Hinks. A Godly preacher and a moderate Independent. Before the restoration he offended the neighbouring ministers and other good people by his vigorous notions and by assisting to raise soldiers for Lambert against Monk. He was also so unhappy as to buy an estate that was Colonel Dudley's, when he absconded for his service to the King. The Colonel returning with the King, denying that the writings produced were under his hand, had his estate again. Mr. Hinks, by raising money for this purchase, had so involved himself in debt that when he was ejected he was utterly insolvent. He had a wife and many children, but God provided for him. His successor, Mr John Taylor, suffered him to live in the Parsonage House upon easy terms, though he preached there in the time of public service. He was afterwards imprisoned for preaching and though before the change of the times he was very hot he then became very cool and moderate. After Mr. Taylor's death he removed to Old Swinford or Stourbridge, and died in great amity with Christians of various denominations."

Previous to this Thomas Gunnes was "minister of Tipton" in 1635, and as such baptised the son and heir of Thomas Parkes, Esq. of Willingsworth, and Rebekah, his wife, on April 1st, the Low Sunday of that year.

In 1669 the Rev Joseph Eccleshall was minister, no doubt succeeding the Rev John Taylor and in 1673 Michael Nickins was chosen minister of Tipton by the "inhabitants thereof." In December, 1699, he married a Mrs. Anne Persehouse, of Sedgley, having buried his first wife in 1693. She was interred at Cannock. Now comes a gap – a century of neglect.

"There [is] nothing farther in either [church] worth recording, and . . . no account of incumbents, except that the present is the Rev. Thomas Shaw Helier." Thus writes the county historian Shaw at the close of last century – this exhaustive and researchful chronicler confesses that such is the poverty of material during the eighteenth century, that even he, a contemporary, cannot compile a list of incumbents!

During the present century the three incumbents before the present holder of the benefice have been – Rev. James Bevan, instituted 11 September, 1812; Rev. Henry Peter Dunster, instituted 2 August, 1847; Rev. William Ker, instituted 19th November 1847; and the patrons were Rev. J. Shaw Hellier, Henry Thomas Dunster, James Shaw Hellier, Esq

In 1851 the value of the living is given as £419, and we are informed that the Prebendary of Prees *was* the appropriator of tithes, but they were held on lease by the executors of the late J. Shaw Hellier, Esq, together with the patronage of the said living.

One curate-in-charge leaves affectionate memorials of services regularly rendered and duties faithfully performed throughout a long period. The text of the following petition to Lord Brougham tells its own tale:—

MEMORIAL OF THE PARISHIONERS OF TIPTON, IN THE COUNTY OF STAFFORD.

To the Lord High Chancellor of England.

We the undersigned being principal inhabitants of the parish of Tipton, in the county of Stafford, in the diocese of Litchfield and Coventry, and peculiar to the Deanesry of Litchfield, which parish, according to the census of the present year, contains 14,951 souls, desire most respectfully to submit to your Lordship. That whereas previous to the year 1803, a resident minister was a thing unknown in this parish within the memory of the oldest inhabitant, the Rev. John Howells has resided as curate from that period to the present time, living in uninterrupted harmony with his parishioners, and discharging to their universal satisfaction the duties of his spiritual cure. That the income of the living, being no more at the first than £23, exclusive of the fees which have been uniformly reserved by the incumbent, the salary of Mr. Howells was first at £20, and so continued till the year 1813, when it was raised to £40 and so continued to 1823, when it was raised to £80 and so continued to the present time, the gross annual value of the living having in the meanwhile been increased to £400, there being no parsonage, and the curate, during the whole period of his residence having had to pay a rent of £60 for his house. That chiefly through the exertions of the Rev. John Howells, four new galleries were added to the parish church, in the years 1813, 1814, to which object he subscribed his salary as curate for four successive years, and that through the same exertions six large Sunday Schools were established, which in the year 1818 were made Day Schools on the Madras system, and now afford religious instruction to about twelve hundred, an account of which schools, as visited by the parliamentary commissioners during the year 1823, is to be found in their report, No. IX page 562. That, through his successful influences as peacemaker, scarce a single lawsuit has occurred during many years in a parish containing so large an amount of valuable and divided property, and that owing to the general respect in which his character is held, he has been appointed though unconnected with the neighbourhood by birth, executor or trustee to no less than twenty-four considerable properties. That in the midst of this ministerial usefulness on his part and affectionate respect on our own, the proprietor of the advowson of Tipton is hastening, in the advanced age of the incumbent, to sell the next presentation and that, as the Revd. Mr. Howells can neither legally become the purchaser, nor sanction, consistently with his views of independence, a projected subscription for that purpose, we are apprehensive of speedily losing the benefit of his farther residence amongst us: under these circumstances we have ventured to lay before your Lordship a case, which, for extent of services compared with deficiency of remuneration, will be deemed, we trust, not unworthy of your Lordship's impartial attention, and it is our anxious prayer in behalf of one who has so long profitably officiated in the parish, that he may be presented with some such Crown living as he might exchange with the purchaser of Tipton, or may be so otherwise provided for as shall to your Lordship seem expedient for the encouragement of patience and diligence and faithfulness in the ministry of the Church.

Dated this 22nd day of October, in the year 1831."

In later times yet another testimony is borne to the faithful discharge of ministerial services performed in the parish; this time to the holder of the benefice. On August 20th, 1866, there was made a presentation to the Rev. W. Ker in recognition of 19 years' arduous labour in Tipton; the present consisted of a purse of 160 guineas, a silver salver, and an illuminated address containing the names of the donors.

* * * * * *

What is known as the "Commonwealth Survey" was made in 1650 by special commissioners, as ordered by Parliament, into the possessions of bishops, deans and chapters, and of all benefices. These records are kept in Lambeth Palace Library. Neither Tipton nor Wednesbury is mentioned, but the Darlaston survey will be found in vol. II., p. 126.

Again, in the same library are found records of the year 1657, when a return was taken as to the Augmentation of Church Lands: Tipton is mentioned in vols 968, 972, 993, 1,004, and 1,018; while Wednesbury is mentioned in the same series, vols. 968, 974, 983, 987, 993, 997, and 1,004.

CHAPTER XXIII.—THE FABRIC OF THE PARISH CHURCH: ITS DEDICATION AND THE WAKE.

The ancient Parish Church at Summer Hill, near Princes End, was long a neglected ruin. Both it and the burial ground were found too small in 1795, when mining operations in this district of rich and varied mineral resources had commenced to attract a larger population of labourers than the agricultural era had ever done previously. For the increased requirements of the parish, and to be more convenient to the growing centre of the population, the present parish church of St. Martin was commenced at Horseley Heath. It was completed in 1797, at a cost of £5,000, including the provision of a large burial ground. It was erected under the powers of an Act of Parliament, which enabled the money to be raised by church rates levied upon the parishioners. Its accommodation was for 1,000, of which 400 sittings are free.

The Act of Parliament may be seen in printed form, a bound copy being safely kept among the parochial documents of the vicar. In the same safe custody is also kept the large parchment already alluded to, by which the contractor, Kyte (of Kidderminster, covenanted to build the church for £1,400. The gallery was put in after the rest of the building as just mentioned. The brick wall was erected round the church yard by the same contractor for £100. The historian Shaw paid his visit of inspection evidently while the process of building was going on. He says: "This [new] church is about seven-eights of a mile south of the old church (situated in a less populous part of the parish, close on the other side of the canal) which, being a square old tower structure of rough stone and plaster, much decayed, and inconveniently situated, was deserted for this modern neat chapel." He adds, respecting the said "neat chapel." "The square of the church is just thirty degrees different from the [compass] dial, which, I believe, is the variation of the needle, so that it stands pretty exact to the cardinal points."

And now to describe the present aspect and appearance of this "neat chapel."

The building has no architectural pretensions whatever, as may be guessed from the fact that the common people have from the very first dubbed it "the pepperbox church," a name not at all unhappily chosen for its terse descriptive powers. The main block is a rectangle, which must be designated the nave, inside which are galleries on three of its sides, the organ being in the west gallery, the front of which is adorned with the royal arms. At the east end a semi-circular arch opens into a very small chancel. There are two porches at this end also. At the west end is a square tower with a domical top—the remarkable feature by which the building acquired its derisive nickname. The vestry is in the tower. There are two other entrances at the west end. The seats are open and have two specially labelled for the wardens, one on each side, a few seats from the back. A plain stone font stands near the N. W. entrance—a whole corner of the building thus doing duty as a Baptistry. There is an octagonal stone pulpit, and an eagle lectern. But by far the most artistic accessory is a tablet on the north wall of the chancel. It is of stone, alabaster pilasters and cornice surrounding a marble panel containing the inscription, which is to the effect that the Holy Table, With its furniture together with all the seats throughout the nave, were given by Rowland Hill, of Denbigh Hall, Tipton (and a nephew of the great Sir Rowland Hill, of Kidderminster) to the glory of God, and in memory of his wife, Eliza Hill, who died in 1887. This desirable alteration in the seating cost about £200, and previously there had been no nave—the seats stretching across the floor from aisle to aisle.

On the same wall there is a memorial tablet to John Davis, a late local surgeon, and to his wife and his daughter.

On the south wall of the chancel is another mural tablet to the memory of Thomas Underhill, who died 1853, and Sarah, his wife, who died in 1852.

Externally the building has been cemented, and has moulded strings and labels, and the whole is supposed to present an appearance in the Italian style; in fact, the plan is in some feeble degree almost that of the continental basilica churches.

It is intended to restore and renovate this church at some future date, when funds can be raised for so desirable a purpose. The work will be undertaken by easy stages for two very good reasons, first, the money may not flow in for the work all at once, but will no doubt flow all the more freely for the completion when the parishioners begin to appreciate the scope and design by which it is proposed to make the parish church worthy of its name and position as such. And secondly, it is thought undesirable that for the prolonged period during which the re-building will be proceeding the congregation should be without the use of its sheltering walls for public worship. One of the most eminent and successful of Birmingham architects is said to have in his mind's eye the model of St. Philip's Church, Birmingham, as the copy for imitation—a handsome type after the style of Sir Christopher Wren.

* * * * * *

Now as to the dedication of the church. St. Martin seems to have been the patron saint of the parish for centuries, the older fabric at Princes End having been dedicated to him; and when that was deserted this new "neat chapel" was dedicated to the same saint. Tiptonians may, therefore, be interested to learn something of St. Martin, his life, and legend.

Saint Martin was one of the earliest French bishops and spent his life fighting against the prevailing paganism of that country. The prettiest part of his legend is that he one day divided his cloak with a beggar, and that soon after Christ appeared to him wearing that half. Another incident—the Emperor Maximus receiving the goblet from St. Martin's hands at a banquet—has made him the patron saint of drinkers. This was by no means an inappropriate connection for Tipton in its old days of bull-baiting and heavy drinking.

Other parish churches in the Midland district—as that at Birmingham—were dedicated to St. Martin. This saint was the first to whom the Roman Church offered public adoration. Martinmas (Nov. 11) is a great rent and hiring day in the north. This was the day on which he was buried A.D 397, at the most ancient abbey in France: but on July 4th, 473, he was "translated"—that is, his remains were removed to a Basilica near Tours, of which city he had been the first bishop,

In the dedication of churches this date (July 4), which in the Kalendar also commemorates the Ordination as well as the Translation of the Saint, was preferred as more suitable for festivals. So in Tipton we find July preferred for the annual festival of the Wake—which was not always a pleasure fair, but special occasion for trading celebrated at first within the precincts of the church and churchyard.

CHAPTER XXIV.—SOME PAROCHIAL ADVERTISEMENTS: THE CHURCH PLATE: THE CHURCH BELLS.

When Tipton had been merely an agricultural community the annual parochial festival had not inconveniently been celebrated in the month of November, when the late autumnal rest had brought the fruitful year to a close, but when Tipton became an industrial community, in manufacturing and in mining, this late period of the year was found most unsuitable for the annual carnival of the wake. And so, as indicated in the last chapter, the broiling month of July was substituted, being better suited to the manufacturing interests, and so much farther removed from the great winter holiday of Christmas. For those were the times before the era of Saturday half-holidays; before trips to the sea-side; and indeed, before even workmen's excursions were dreamt of. There were no Factory Acts in those days, and nailers and small outworkers slaved in unsanitary smithies, early and late, from week-end to week-end. And when the wake game, it was indeed a holiday; something to be observed and well marked in the year's calendar of events. It cannot be wondered at that men went to excess, when their lives were so monotonously often made up of toil and unrelieved labour. Tiptonians, therefore, were not averse to changing the date of this great local holiday which was so markedly their own, and when overflowing hospitality and unbounded welcome was so unreservedly extended to all who visited their parish on that festive occasion. Besides, being notorious good livers, they were not averse to change the wake dinner from the customary goose, which in November was neither a green or stubble bird, nor yet a fattened Christmas goose, for the more succulent delights of a couple of fine young ducks in their first feather, as the month of July could always provide. Taking all these things into consideration, the following advertisement, which appeared in *Aris's Birmingham Gazette*, July 16th, 1792, will commend itself to our better understanding:—

"TIPTON WAKE.

"Tipton Annual Festival or Wake, having for many years been held at the latter end of November, and that time of the year for such festival being now found highly prejudicial to the Coal Trade and Manufactories in the Parish and Neighbourhood, as also injurious to many poor families of the same, their work being much wanted at that season: the Gentlemen and other principal Inhabitants thereof think it advisable to alter the said Festival or Wake to the Sunday before the 24th of July, unless the 24th be on a Sunday, and in such case it will be held on that day.

"The 22nd of July being the Time appointed for the celebration thereof this present year, a Charity Sermon will be preached in the Parish Church of Tipton, in the Afternoon, by the Rev. A. B. Haden, clerk, for the Benefit of four Sunday Schools belonging to that place. Service to begin at 3 o'clock.

"Tipton, July 13th, 1792."

This Rev. A. Bunn Haden was Vicar of Wednesbury, an absentee and a pluralist, and one who had allowed his church to fall into such a state that the rain streamed on the preacher as he stood in the pulpit!

Another parochial advertisement may now be quoted. It appeared in the same newspaper in the issue of Monday, April 20th, 1795:—

"VOLUNTEERS FOR THE NAVY.

"Wanted, by the Parish of Tipton, in the County of Stafford, three men to serve as Volunteers in His Majesty's Navy during the War and no longer. Such able-bodied men from the age of 18 to 45 as are disposed to engage in this honorable service, shall receive Twenty Guineas Bounty, and Five Shillings to drink His Majesty's Health, by applying to the churchwardens and overseers of the parish of Tipton."

Inland towns and parishes like Tipton were not exempt from supplying blood and sinew to the naval service during those protracted struggles with France; and this year (1795) when Tipton advertised for its quoto was the year after Lord Howe's great victory off Ushant, and the same year in which Bonaparte became the most conspicuous figure in European politics.

Yet another advertisement in *Aris's Gazette* throws a side light on Tipton's parochial history at this momentous period, It appeared January 29th, 1798, and ran—

"BUILDING MATERIALS.

"At the next Meeting of the Trustees for taking down and rebuilding the Parish Church of Tipton in the County of Stafford, to be held at the house of William Short, Innholder, in Tipton aforesaid, on Tuesday, the 6th of February next, at 3 o'clock in the afternoon, will be sold by Auction by Edward Jessop, all the Materials of the Old Church (except Monuments, printed Tables, Bell, and Appurtenances) comprising a Quantity of Good Bricks, Tiles, Stone, Lead in the Tower, Timbers, Glass, Pews, &c., with a large Painting of the King's Arms, and which will be sold in distinct Lots.

"For View of the Premises apply to Mr. Edward Fisher, or Mr. Joseph Smith, churchwardens."

QUERY.—What became of the old monuments, &c,? It may be noted that it was then compulsory to display a copy of the Royal Arms in churches as indicative of the king's supremacy as head of the English Church

* * * * * *

Of the altar plate of Tipton Church two pieces only are of sterling silver, one antique and the other modern.

The chalice, weighing 9¼oz,, bears the inscription—

"John Nightingale of Tipton
Churchwarden, Anno 1667."

The patten about 4oz. in weight, bears the inscription—

"The Gift of Rowland Hill,
Denbigh Hall, 1889."

The remainder of the service consists of five pieces of plated goods. There is another chalice, electroplated, manufactured by Elkington and Co., of Birmingham. The flagon is merely inscribed "Tipton Parish Church." A large salver bears the inscription—

"The Gift of Mrs. Dixon,
of Horsley House.
To Tipton Church."

A small salver bears an exact repetition of this inscription. Another small salver, not in use, is of Elkington and Co's workmanship.

* * * * * *

In the old church tower at Princes End were three bells—probably the same three mentioned in the "Reformation Inventory." These were sent to be recast when the new church was built, for insertion therein. The receipted bill of the bell-founder (Thomas Mears) is still to be found in the parochial documents carefully preserved by the vicar. It is under date 1799, and refers to an enlarged peal of six, the items being—

	£	s.	d.
Bells	145	10	8
Hanging same	68	12	0
	£214	2	8

For at the erections of the new parish church the peal was increased from three to six bells, of which the present treble and No. 2 formed a part. The bells are now eight in number, the weight of the tener being 12cwt. 251bs, and they are all hung on one level in a circular tower of 12ft. 6in. in diameter. It appears that in 1848 the tenor of the ring of six got broken and had to be re-cast; bells Nos. 5, 4, and 3 were also re-cast at the same time and two new bells were added, thus bringing up the number of the peal to eight, as it stands at present. After the re-hanging the first peal of Kent Triple Bob Major, 5,056 changes, was rung by a band from Birmingham, conducted by Samuel Marsh, on February 22nd, 1852. After this no change ringing was attempted until November 16th, 1884, when a peal of Grandsire Triples was rung. Now, under the leadership of an enthusiastic and thoroughly practical campanologist (Mr. J R Small) Tipton possesses an admirable band of change ringers and the belfry walls are now adorned with tablets recording their various campanological feats including one of which they are justly proud, a peal in Steadman's intricate and musical method.

The inscriptions on the bells are as follows:—

Tenor.—"C. and G. Mears, Founders, London, Rev. W. Ker, Incumbent; Messrs. Haines and Hickman, Churchwardens, 1848."

No. 7.—C. and G. Mears, Founders, London, 1848.

No. 6.— ,, ,, ,,

No. 5.— ,, ,, ,,

No. 4.— ,, ,, ,,

No. 3.— ,, ,, ,,

No. 2.—The gift of William Underhill, Churchwarden; Thos. Mears, of London, fecit 1797."

Treble.—"The gift of James Fisher, Ironmaster Thos. Mears, of London, fecit 1798."

A tombstone inscription sets forth that Edward Fisher (born 1751 and died 1810) who was 14 years churchwarden of Tipton, was the donor of bell No. 5.

CHAPTER XXV.—TIPTON PARISH REGISTERS.

The condition of the older Parish Registers of Tipton has already been alluded to in Chapter xviii. The modern ones are well kept, and may afford good and reliable material for the genealogist, but for the historian the older ones may be searched with very much more interest. All are kept in an iron safe (in the vestry), which is fairly strong, but seems scarcely likely to resist fire.

The first register, in its earlier pages, seems to have been a transcription; probably in accordance with a peremptory mandate of the year 1597, ordaining that parchment registers should be purchased at the expense of each parish, and that all the entries from the older books, mostly of paper, should be therein transcribed from 1558.

In the older registers of Tipton an ink line roughly drawn down the side of each page of the skin, gives a narrow margin for three initial letters—C or christening, B for burial, and M for marriage. During the Cromwellian period it is noted that the entries mostly take the form of "Born," and do not indicate a "Baptism." From this it may be inferred that an Anabaptist was in possession of the benefice. During this period we note (in September 1647) that a baptism of an infant was performed in private, as evidently the doctrine of infant baptism was in dispute in Tipton and Nonconformity shows undiminished strength in this parish at a much later period—namely in December, 1728, when there is record of a baptism performed at "a Meeting House."

But going back to the troublous times of the civil strife and puritanical supremacy, we find significant entries:—

In 1649, "Thomas Nocke marrd. lots of the parish about 14 dayes before Micaeltide." Was this a Justice of the Peace usurping clerical functions wholesale?

Again, "Jas. Warham, marrd to Martha Callaway by John Wilmore"—a magistrate from Dudley—"in the house of William Buxton"—the religious service was here superseded without doubt. And in 1650 are recorded the civil marriages of John Mallen and Joseph Darbie, "wher I know not." Laconic, but full of meaning!

The second register ends with the following memorandum:—"There are 30 leaves in this booke, 20 Feb., 1711 Witness, JON HIGGINSON." Careful as this scribe was, such a useful memorandum could not correct previous errors, and probably it was left unheeded by those who made subsequent entries in the registers.

Discrepancies in the register may sometimes be detected, showing that entries have been interpolated at a much later date. In 1604 there would seem to have been a remarkable amount of mortality in the family of the Nightingale's, even if an epidemic had been then raging in Tipton, no fewer than 11 deaths under this name being entered in the two months of August and September. Other familiar names as that of Nightingale occur at frequent intervals.

In 1667 a baptismal entry of Gerrard (son of a Gerrard) shows that the family of Whorwood was still connected with the parish. Then we have the surnames of Wyrley, of O'Kell (a yeoman family to be mentioned in a subsequent chapter), of Moxley (a surname evidently acquired from its place of origin), and of Ansbrock, which Mr. T. Cooper supposes to represent the family of Addenbrook. Then as to Christian names:

Christian names often run in certain families with bewildering frequency. In the Whitehouse family Mordecai was once a favourite, as was Eutychus in the Fisher family. This use of Biblical names savours strongly of Puritanical tendencies.

As to the due publication of banns, we have also, interesting records.

Of the marriage of Dorothy, daughter of Paul Stanley, to Thomas Winnington, August 8th, 1658, it is noted that it "was published immediately after morning exercise."

Again in 1653, "the purpose of marriage" between two parties, one a parishioner and the other of Birmingham, "was published in the public meeting place at Tipton 3 Lord's Daies, the last whereof was ye 27th day of November, and being without contradiction." So much for carefulness and accuracy. Now for carelessness and glaring neglect.

In 1724 we have an entry of a marriage by license which had been performed four years previously, and "the reason why they were registered here was they had a desire it should be kept private for some time and forgetfulness was the reason they were not registered in order."

Legislative wisdom on the part of our ancestors once exhibited itself in an attempt to bolster up a decaying industry—the great wool trade of England. In 1678 an Act ordered that the dead should be buried in woollen shrouds; and in that year the Tipton registers chronicle such a mode of interment.

Of the natures of Peculiars we have already treated (see chap. xxi). At Tipton Church, January 5th 1675, It is recorded that a marriage was performed by a license from "Mr. Mallet, Official of ye Peculiar Exempt Jurisdiction," of Tettenhall.

BRIEFS are another interesting form of entry to be found in Registers. Royal Letters Patent authorised collections to be made in churches, after the Reformation, for the repair or re-building of churches and other purposes. In the middle of the last century, owing to the growing frequency of these Briefs (issued from the Court of Chancery), it was ordered that they should only be granted on the formal application of Quarter Sessions. In the Tipton registers we have examples of these briefs:—

1657, January 17.—"Collected in ye parish of Tipton in the co of Stafford for ye relieffe of ye inhabitants of Desford in the co. of Leicester towards their losses sustained by fire (according to his Highness his letters pattent) ye some of 7a. 10d."

1659, September 4.—"Collected in the parish of Tipton &c.... the sum of 12s. 4d. for the town of Southwold otherwise Soulbay in co. Suffolk."

1661, June 30.—"Collected &c, ... the some of 4s. for ye reliefe of Drayton in co. of Sallop—8d layde out of my purse."

On July 7th of the same year there was another collection for "the relieffe of Oxford"; and in August 5s. was collected for East Hogborne, in Berks; and later 7s. for Chichester.

On the last page of the first register another Brief records the collection of 3s. for the "relieffe of ye inhabitants of Milton Abbey, in co. Dorsett," on the 8th September, 1661.

The transcript of the Tipton parish registers kept at Lichfield date only between 1672 and 1812, and even the years 1705-1710 and 1732-1734 are then missing from these. This is owing to the laxity with which was carried out the injunction (1597) to forward duplicate registers to the episcopal registrar.

Local genealogists will find much more material than can be given here by reference to the extracts of Tipton Registers published by Mr. Thomas

Cooper, of Dudley, to whom reference has already been made. His work, carefully arranged in chronological order, and judiciously selected, was printed some time ago among the "Notes and Queries" in the *Birmingham Weekly Post* (Notes 2,283, 2,333, and 2,337)

Up to the beginning of this century we might classify the volumes of registers after the following arbitrary arrangement:—

VOL.	DATE.	CONTENTS	REMARKS
I.	1573—1664	C. M. and B.	Parchment.
II.	1664—1697	,,	Ditto:
III.	1697—1736	,,	Ditto: on a paper flyleaf is a list of prominent inhabitants in 1700.
IV.	1736—1769	,,	Parchment: duplicates after 1754 most of the marriages with the same entries in the printed-form register.
V.	1754—1804	M. only	Paper, with printed forms as ordered by Act of Parliament.
VI.	1770—1808	General register	Duplicating many marriage entries.
VII.	1805—1827	M. only	Follows vol. V.
VIII.	1809—1812	General	Plain paper; many leaves left blank at end, because the separate registers are to be commenced from this date.

From 1812 we get the three classes of registration separated in consequence of the passing of George Rose's Act (52 Geo III, cap 146): and (1) the BAPTISM Volumes run, on the proper printed form—

Vol	I.	1813—1819
,,	II.	1819—1824
,,	III.	1824—1830
,,	IV	1830—1837
,,	V.	1837—1847
,,	VI	1847—1870
,,	VII.	1870—1889
,,	VIII.	1889—current.

Then (2) the BURIALS also from that date run on in the printed forms, as ordered—

Vol.	I.	1813—1826
,,	II.	1826—1835
,,	III.	1835—1850
,,	IV	1850—1865
,,	V.	1865—1882
,,	VI.	1882—1891

The interments have necessarily been few since the cemetery was opened. There is a register of the vaults and brick graves in the churchyard, but it has been neglected as regards its legitimate purpose, and some bygone minister has evidently utilised its pages for jotting down the heads of sermons while he was probably awaiting the arrival of the funeral procession. And (3) continuing the separate register for MARRIAGES there are—

Vol.	I.	1813—1823
,,	II.	1823—1834
,,	III.	1834—1837 blank at end

The blank pages denote the appearance of a new form of register—in fact, the first of the Registrar General's book-forms—which run on in numerous volumes, dated as follows:—

1837—1840	1855—1859
1840—1843	1859—1862
1843—1845	1862—1865
1845—1847	1865—1870
1847—1850	1870—1874
1850—1853	1874—1880
1853—1855	1880—1888

And the current one from 1888 is in duplicate, for the purpose of supplying the second copy to the Registrar. There are also the usual Banns Books for the "better prevention of clandestine marriages."— 26 Geo. II.

CHAPTER XXVI.—TIPTON CHURCH ACT, 1794

The full title of this piece of local legislation is "An Act for taking down and rebuilding the Parish Church of Tipton, otherwise Tibbington, in the County of Stafford, and for Enlarging the Cemetery or Burial Ground thereto."—34 George III. The preamble sets forth that the said church was a "very ancient fabrick in so ruinous a condition that it is become dangerous for the Inhabitants to attend divine service therein, and cannot be effectually repaired, but must be taken down, rebuilt, and enlarged."

The Trustees empowered to carry out the work were numerous and influential, and included some of the best known names, not only in Tipton, but in the whole vicinity round about. There were, *ex-officio*, the clergy and the churchwardens: then among others.—

William, lord viscount Dudley and Ward,
Hon Edward Foley,
George Birch, Esq (lord of the manor),
Jervoise Clarke Jervoise, Esq. (of West Bromwich manor),
Rev. Alexander Bunn Haden (vicar of Wednesbury),
Rev. Luke Booker (of Dudley),
Rev Jno. Best (vicar of Sedgley),
Rev. John Dudley (rector of Himley),
Thomas Dudley, Esq.,
Joseph Scott, Esq.
Edward Whitby, Esq.,
Thos, Holbeche, Esq,
Ed. Dixon, Esq,
Ol. Dixon, Esq,
Jos. Amphlett, Esq.,
Wm, Bedford, Esq.,
Richmond Aston, Esq.,
James Keir, Esq.,
John Dumaresq, Esq,
Richard Jesson,
Isaac Whitehouse,
Wm. Underhill (first churchwarden of new church),
Wm. Cotterill,
Bailey Caddick, jun.,
James Fisher,
Edward Fisher,
Wm Nicklin
William Mee, &c, &c., &c.

These Trustees were sworn to execute the work imposed by the Act, faithfully and honestly, and to the best of their skill and judgment, five to form a quorum, and new trustees to be elected to re-fill vacancies caused by death or by refusal to serve.

They had power to raise money for their purpose by rates, not exceeding any year 6d in the £; and their executive officers were a treasurer, a clerk, an inspector of works, and, lastly, collectors of the rates (not being of the people called Quakers) who were bound to serve under a penalty of £20. The rates were to be collected in full from tenants; but they had the right to deduct one half of the rate from their rents. The whole sum to be raised under the Act was £2,000 (beyond the cost of obtaining the Act), repayable in 30 years; money was borrowed on the security of the rate, or raised by annuities. Many clauses regulate the financial part of the scheme, define legal meetings, give power to enforce contracts, and lastly, to rebuild the church on a different scite (*sic*).

The first general meeting of trustees was held in Tipton on June 24th 1794, at the house of William Short, inn-holder, when twenty-five members subscribed to the oath. The Rev. T. Shaw Hellier (incumbent) presided. On July 22nd, at the second meeting, thirteen more trustees qualified, and five more on September 22nd, 1795.

At the first meeting Messrs. Hancox, Aston, and Hodgetts, of Dudley, bankers, were appointed treasurers, John Willim, attorney, of Bilston, was appointed clerk, while Edward Crowther, of Bescott, and William Underhill, of Tipton, were the first assessors for the rate of 6d in the £. The election of collectors was fixed for the Easter Friday following (1795). In July, 1803, Edward Dixon and Son, bankers, Dudley, became the treasurers to this trust. Borrowing powers were limited to the said £2,000 odd, and the whole principal and interest was to be repaid within 30 years. The first rate was made 25th August, 1795, and on the credit of that the first loan was raised on September 22nd.

Difficulties in carrying out the work were as frequent as the means were sometimes costly. At the close of 1809 it was reported that the Birmingham Canal Company refused to pay £54, the amount of the levy due from them for three years. In August 1813, one of the rate collectors, named Henry Proctor, a mercer, became insolvent, and presumably absconded, as his security (£50 14s. 7d.) was attached. It is interesting to note that the name of his fellow collector is written down as "Philip Williams, forgeman."

While the building of the church was in progress all Tipton banns were published, and the marriages were solemnised, in the neighbouring parish church of Dudley, but the fees were received by the curate and clerk of

Tipton. No interments were to be permitted within the walls of the new church; but the trustees were to purchase a new burial ground.

Negotiations were entered into for eligible sites, and the old building was not to be disturbed until such time as the new church was quite ready for the performance of divine service. It was November 3rd, 1796, before the new erection was reported to be wallplate high. The building operations had then been about 12 months in hand, the site (including burial ground) being nearly two acres, purchased at a cost of £189 14s. The deeds of lease and release from Dixon Amphlett, and Bedford, dated respectively 2 and 3 August, 1797, were ordered to be enrolled in the High Court of Chancery, and registered in the Consistory Court at Lichfield.

[THE CONSISTORY COURT.—The Dean and Residentiary Canons constitute the "Chapter," and occasionally hold their Court in the Chapter House, to hear and determine "causes of instance," &c. For the general regulation of the Church weekly "hepdomedary chapters" are held. In all disputes arising within the Close, an appeal lies from them to the Bishop, but to no one else beyond, the Church and the Close being governed by local statutes confirmed by Edward IV and others, including Wolsey as Pope's Legate. The Register Office, where wills are deposited, is in the Close.]

Proposals to insert north and south galleries to correspond with the west gallery were first made in September, 1808, but owing to the opposition of Rev. T. Shaw-Hillier, the work was not actually accomplished till 1813-4, at a cost of £310, the income from the seats, when they were placed therein, very materially increased the stipend of the Rev. Mr. Howells. His salary, however, was eked out by the well-patronised middle-class school which, through the kindness of his many friends in and around Tipton, he had been enabled to establish near the church.

Smaller galleries, presumably for the school children, were decided upon in February, 1824.

We now come to the allotment of pews to those claiming a right thereto in the parish church. As these "faculty pews" were somewhat numerous in the case of Tipton the state of the law on this matter may be interesting. The question naturally arises—"How could any one acquire property in a church pew?"

A prescriptive right to a pew in a church as appurtenant to an ancient messuage may be established by immemorial use and enjoyment from which a faculty is presumed, and there is no necessity that the house should be within the parish. But if the plaintiff claims a prescriptive right, and allows the commencement of it in very modern times his claim will fail. Where a pew in the chancel belonged to a person in respect to the ownership of an ancient house it was held that the tenant of the owner obtained a sufficient title by occupation to justify an action in the Ecclesiastical Court for perturbation of a pew.

Pews in a church are somewhat in the nature of an heirloom, and may descend by immemorial custom, without any ecclesiastical concurrence from the ancestor to the heir.

The right to sit in a particular pew in the church arises either from a faculty or grant from the Ordinary, for he has the disposition of all pews which are not claimed by prescription.

In an action upon the case for the disturbance of the enjoyment of a pew, if the plaintiff claims it by prescription he must state it in the declaration as appurtenant to a messuage in the parish. This prescription may be supported by an enjoyment of 36 years' standing, and perhaps any time beyond 20 years. But in such action against the Ordinary, the plaintiff must both allege and prove repairs to the pew. Perhaps when pews were alloted in the first instance by the vicar and wardens, the squire's pew-room would be more than the farmer's because of the larger amount of pecuniary support from the former for alterations or rebuilding. Or, if pews were bought out and out, the squire would perhaps pay more than the farmer, and more setting room would in consequence be alloted to the squire's family than to a farmer on any of his holdings.

Faculty pews are getting rarer and scarcer each year. At Wednesbury they have been sold by auction within the present century. A large pew in Wednesbury Old Church, attached to the freehold of an old hostelry on the way to Walsall, and still known by its ancient sign of "The Old Leathern Bottle," was sold for £40, while another sold at the Turk's Head Hotel fetched £32.

Now to relate the circumstances of the allotment, or re-allotment at the re-building of Tipton Parish Church.

Old claims to pews were first respected: at the preliminary allotment the owners of pews in the old church had seats alloted to them in the new building. Pews in the galleries were to be for general use, and unappropriated, so far as the free seating was demanded by the stated requirements; but any pews or seats beyond this fixed number were to be let, and the money thus raised by pew rents was to be applied to paying the annuities already mentioned; and any sum beyond this was to go to the augmentation of the curate's stipend.

A public advertisement published in a Birmingham newspaper in April, 1797, 'required all persons claiming pews in the new church (1) by any right or interest in pews in the old church, or (2) in respect of having farms in the parish, to send in their claims in writing, stating their rights, and, in the case of farms, giving the situation, extent, and names of the occupiers.

Some larger pews being in demand an order was given to make 12 double pews instead of 24 single ones.

On June 23rd the trustees proceeded to their first allotment, which was made as follows:—

NORTH AISLE.

No. 7 To Robert Moore
,, 8 John Smith
,, 11 Richard Nightingale
,, 12 Henry Worsey
,, 13 Devisees of Richmond Aston, deceased
,, 14 James Fisher
,, 16 William Mills and Joseph Smith
,, 18 Heirs of John Taylor, deceased
,, 19 [Christening and Churching Seat]
,, 20 Trustees of late John, Lord Viscount Dudley and Ward.
,, 21 George Birch, Esq.
,, 22 Lord (William) Viscount Dudley and Ward
,, 23 Francis Stokes, Esq.
,, 24 William Nicklin, carpenter, and William Nicklin, maltster
,, 9 Assignees of Samuel and John Hallen

SOUTH AISLE.

,, 43 To William and Danl. Wright
,, 44 George Parker ,
,, 45, 46 Messrs. Dixon, Amphlett, and Bedford
,, 47 Lessees of the Prebend of Prees
,, 51 Mrs. Whitby, Mrs. Feley, and Mrs. Townsend
,, 52 Edward Fisher
,, 53 Rev John Best
,, 54 Messrs. Dixon, Amphlett, and Bedford
,, 55 Mary Alexander
,, 56 John Hodgkins
,, 57 Joseph Pemberton

Allotted to the general congregation—
North Aisle: Nos, 1, 2, 3, 4,17, 33
South Aisle: Nos 34, 50, 63, 64, 65, 66

Further allotments were made July 18th, to owners of farms, as under—

NORTH AISLE.

No. 5, 6 To George Birch, Esq
,, 10 John Hateley (Puppy Green Farm)
,, 15 Trustees of late John, Viscount Dudley and Ward
,, 25 Bayley Caddick (of Toll End)
,, 26 William Wright and Benjamin Stokes
,, 27 William, Lord Viscount Dudley and Ward
,, 28 Owners of Bloomfield estate*
,, 29 Miss Fleeming 5 sittings and Joseph Whitehouse 2 sittings

* A 99 years' lease (79 unexpired) of this colliery and farm house, on about 42 acres, was advertised for private sale in *Aris's Gazette* on April 27th, 1795. Applications to Rev. John Taylor, Birmingham, &c.

SOUTH AISLE.

No.38 To James Keir, Alexander Blair, &c.
,, 39 — Green (Horseley Heath Farm) and to Walsall School Farm, in halves
,, 40 Isaac Aston 4 sittings, and John Nock, of Great Bridge, 3 sittings
,, 41 Patricia Mee, widow (Dudley Port Farm)
,, 42 Thomas Fletcher (Fletcher's Farm)
,, 48 J. Dumaresq and Co. (Gospel Oak Farm)
,, 49 Benjamin Parker (Brickkiln Farm)
,, 58, 59, 60 Dixon, Amphlett, and Bedford
,, 61 Bayley Caddick (Brookhouse Farm)
,, 62 Joseph Stevenson

In 1799 a further small allotment was made. And in March, 1822 pews Nos. 34 and 35 were converted into one and alloted to the Rev. James Bevan, while Nos. 33 and 34 in the other aisle were set apart for the wardens.

Now as to the financing of the scheme: Interest at the rate of five per cent. per annum was paid (half-yearly) on all the sums borrowed, except that the sum of £189 14s. for the site, secured on the bond of the trustees of the church, was paid off by fixed instalments. Scheduled in tabular form, the following is a memorandum of the mortgages made pursuant to the provisions of the Tipton Church Act:—

DATE	MORTAGES.	SUMS BORROWED	ANNUAL PAYMENTS.	WHEN PAID OFF
1796 April 22.	Daniel Moore, of Tipton, iron-master.	£100	£5	
1796 July 15.	William Jennings, of Bilston, chape maker.	£100	£5	4th Sept. 1807.
1797 April 21.	Ed. Hancox, Elz. Aston, John Laugher, and Moses Warr, of Dudley, bankers.	£500	£25	By instalments.
1797 Aug. 3.	Ed. Dixon, Joseph Amphlett, and William Bedford, of Tipton.	£189 14s.		10th Nov. 1815.
1799 April 29.	Joseph Amphlett, James Fisher, Zachary Parkes, Benjamin Parker, and Bayley Caddick, jun., trustees of the Parish Leasow.	£500	£25	(? 1824)
1806 June 20.	Same trustees.	£552	£27 10s.	

With regard to the dept specially mentioned, it may be noted that

£189 14 0		(Purchase money)
170 14 4		(18 years' interest)
360 8 4		Altogether

was ordered to be paid to William Bedford, the survivor, on the aforementioned date (10 Nov. 1815).

Reference has been made to the second method of raising money by annuities in pursuance of the Act. Here follows a memorandum of the said grants of annuities, at the rate of 10 per cent. per annum, and on some of which—long-lived annuitants—a loss was sustained; while on the short-lived annuitants the gain was as material as it was immediate:—

DATE	MORTAGES.	SUMS BORROWED	ANNUAL PAYMENTS.	WHEN PAID OFF
1796 April 22.	Ann Portray, of Darlaston, spinster.	£100	£10	Died about June, 1797.
July 15	Edward Plews, of Walsall, gentleman	£300	£30	
1796 June 23	Nancy Moore, of Tipton, spinster	£150	£15	Died 14th April, 1802
July 18	Daniel Moore, of Tipton, iron-master, for the life of Martha Willett, Spinster.	£100	£10	

CHAPTER XXVII.—TIPTON BENEFACTIONS: LOST CHARITIES: SHELDON'S DOLES: WOODHALL'S SCHOOL ENDOWMENTS.

It was at the instance of Lord Brougham that the first Charity Commission was appointed in 1818. At this time the grossest abuses existed, often with the connivance of high public functionaries. Doles and charities afforded a wide field for corruption to work in. The most striking evil which then existed was the unblushing effrontery with which the charities were diverted from public to private objects. It is clear that robbery on a large and systematic scale went on for years, or what, for instance, became of the following Tipton Charities, the product of the 16th, 17th, and 18th centuries, reported up thus:—

LOST CHARITIES.

"There was a table of benefactions in Tipton Church, which stated as follows:—

Mr. Edward Nightingale, in 1594, gave two pounds per annum for ever.
Mr. Edward Nightingale, in 1604, gave five shillings per annum for ever.
Mr. Edward Dudley, in 1687, gave two pounds per annum for ever.
Mr. John Jeavon, in 1687, gave five shillings per annum for ever.
Mr. Thomas Nock, in 1688, gave ten shillings per annum for ever.
Mr. John Nightingale, in 1688, gave five shillings per annum for ever.
Mrs. Jane Nickens, in 1727, gave the interest of twenty pounds for ever.

N.B.—All the above gifts are to be distributed to the poor of this parish yearly (viz.,) the one half to be given on Midsummer Day and the other half on St. Thomas's Day.

This table was taken when the church was rebuilt in 1796, and is now lost; but a copy of this was taken, which has since been printed for the information of the neighbourhood, and in the hope of recovering some of the charities. There is only one person, an old man, who ever remembers any of these charities to have been in existence. He states that he recollects money being distributed to poor people, and that he himself has assisted in the distribution. He says that the overseers supplied the money, but he does not know from what source they obtained it, nor does he know to what amount money was distributed.

The Rev. Mr. Helliar, who was incumbent for near 40 years, and who died in 1812, is stated to have frequently made inquiries as to these charities, and to have exerted himself for their re-establishment, but without success."

* * * * * *

We find, however, that one benefaction in this parish has been well managed. In the last chapter it was recorded that on April 29th, 1799, the church rates (under the Act) were mortgaged to the trustees for poor widows in the parish, for the sum of £500, proceeds of the sale of the mines under the "Parish Leasow." This land is the charitable bequest of one Josiah Sheldon, and the income of the whole charity has been about £57 a year, affording more than a pound a week, distributed in doles of bread to poor widows not receiving parochial relief.

The Government report of 1823 runs as follows:—

SHELDON'S CHARITY.

"Josiah Sheldon, as stated in the recital in the indenture hereafter abstracted, by will, about the year 1722, gave the rent of a certain piece of land, to be distributed weekly at Tipton church in bread, to 12 poor widows who receive no collection or relief from the parish rates. The land consists of about 2½ acres, and the rent need always to be applied in purchasing bread to be given to poor widows. In 1797 the coals under this land were sold for £1,052. The land was not sold; but the coals demised for 21 years, the lessees paying five guineas yearly for the upper soil, as appears by the following deed:—

By indenture, dated 23d June, 1797, between Joseph Smith, and three others, churchwardens and overseers of Tipton, of the first part, Moses Warr, and two others, executors of Richmond Aston and Daniel Moore, and John Beaumont, of the second part; and Joseph Amphlett, Esq., and four others, of the third part, reciting the gift of Josiah Sheldon, as above; and reciting, that the rents of the said ground had been disposed of accordingly; and reciting, that there was coal under the said ground, which it was desirable to sell, and that the same had been sold by auction in 1795, at the price of £1,052, to the said Richmond, Aston, Moore, and Beaumont; it is witnessed, that in pursuance of the said agreement, and in consideration of the sum of £300 then paid, and in consideration of the payment of the residue at the times therein specified, the said Joseph Smith, and others, demised to the said Warr, and others all the said piece or parcel of ground, with all coals, &c., under the same, with power to erect engines, &c, upon the same ground; to hold for 21 years, from the 23rd June, 1797, paying yearly £5 5s. as a surface rent. The lessees covenant, at the expiration of the term, to leave the soil in a husband-like condition. And it was agreed, that the said Joseph Amphlett, and others, and the survivors and survivor of them, and the executors and administrators of such survivor, should stand seised of the said £1,052,

When received, in trust, to place out the same in the three per cent. consols, or on the fund for re-building Tipton church, or on mortgages, or real or Government securities, upon trust, to indemnify the trustees from any damage they might receive from the contract. And upon further trust, to pay the dividends and interest of the said stock, or other securities, to the churchwardens and overseers of Tipton, to the intent that the same might be applied for the same purposes as the rents of a piece of land thereby demised, were by the said will of Josiah Sheldon, made subject to; provided, that when the trustees should be reduced to two, the major part of the parishioners of Tipton, in vestry assembled, should appoint other fit persons residing in or near Tipton, to make up the number five, who should transfer the trust property, to hold to such new trustees jointly with themselves. By indenture, dated 6th July, 1821 the premises were conveyed to four new trustees, upon the trusts declared in the deed of 1797.

The sum of £1,052, when received, was advanced to the churchwardens under the power of an Act of Parliament, passed in 1795, for taking down and rebuilding Tipton church at five per cent interest. Of this sum £400 has been repaid, and is now in the hands of Messrs. Dixon, Dalton, and Co., bankers, at Dudley, who do not allow interest for it. The remainder (£652) is secured on the church; but the trustees for re-building the church have offered to pay off a part this, and are obliged, by their Act, to pay all the money borrowed within 30 years, which term is within a year or two of expiring. The trustees of the charity have not decided how to dispose of the money when paid off. The leasees under the lease of 1797 did not get out all the coal within the term, and a second sale by auction was made of what might remain, about three years ago, when the sum of £165 was bid, and the coal was sold at that price. Since the sale it has occurred to the trustees that it might be advisable to invest the trust-money in building houses on the land, and with that view the contract has not been confirmed, the purchaser having consented either to confirm or rescind the bargain, as the trustees should; on further consideration, think best for the interest of the charity. For this reason no rent has been received for the upper surface for the three years that this business has remained undecided.

The interest of the money secured on the church was divided yearly, in eightpenny or ninepenny loaves, amounting nearly to a pound a week, till the £400 was paid off. The distribution was strictly confined to widows not receiving relief. The bread was given out at the church, and the distribution was managed by the church committee; and on balancing the account with them a short time ago, it appeared that there was an arrear of nearly £100 due for interest. It is intended to add this to the principal, and a meeting of the trustees will be held immediately to consider of the best means of investing the trust money, and of the propriety of confirming or rescinding the contract for the second sale of coal."

Bearing on this benefaction, and some of the details already given on it, are to be found some records of the Parish Vestry proceedings.

Minutes referring to the Parish Leasow inform us that John Beaumont surrendered the lease thereof in February, 1819, leaving the shaft, the use of which was granted to Thomas Morris for six months, at 20s. per month, the ungotten mines to be advertised in the meantime, but in 1830 the trustees of the Leasow were asked to confirm and complete the sale of the lower mines to the same Thomas Morris for £165. New trustees elected in March, 1821, were Rev. James Bevan (of Wombourne), Perpetual Curate of Tipton; Rev. John Howells, the resident curate, William Turton, of West Bromwich; and William Yates, of Tipton.

* * * * * *

Lastly, we have the chief glory of Tipton's charities in Woodhall's bequest. If, however, the income had been applied to higher or intermediate education, and the care of the elementary education left in the hands of the School Board, its results might have been even better than they are. "Solomon Woodhall, by will dated 14th April, 1796, gave and bequeathed to the Rev. Thomas Shawe Helliar, the Rev. Joseph Cartwright, and nine others, £650 upon trust, to invest the same in funds, and there keep the same until the same should be repurchased or redeemed, and as soon as the same should be repurchased or redeemed, to apply the money received in consideration thereof, in purchase of stock of the same or like nature, producing as near as might be a like interest, and apply a competent part of the dividends for supporting and establishing a school at or near Great Bridge, in the parish of Tipton, for educating boys, being the children of poor persons, parishioners of the inhabitants within the parishes of Dudley, Tipton, West Bromwich, and Wednesbury, in reading, writing, and arithmetic; and when there should be any surplus of dividend, to invest the same in the purchase of the like stock; and he directed that his trustees should purchase such books, papers, and slates as they should deem requisite, and should elect some proper person of the Established Church of England to instruct the boys, with a power to remove and displace the master as often as they should think fit, and to impose on the master the terms of renting at his own expense and residing in such house at or near Great Bridge as they should think fit and convenient for a school, allowing him such salary as they should think proper. The master to take the boys to church on Sunday and Christmas Day, the number of boys not to be less than 30 or more than 40, to be admitted between seven and eleven years old, to be chosen by the trustees, and to remain four years only; the trustees to choose a treasurer to manage the school, and receive the dividends, and pay the master, and to be allowed such salaries as the trustees should think proper; the trustees to meet 21st December yearly, to settle the accounts. Trustees ceasing to be resident in Dudley, Tipton, West Bromwich, and Wednesbury to cease to be trustees, and when the trustees should be reduced to six, the survivors to nominate five others and transfer the trust property to them.

Mr. Woodhall died about the year 1800, and the £650 left by him remained for some years partly on private trust and partly on the security of a turnpike trust. In the year 1804 Isaac Hawkins Browne, Esq. and the Rev. Thomas Gisborne, the executors of Mr. Isaac Hawkins, of Rurton (who left a large fund to be applied by them to pious and charitable uses), contributed a donation of £100 in aid of the objects of Mr Woodall's will. This also remained for some time on private security, till the whole was gathered in about the year 1820 and invested in the purchase of £1,102 18s. 9d. 3 per cent. consols, in the names of the Rev. John Howells, James Bourne, George Dalton, and Joseph Green Bourne. When this legacy came into possession a school was established in Tipton, to which 10 children were appointed from each of the four places mentioned in the will. None of those appointed from Dudley ever attended. Some came from West Bromwich and from Wednesbury for a considerable time, but schools have been established in those two places which are more convenient for the children to attend, and they have ceased to come to the Tipton school.

The interest of the stock above mentioned has been combined with other funds consisting of the interest of a legacy of £100 old South Sea annuities, left by Miss Catherine Nickens, and of subscriptions and collections after sermons, with which three schools, established in different parts of this extensive and populous parish, through the exertions of the Rev. John Howells, are aided viz., at Tipton Green, Ocker Hill, and Horseley Heath, containing 500 children, boys and girls in each. Every child pays a penny a week to provide writing materials and firing, and to pay the expense of the repairs of damage done to the school. These three schoolrooms were built entirely by subscriptions of the parish."

The foregoing extract is taken from "The Endowed Schools of Staffordshire," by George Griffith (1860).

The Rev. John Howells was, of course, the curate of the parish. The report of 1823 gives the following statistics:—

Day scholars, Boys	414
,, ,, Girls	370
Sunday scholars (not included above), Boys	18
,, ,, ,, Girls...	115

It says further—"These schools are all conducted on the Madras System, and are in union with the Central Society, and the governors have the advantage of getting books at a very moderate rate from Bartlett's Buildings Society."

The Central Society aided the erection of the schools by a donation of £200 in the year 1818. The Madras System, here alluded to, was introduced into England from Madras, by a Scotch teacher, named Dr. Bell, and was adopted by the National Society (Church of England), and hence the term "National Schools." Soon afterwards, this monitorial, or mutual system of instruction, was modified by Joseph Lancaster, a Quaker, and being adopted by the British Society, originated the British Schools (where the Bible was read without note or comment, and no distinctive religious teaching was allowed).

A return published in 1831 states that 1,000 children were attending Tipton National Schools. A printed return of the Council on Education, of inspected schools in 1844, makes no mention whatever of these Tipton schools, although we find the names of Wednesbury Church Schools. St. Leonard's Schools Bilston, Trinity Schools, West Bromwich, and others in the immediate neighbourhood. Evidently they were not yet under Government inspection.

CHAPTER XXVIII.—CHARITY LANDS: TRUSTEES UNDER THE ACT, AND THE CLOSE OF THE TRUST: OLD CHURCHWARDENS, &C.

At a recent return the income of the Tipton endowed charities was said to be £101 6s. 8d. per annum, of which £42 12s. 1d. was devoted to education, and the rest expended in doles. These doles of bread are not now the exclusive privilege of the mother church of the parish (St. Martin's), but are shared with the daughter churches that have grown up within the last half- century. This distribution of the doles over the wide area of the whole civil parish is due chiefly to the exertions of the Rev, A. Solari, late vicar of Ocker Hill Church.

Considering that the authorities of Lichfield Cathedral, and the Ecclesiastical Commissioners, have together reaped a harvest of not less than £100,000 from lands in Tipton—from the mineral wealth below the surface, of course—it is not very creditable that the church accommodation within the parish should exhibit itself with so much meanness.

The following is an extract from a report presented at an Archidiaconal Conference, held at Stafford in 1869:—"The old parish of Tipton contains 21,000 people, and is divided into four districts, with four clergy and four churches, containing 3,000 adult sittings, of which 1,700 are free, there are no mission rooms. One district has 3,000 people, one clergymen with £50 a year, no parsonage, and a church wretchedly poor and mean, in a most unseemly position. Three new districts might at once be marked out, each with about 3,000 people, and mission work be commenced, with a view to the provision hereafter of more complete parochial apparatus."

It was about this time that Bishop Selwyn took charge of the diocese, and threw into his work all that energy and thoroughness which had characterised his spiritual labours at the Antipodes. In Tipton Bishop Selwyn found a parish of neglect and poverty, worthy of his attention.

But before leaving the subject of the charities it may be useful to quote the record of those Tipton lands, which proved so beneficial and so advantageous to the neighbouring town of Walsall.

Certain lands in Tipton, belonging to Walsall Grammar School, are thus mentioned in the Charity Commissioners' Report, 1823:—

"Under the land at Tipton there are coal mines, which have been sold under the authority of the Act (1797), by public Auction, to Charles Poolton, Samuel Proud, Thomas Price, and John Law, for a term of 42 years, at £505 per acre, amounting in the whole to £12,243 1s. 10½d. (see Chapter XII).

"By the contract entered into on this occasion which is dated 24 March, 1800, the governors of the school covenanted to convey to the lessees, &c., all the mines and veins of ironstone under those ten closes near Princes End, in the parish of Tipton … and under the Birmingham Canal passing through … containing 24 acres 39 perches (survey of 1784) and to make cuts and canals … to set up engines …; in consideration thereof the said Poolton and others … to pay £1,638 1s. 10½d. and £505 yearly until the whole should be paid; the leasees to fill up the cuts, drains, &c., and make the whole fit for tillage before 25 March, 1842.

"And the governors further covenanted that they would demise the said closes, to hold to the said lessees from 25 March next after the death of Daniel Whitehouse, for 21 years, at the Rent of £30.

It appears that Daniel Whitehouse died about 1801 having before that held the land on lease at £12 a year."

These Tipton lands, forming part of the Walsall Grammar School endowment in 1554, were not "pastures" in 1819, as they were when originally described in the Charter, but were then scheduled as—

	a.	r.	p.
Tipton Farm in the Parish of Tipton	23	1	11
Of which 1a 1r. 35p. now forms part of the line of the Birmingham Canal and tow path.			

Another schedule in the Charity Commissioners' Report of 1823 sets forth the rental—

	£.	s.	p.
The Tipton Farm, with a house and buildings let to Poolton, Price, and others, on lease for 21 years, from the 25 March after the death of one Daniel Whitehouse, which took place in 1801, is now held by Thomas Price and Samuel Proud, at the yearly rent of....................................	30	0	0

* * * * * *

Beyond the list of original Trustees under the Tipton Church Act, other names deserve to be placed on permanent record. Vacancies in the body of Trustees caused by death, &c., had to be filled up co-optatively. The following is a list of the vacancies so filled, compiled by Mr. Richard Haines, of Hill House, West Bromwich:—

DATE	TRUSTEES ELECTED	IN ROOM OF TRUSTEE DECEASED.
1974		
June 24	Abiathar Hawkes	Edward Whitby
1795		
Aug. 25	John William (clerk to Trust)	Edward Harper
1796		
Apr. 1	Richard Edwards	Richmond Aston
1797		
Sept. 22	Joseph Stevenson	Wm. John Banner
1803		
Apr. 15	Edward Elliott	Joseph Amphlett
,,	William Persehouse	Francis Stokes
,,	James Whitehouse	John Hateley
,,	Jeremiah Willett	Daniel Moore
,,	John Gwinnett	William Short
1805		
Nov. 22	Rev. John Howells	John Dumaresq
,,	John Hodgkins	William Mee

1807		
Sept. 4	Edward Dixon	Edward Dixon
1810		
Apr. 27	Wm. Nicklin (maltster)	Edward Whitehouse
1812		
Mar. 15	Henry Golding	Edward Foley
,,	Thomas Hood	George Birch
,,	Joseph Bourne	Jervoise Clarke-Jervoise
,,	Charles Jeavons	Rev. Wm. Perry
1813		
Jan. 5	Edward Fisher	Edward Fisher
May 22	Obadiah Moore	Thomas Holbeche
,,	Philip William	Oliver Dixon
Sept. 24	Richard Smith	William Cotterill
,,	William Turton	Rev. T. Shaw-Hillier
,,	John Bissell	Wm. Pitchfork
,,	John Holland	Richard Jesson
1815		
Mar. 3	Simeon Bissell	Rev. Joseph Cartwright
,,	James Nock	Rev. John Best
1819		
Apr. 25	William Yates	Isaac Aston
,,	Aaron Manby	Richard Mee
,,	William Turton	Peter Fisher
,,	Thomas Hill	Zachary Parkes
,,	Joseph Hateley	Benjamin Parker
1820		
Jan. 7	Thomas Price	James Fisher

Among some of the more prominent churchwardens of Tipton may be noted the names of—

1553, Edward Nightingale and William Thornton.
1657, John Nightingale.
1683, John Nightingale and William Clare.
1797, William Underhill and Joseph Smith,
1798, Edward Fisher and Joseph Smith.
1799, James Fisher.
1848, R. Haines and Hickman.

The name of Clare has been noted in chapter xix, as that borne by the Cromwellian cornet, and the names of the overseers of the poor in 1646 have also been recorded in the same chapter.

Casually may be noted also the names of a few clergymen who have been curates in the parish, namely, the Revs. G. H. Colton (1834), John L. Ison (1837), Horace F. Gray (1840), F. S. Bradshaw (1843), and Augustus Davis, B.A. (1844).

Some of the trustees originally appointed under the Act never qualified, and those elected during the last 20 years of the Trust may be deemed to have been the principal inhabitants of the parish.

On July 6th, 1821, John Willim resigned his post as Clerk to the Trustees, and Simeon Bissell was appointed in his stead. In October, 1823, this latter official was made governor of the workhouse in place of the matron, Elizabeth Horton, retired, and in 1828 his salary was raised to £120 as assistant overseer.

The Trust terminated gradually as liabilities were paid off, and towards the end Government annuities were purchased for those having just claims against the Trustees. As times advanced the objection to Church rates—on which the Trustees had been mainly dependent—gathered strength. It was fortunate that the liabilities incurred under the Act were liquidated before these objections took an active and aggressive form. A meeting, attended by 51 parishioners, was called for the purpose of enforcing the payment of the church rate granted July 2nd, 1832; this was more than a year after, namely, October 4th, 1833, so that the rate had not been collected in that time.

Opposition grew and became more active. A contest about the Church rate set in on November 29th, 1844, when a motion for a 5d. rate received 73 votes, and a strong minority of 62 for a farthing vote demanded a poll. The election for a people's warden on the 25th March following turned upon this question, the candidates being William Sheldon and E. L. Cresswell.

CHAPTER XXIX.—ST. JOHN'S CHURCH: THE ORIGIN OF THE TIPTON SURNAME OF "WHITEHOUSE": ST. PAUL'S CHURCH.

From the old Vestry Minute Book we gather that in March, 1816, the old church tower was occupied, that interments were made in the burial ground, and that one Charles Kemp was rated as in occupation of the premises, although the rate on that occasion was excused. And it was not till 6 March, 1820, that all deeds and papers relating to the demolition of the old fabric were ordered to be deposited in the safe in the vestry of the new church.

The old tower of.the ancient parish church stood desecrated till 1850, when to meet the still growing needs of the population a chapel of ease was erected in attachment to it. This was done at a cost of £750, raised by subscription, and it provided 500 sittings. The original building to which the tower was attached had been dedicated to St. Martin; but the name being appropriated by the modern parish church, the new church on the ancient site was dedicated to St. John.

But before this could be done some difficulty with the tenant of the old tower had to be overcome. It was then occupied as a dwelling-house by an eccentric individual who had reared a family of children there. He is said to have been a barrister, or at least a man of superior education, living in reduced circumstances. By what right he claimed the old tower is not quite known but it is a fact that before anything could be done with this old site the freehold had to be purchased from him for a sum of £30. To the tower was attached the new building—a mere rectangular room, in common blue and red bricks, and not too high in the roof. The tower is used as the vestry. No further mention is deserved by the fabric of the body of the church. But the old tower is interesting from its age, although it is comparatively modern. It is a square embattled tower of roughly coursed stonework in three stages, and now reaching to a height of 30 or 40 feet. On the east side of the lowest stage is inserted a pointed window of doubtful age. In each of the four sides of the top stage is a coupled louvre window, with stone mullions and trefoil heads enclosed by a circular head without labels. The two string courses which divide the three stages are simply hollowed out and these again possess no distinctive characteristics as to period. But the peculiarity of this tower is that although the bottom stage is perfectly vertical, above each string course the stonework is made to batter (or taper) slightly upwards so that the whole structure gets a little narrower towards the top. On the north and south sides of the lowest stage are two very narrow openings which have been rudely filled in with masonry, seeming to indicate the former position of two narrow lights, and therefore tending to show that the stage of the tower was not formerly the bottom one. On the south side, in the middle stage, is the face of a stone sun-dial. The rounded head of this tablet evidences its late period—almost Annean as its date declares, for the inscription in the semi-circular heading of the dial runs thus—

THIS
STEEPLE WAS
BUILT ANNO DOMINI
1683
JOHN NIGHTINGALE
WILLIAM CLARE, CHURCH-
WARDENS

Of course the steeple disappeared long ago, when the body of the old church fell into such ruinous decay.

The few interments since made in the burial ground were allowed under very special circumstances. All the old graves and vaults (like the tower) are said to have sunk quite 20 feet below the level of the present surface and with regard to the extent, the present enclosed and unused site is but a small portion of the ancient burial ground, which is said to have reached on the north side as far as the Gospel Oak Ironworks, and on the east side beyond the present line of canal.

And only in recent years has the street frontage to Church Lane been open. A public-house and some cottage property actually shut in the church and its grounds from view; and at the present time, although a pair of open iron gates and a well-kept path may attract the attention of the passers by, it is still quite possible for the stranger to pass along the street without ever discovering St. John's Church. Well may Bishop Selwyn describe the position as "unseemly" for a church—stuck out of sight behind an inn! The site of the ancient parsonage house (mentioned in chapter xxii) is said to have been near the end of Church Lane, somewhere near where Princes End railway station now stands. The present parsonage house is a small but comfortable cottage, erected through the exertions of the Rev. S. T. Tozer, but also hidden away from the front street behind some cottages next the aforementioned gates. However, it is convenient for its proximity to the church and the schools; and this, in the eyes of the late Bishop Selwyn, was always the main object. Previously Mr. Tozer had resided out of the parish. It is only by courtesy that the title of "parsonage" can be extended to this cottage residence, in the same way that the saved building itself is dignified with the title of "church."

Along the south wall of the churchyard Mr. Tozer has carefully arranged the few gravestones left on the spot. They are broken and nearly obliterated by age and the weather. So far as they can be deciphered they are somewhat interesting. One of the latest put down was that of William Elwell in 1792; whilst those in the worst state of preservation belong to the two wives of Josiah Sheldon (? the benefactor of the parish). There is a stone to one Iosiah Sheldon, 1624. Others record the deaths of—

Thomas Nock, Oct. 26th, 1688.
Ioane, wife of John Nightingale, 1678.
Thomas Nock, May, 1768.
Daniel Round, March, 1780.

Two others bear the name of Clowes, and both show the heraldic fleur-de-lys and the heraldic rose.

Then there are stones to—

Diana, wife of Joseph Parkes 1743.

Mary, wife of William Mills, 1751.

Elizabeth, wife of Solomon Woodall, 1793.

But the most curious of all is a gravestone to one Elizabeth, wife of Richard Timmins, aged 27. The lettering of this—dating from about the middle of the last century—is not only unconventional from the awkward parting of the words at the end of the lines; but the semi-circular panel at the top of the stone contains a queer design, evidently an implement or instrument of some kind. Rude devices of trade symbols are sometimes met with, indicating the nature of the employment of the deceased. The nearest guess that can be hazarded in this instance (for the stone is worn and partly obliterated) is that the carving represents an old-fashioned box-iron and its oven, evidently lying on its side from the position of the charcoal flue—perhaps the artist found it easier to get it in thus.

* * * * * *

No doubt in erecting this new church of St. John traces were laid bare of the ancient foundation dedicated to St. Martin—stones that call for the reverence and respect of all Tiptonians who venerate the traditions of their past. For here may be given a theory of a somewhat legendary character respecting the erection of a christian church on this venerable site. In the early centuries of the Christian era, the North of England Pagans were converted by the preaching of St. Ninian, "a most holy man," and a reverend bishop of the British nation, whose See was named after St. Martin, and who built a stately church. "The place belongs to the province of the Bernicians, and is generally called the White House, because he built there a church of stone, which was not usual among the Britons"—the "Britons" being Christians, as opposed to the "English," who were Pagans (see *Bede's Ecclesiastical History*, Bohn's edition, p. 113).

St. Columba, who laboured so zealously for the conversion of these southern Picts, was succeeded by many equally zealous workers, who perhaps rescued the said stately church, and made it the head quarters of a mission settlement. From this issued forth, among other noted successors of St. Columba, the great missionary, St. Chad, who came into Mercia (this Midland district), and is said to have erected a mission church in this immediate vicinity. Now the theory is that the site then selected was the very spot on which St. John's Church now stands. In support of this we have to note the following circumstances.

The Midlands were then well-wooded, and churches were always placed in groves of trees, generally oak. (Is not the word "Kirk" said to be derived from *quercus*, an oak?) Then the white limestone was here ready to the hand of the builder—perhaps it was the very presence of this stone that reminded the missionaries of the white edifice left behind in the woodlands of their beloved northern home. And when their new white house of God was erected they dedicated it to St. Martin, in fond recollection of that mother church in Bernicia. Perhaps this affectionate remembrance accounts also for so many dedications in this Mercian district to St. Martin; but that the St. Martin's of Tipton was the original white house of St. Chad and his colonizing priests is thought to be so from the fact that in this parish the most common surname is Whitehouse. To this day the Tipton pronunciation of the name more nearly approximates that of the original Anglo-Saxon than the proper and accepted pronunciation, especially the final syllable as "hus." Of that ancient structure all traces have long since disappeared; but the fact that the church possessed a tower is itself another piece of evidence favourable to the theory set up here—for in the earliest times of the Christian era a tower was absolutely necessary to a church, as a place of safety and defence against the fierce attacks of Pagan neighbours. That in after years a spire was superimposed, was simply the utilisation of a base, whose defensive use had become obsolete in the more peaceful times of an undisputed Christian sway, for an architectural feature to point men's thoughts heavenwards.

* * * * * *

The population of St. John's ecclesiastical parish was last returned at 3,896. The living, a new endowment by the Ecclesiastical Commissioners, is now valued at £280 per annum. When the Rev. S. T. Tozer first accepted the living it was but £10 a year!

The only vicars of the parish have been—

Rev. —. Herbert, 1850.

Rev. S. T. Tozer, 1863.

* * * * * *

St Paul's Church, in Owen Street, is the most centrally situated church in Tipton, standing in the midst of a thickly grouped industrial population. It is a large brick structure, ugly but massive, and as substantial as it is plain. It has a tower, through which it is entered from the street, and which contains one bell. From this spacious entrance there is an extremely wide nave between the seats, straight through to the altar, and into which forms may be carried on the occasion of a crowded congregation. The numbered pews are the old-fashioned high box pews, while at the rear of the church the seats are mere benches with backs, and arm-rests at each end. There is a gallery running round three sides of the building, and the original seating accommodation was for 1,322, of which 744 were to be free. What income is derived from the pew rents is uncertain. All the wood-work is painted and is of the very plainest description, and the whole of the interior needs renovation. There is no burial ground, but under the building are a number of vaults intended for sepulchral purposes, which, however, have never been used. The earlier registers are not well kept, and the first is missing altogether. The structure was erected in 1838-9, at a cost of more than £5,000 raised by subscriptions and grants.

The living was first known as a "perpetual curacy," and valued at £150 a year, in the patronage of the incumbent of St. Martin's Church, Tipton, and originally the population was over 10,000 souls. But St. Paul's parish has suffered very considerably since St. Matthew's ecclesiastical district was carved out of it, and the population is given (1881) as only 5,500. The living is now worth about £300 per annum. There is a vicarage house in Canal Street close at hand, but it is very inconvenient and altogether unsuitable for such an official residence. Some 17 years ago a sum of nearly £1,700 was raised for the purpose of building a new vicarage, and Sir Horace St. Paul offered a site; but as this was a long distance from the church the scheme fell through, and the money has since been invested by the Ecclesiastical Commissioners, and the interest on it augments the annual value of the benefice.

Among those instrumental in forming St. Paul's parish is said to have been the Rev. J. L. Ison, a curate at the Old Church. The living has been held by the Rev. E. H. A. Gwynne, B.A. the Rev. Wyndham M. Hutton, Rev. Thomas Henrey, and the present vicar, instituted St. James' Day, 1873, is the Rev. W. Cornwell, a brother of the writer of the well-known educational text-books.

The collecting plates, which are of pewter, bear the date 1861, and the names—

William Howells } churchwardens.
Simeon Round }

CHAPTER XXX.—ST. MARK'S CHURCH, OCKER HILL; ST. MATTHEW'S CHURCH, AND TIVIDALE CHURCH.

St. Mark's Church, at Ocker Hill, was erected 1849-50, at a cost of about £2,500, raised by grants and subscriptions. As a district for ecclesiastical operations the parish was formed in 1846, and included Ocker Hill, Toll End, and Lea Brook, and the adjacent parts of Tipton parish. The population in 1881 was returned at 4,111, and the number of sittings provided in the church is 600.

The style of this church is early decorated Gothic, in blue bricks, with plentiful stone dressings, even the buttresses having stone weatherings. There is a nave, with a clerestory lighted (somewhat inadequately) with trefoils. There are two aisles, but neither tower nor spire. There is a large three-light window at both the eastern end and at the western end; that at the eastern extremity being surmounted by a rose (or wheel) window, and that at the western end by a vesica window. The west end also has a good doorway, with stone shafts, and a moulded arch with corbel terminations.

An exposed bell, under a bell-cote, hangs at the western end of the south wall. The organ is still in the small western gallery, although a new organ chamber has just been added at the south-east of the building. It is intended to add a new vestry and a narthex. At present there is a small vestry on the north-east. The churchyard was extended about seven years ago, and is still used for interments. The register dates from 1850.

The benefice was, in the first instance, a perpetual curacy, valued at £150; it is now described as a vicarage, and worth £250 per annum, in the gift of the Crown and the Bishop of Lichfield alternately. The incumbents have been—

1850-1854, Rev. Lionel W. Stanton, B.A.

1854-1888, Rev. A. A. N. F. Solari.

1888, Rev. E. J. Norman.

Within the last two years a sum of £700 has been raised towards church restoration and improvement, and a further sum of £1,000 is still needed for very necessary repairs. A hot-water heating apparatus has been put in, and altogether Mr. Norman is as indefatigable as his well-known predecessor.

For more than 30 years the form of the Rev. Angelo Solari was a familiar figure in the district, as he day by day and year by year moved about unceasingly in his ministrations among the poor. And at one time when he bestrode a remarkably small and very shaggy pony, he presented a picture as quaint as that of a mediœval monk mounted on a mule. The little animal, too, seemed endowed with his master's never-failing spirit of meekness and all-enduring patience, and was popularly supposed to derive the chief of his sustenance by browsing around the gravestones in the little churchyard!

With a singleness of purpose the good man devoted his life to ameliorating the condition of the very many poverty-stricken parishioners to be found in that portion of Tipton parish. In exceptional times, when privation and hunger were more than usually rampant, his appeals to the public were as regular as the responses thereto were hearty—for his self-denying ministrations were in time generally known abroad throughout the whole wide district. Even tramps secured his ready sympathy, and children with equal readiness confided in him without reserve.

Whether the constant strain of this never-ending conflict with poverty and ignorance was too much to be borne by the single strength of one champion for the long period stretching over a third of a century it is certain that at last something gave way with startling suddenness, for the surrounding district was shocked and horror stricken to learn that Mr. Solari had committed suicide by cutting his throat in his room, on that dread 8th day of March, 1888. Never was anything so difficult to realise, and seldom indeed has a clergyman passed away so universally beloved and so widely regretted.

Many are the anecdotes related of this simple minded minister of God. A few years ago he was invited to a semi-public banquet at Wednesbury, All in good time he put in his appearance, and was just shaking hands at the dining room doors with the official in charge of the arrangements, when he caught sight of the clerical garb already seated at the top of the table. "Who is that clergyman seated there?" inquired Mr Solari. "Oh!" was the reply, " that is the new vicar we wish to publicly introduce on this occasion." "Ah! then good day. One of us is quite enough," and seizing his hat, he had disappeared before the astonished official could recover himself.

* * * * * *

St. Matthew's Church, on the Dudley Road, was erected in 1881 to meet the requirements of the outspreading population of St. Paul's parish, The cost, which was nearly £6,000, was borne in a great measure by the liberality of a few large subscribers, aided by the ready response of very many smaller contributors all worked up by the indefatigable energies of Mr Edward A. Spurgin, who acted as secretary to the fund. Of course there were the usual grants from the various church societies and other bodies connected with the Establishment. The exact amount paid to the contractor, including his "extras," was £4,868 4s. 9d.; legal, ecclesiastical, professional, and other charges brought up the amount to £5,877 7s. 3d. A balance of over £25 was then left in the hands of the honorary secretary, who thereupon placed this sum to the credit of a new parsonage account (December 1881), and made an appeal for further funds. To the church building account Lord Dudley had given £900 plus £500 for erecting the tower. Mr. William Roberts gave £705, plus £300 to the tower fund. Mr Alfred Roberts and Sir Horace St. Paul gave each £705. These are but the few larger subscribers. Then to the new parsonage account Lord Dudley gave £100, while £50 was forthcoming from each of these three munificent donors—Sir Horace St. Paul, Mr. William Roberts, and Mr. Alfred Roberts. The appeal asked for £700 to meet certain grants, but the total expenditure on this handsome official residence (which stands beside the church), and the erection of boundary walls and certain provision to meet other incidentals, was about £2,000. The appeal stated that house-rent was then being paid for the vicar, while in return the living produced only the interest on £1,000 endowment, £40 in offertories (in lieu of pew-rents), and about £40 for tithes. The Incorporated Society had stipulated for 265 free seats, which the architect met by providing sittings as follows:—

Nave	196
,, free	214
Gallery, free	68
	478

The population is estimated at about 4,000, and in the vestry hangs a handy map of this district parish, showing how its ecclesiastical limits are bounded by the parishes of St. Edmund's, Dudley (diocese of Worcester); St Peter's, Upper Gornal; Sedgley; Coseley; St. John's, Tipton; and St. Paul's, Tipton.

The living, valued at £270, has been held from the first by the Rev. Robert Street Keitch, of St. Aidan's; it is in the gift of the Simeon Trustees.

This church is as neat a structure as any in the district, and in the matter of taste and judgment reflects the highest credit upon the architect and the Building Committee. It is of good red brick, substantially built, and is as effective as any modern building can be in the Early English style. It consists of a wide nave and two small aisles, approached from the street through a narthex, while the vestry occupies the north-east and the organ chamber the south-east, having the chancel between them, which is terminated by a sacrarium with an angular apsidal end. The choir stalls are on each side of the chancel for antiphonal singing. The pulpit is of stone, the gift of Dr. W. L. Underhill. A stone font stands at the south-west of the nave, and near the entrance, the position of the baptistry rightly symbolising that baptism is the method of entry to the Christian Church. There is a small gallery at the western end. The aisles are mere passages for approaching the pews in the nave, and the nave arcading is in six spans, carried on bold stone circular pillars with brick arches, and a clerestory with triple lancet lights. The windows of the aisles are coupled lancets. At the western entrance is a good doorway with stone shafts and a tympanum, the carving of which gives in relief the appropriate subject of the church's patron, St. Matthew. On the south-east is a massive tower, with buttresses and four pinnacles, and containing one bell.

The Vicarage House is as well built as the church, its fittings being replete with every convenience, and is quite value for the £1,600 expended upon its erection.

* * * * *

Tividale is, to all intents and purposes, in one and the same industrial centre with Tipton. To supply the spiritual needs of this district an ecclesiastical parish was formed here in 1879, with an area of 1,000 acres, and a population of 4,800. Of this new district one-sixth of the population and one-fourth of the acreage were in Tipton civil parish, the greater portions of each being in Rowley Regis parish. But previous to this a mission room had been established under the charge of the Rev. A. O. Cherrington whose stipend was paid by St. Michael's, Paddington. This mission room certainly was but a very humble affair, made by converting two cottages to the purpose, a good work in which the late Mr. William Williams and Mr. Charles Bradley took an active part. As soon as this was in successful working order a committee was formed (December, 1874), to promote the erection of a church. Among the names first appearing on the committee were those of Rev. A. O. Cherrington, Messrs W. Williams, C. Bradley, W. Bradley, E. Yardley, A. Hand, T. Shorthouse, W. J. Hayward, Round Bros, J. R. Wainwright, G. Barklam, &c, &c. It was at first intended to build on the site opposite the offices of Messrs J. and C. Holcroft, but this land was eventually sold to that firm and the present site was purchased. Messrs Davis and Middleton were appointed architects, and in October, 1876, the contract was placed with Mr Everall, of Malvern, at the following price:—

Church	£5,500
Tower	2,500
Total	£8,000

The Earl of Dudley munificently paid for the tower and gave £3,000 towards the church as well. The memorial stone was laid January 8th, 1877, by the Rev. G. F Prescott, of St. Michael's, Paddington, whose congregation afterwards contributed a repair fund of £439 9s. 8d. Here was a bright example in the history of the English Church—a wealthy London congregation, intent on doing good outside their own parish, sought for some poor district in which to work off their superfluous energies, and to lay out their surplus money in propagandism and home mission effort to the very utmost advantage. And where was to be found a more deserving district than Tividale?

The parish is in the centre of the Black Country, its population being chiefly workers in collieries, ironworks, and brickyards. Rowley belongs to the diocese of Worcester, while Tipton is in that of Lichfield; and no one took a more intense interest in providing this new church than Bishop Selwyn, who had been present at the stone-laying; and but for death would have been delighted in taking part in the consecration ceremony, which had been fixed for April 24th, 1878. This much-beloved Bishop, however, died on April 11th, and the consecration, which took place on July 13th, was the first public episcopal act of his successor, Bishop MacLagan. The church was dedicated to St. Michael, after its foster-mother church at Paddington.

The building is said to be one of the best modern erections within the diocese of Lichfield. It is in the Early English style, and consists of nave, aisles, chancel, and a tower. The nave is 100 feet by 59 feet. A vicarage, adjoining the church, was built later on, and both church and vicarage were free from debt before the first vicar left. The living, in the gift of the Bishop of Lichfield, is worth £200 with a residence. The second vicar, the Rev. S. A. Smith is now vicar of All Saints', Birmingham. The present vicar is the Rev. G. R. Wynn-Griffiths, who received a very fitting preparation for his ministry in this unlovely industrial parish at the same school of training which had produced the Revds. Canon Body and Canon Bodington—the curacy at St. James's, Wednesbury.

For this much needed church the subscription list contained the offerings of the rich and poor in the parish, the Church Building and kindred Societies.

The church now contains the following interesting gifts:—

Marble Font, Ch. Prescott, Esq.
Litany Desk, G. Rowland, Esq.
Communion Plate, Books, Vases, &c., P. Parkes Esq.
Chancel Windows (four lights), Mrs. S. Bradley
Brass Altar Rail, T. Sheppard, Esq.

Brass Lectern, Mrs. Fordati.
Kneeling Rug, Mrs. Prescott.
Handsome Pulpit, J. R. Wainwright, Esq.

A new organ, valued at £660, is to be opened in July next (1891). There are 800 seats, all free. The register dates from 1878, although the mission work by which the Rev. Arthur O. Cherrington endeared himself to the parish began in 1874.

CHAPTER XXXI.—HISTORY OF NONCONFORMITY FROM PURITAN TIMES: PRESBYTERIANS, INDEPENDENTS, AND BAPTISTS IN TIPTON

Having now completed—as fully as the material placed at our disposal will permit—the ecclesiastical history of Tipton so far as it is connected with the Established church, we proceed at once to give the further history of religious thought within the parish so far as it is concerned with Nonconformity and Dissent, and so far, also, as the material and detailed information supplied by those who have it in their possession will allow.

Passing allusions have already been made to these subjects, particularly in those chapters on the Advowson and on the Parish Registers respectively. The Reformation had scarcely separated the Protestants from the Romanists before the former developed an offshoot party commonly called the Puritans. These were for a long time embraced within the body corporate of the Anglican Church; it was only when uniformity of public worship was rigorously insisted upon by various Acts and authorities that the line of cleavage became an actual split. Puritans then divided themselves into Presbyterians, Independents, and Baptists.

Roman Catholicism does not seem to have flourished in Tipton—religious thought seems to have advanced too far at the Reformation. Anyway, they are not even now so strongly represented as to be able to maintain any place of worship within the confines of the parish.

Presbyterianism established itself chiefly in Scotland; the Independents parted from them when they had gained political ascendancy and by ordinance had supplanted the Book of Common Prayer by a Directory, August 23rd, 1645. However much the Independents might have acquiesced in the removal of the Prayer Book from the parish churches they could not agree to submit themselves to the government of the Presbytery.

In Tipton records we have already found allusions to both Independents and Presbyterians; but perhaps the latter term may have signified the former denomination. In chapter xxii. we noted the troubles which befel that "moderate Independent," the Rev. Richard Hinks, who was driven from the living of Tipton by the Act of Uniformity in 1662.

A Presbyterian Conventicle at the house of William Clare, at Tipton, 1703, was also mentioned in chapter xix. Whether this William Clare, the "Oliverian Cornet," was the same William Clare, who was churchwarden of Tipton in 1683 it would now be difficult to decide. The probabilities are naturally against such an assumption. But it is interesting to note that one William Clare was married at Tipton on Christmas Day, 1693, to Mary Liesse, of Wolverhampton, "by license from Mr. Nicholls." And further, some riots, which took place in 1715, we shall also observe seem to have been directed against local Presbyterianism.

The riots spoken of, half political and half religious commenced at London in the first instance. On Queen Anne's birthday (April 23), in 1715, the smouldering fires of political unrest and disturbance broke out, by the Tory "Jacks" (*i.e*, Jacobites) raising a cry of "God bless the Queen, High Church, and Sacheverell!" Dissenting places of worship were attacked, and the Pretender's health was publicly drunk in the streets. These Jacobite riots and tumults spread to the provinces, some occurring at Lichfield, Wolverhampton, Stafford, Leek, &c., &c. At Wolverhampton the cry was "Damn King George and the Duke of Marlborough!" All these tumults called forth the passing of the Riot Act. "No George!" was the cry in Wednesbury and Tipton a district not slow to take up the wave of disturbance and pass it on from Wolverhampton side towards Birmingham. In July a Wednesbury Jacobite named Stone harangued the mob, and on the 15th of that month an attack was made on a Presbyterian meeting house at West Bromwich, when Cornet Lowe, a Whig gentleman residing at Charlemont Hall, near Wednesbury, shot and killed two of the rioters—a Thomas Royston, of Wolverhampton, and a Francis Gibbons, of Sedgley. These "Church and State" tumults were not quelled until the military had been called out and had scoured the district.

From this date a very wide gap appears in the history of Tipton Independents, owing to the neglect of those in authority to keep proper records. Earlier in this century the denomination seems to have possessed no less than three places of worship, including the one in Sheepwash Lane, which is in West Bromwich parish. In accordance with a custom of the denomination existing in the latter end of the last century and the commencement of the present each chapel had a distinctive name. Evidently this was an outcome of their dominant idea of Church government that each congregation was a separate and distinctive and a self contained body in itself – hence the alternative name of "Congregationalists" applied to this denomination. The chapel at

Sheepwash Lane was called "Salem," signifying "Peace." The present Ebenezer Chapel in Union Street was established in 1830 through the efforts of some of the friends, chiefly those resident in Tipton, of the Dudley King Street Church. At first meetings were held in a house in Union Street, which was altered so as to afford as convenient and as commodious a premises as possible. The meetings were conducted here till about the year 1840, when the present building was erected and called Ebenezer —"the stone of help." A few years later the chapel was enlarged, and a school room was erected. Again about the year 1859 galleries were put round three of the interior walls, and on the re-opening a sermon was delivered by that famous preacher, the late Rev John Angell James, of Birmingham. About 17 years ago the present large organ was substituted for a much smaller instrument which had previously done duty.

This chapel was evidently not the first Meeting House in Tipton, but a second one was established about the year 1865, namely, the Zoar Chapel, in High Street, which was a daughter to the mother church, Ebenezer. The two congregations, however, amalgamated again about 1872, and the Zoar Chapel was dismantled, and has since been utilised as a warehouse.

Of the Baptists it will be merely necessary to recall the fact that their existence as a body militant (1647) was strongly surmised in chapter xxv. Their strength morally, if not numerically, will also be further evidenced when the subject of Wesleyanism comes to be treated; for we shall find they did not fear to withstand the great John Wesley himself in 1751, so as to compel him to go into theological argument against them. He certainly spent but a very short time in controversy, from which it may be inferred that this great revival movement of the eighteenth century was accomplished like all similar movements—by appealing to the emotions, and not through the argumentative faculties. Hence Wesley's great success among the illiterate masses of this Black Country region. The history of the Baptists in Tipton since that time has not been very exciting. Between 50 and 60 years ago a few Baptists, said to have been previously connected with the Coppice Chapel, Coseley, established a meeting room for worship at Summerhill, and a church was formed; two or three years later a small chapel was erected, of which a Mr. Parsons was the first minister. After his death Mr Yardley was for some years the pastor. In the year 1846 this little community, strengthened by the dismission to their fellowship of several members of the church at Darkhouse, Coseley, left Summerhill for a new chapel erected in High Street, Princes End. This chapel, in accordance with a custom already mentioned—for the church government of the Baptists is almost as free and untrammelled by central authorities as that of the Congregationalists—designated their home and habitation "Zion."

Here for two years the Rev John Stent ministered. He was succeeded by the Rev. James Voller, who, after five years ministry, removed from Princes End to undertake the pastorate of a church in Sydney, in 1853. After Mr Vollar's removal the Rev R. Nightingale became Pastor, and remained for 16 years with the church, till the summer of 1869, when he emigrated, with his family, to Nebraska. So that this Tipton community received two accessories to its membership from Coseley, and sent out two enterprising ministers to the colonies—perhaps a welcome change after the insalubrity of Tipton. During this last pastorate it was found necessary to add galleries to the chapel. In 1870 came the present pastor, the Rev, J. Cecil Whitaker; and in the following year it was deemed absolutely necessary, in consequence of mining operations having endangered the safety of the chapel, to move to another situation. So High Street was deserted for the present site in Newhall Street. The memorial stones of this new chapel were laid by Mr. W. P Greenway, of Coseley, and Mr. M. A. Bass, M.P. (now Lord Burton) on November 28th, 1871. The building was opened the following July. There is a convenient schoolroom adjoining the chapel.

In the same thoroughfare (New Hall Street) has recently been erected the Salvation Army Barracks (1887), the meeting place of the newest and noisiest denomination.

CHAPTER XXXII.—THE HISTORY OF WESLEYANISM: PARK LANE CHAPEL: GREAT BRIDGE CHAPEL: DUDLEY PORT CHAPEL.

There is in existence a very rare pamphlet published in 1744 under the following title:—Some Papers giving an Account of the Rise and Progress of Methodism at Wednesbury in Staffordshire, and other Parishes Adjacent: as likewise of the late Riots in those Parts. London: Printed for J. Roberts in Warwick Lane 1744." It chronicles the advent into those parts of Charles Wesley in the November of 1742, showing how he preached in streets and in fields, and how John Wesley appeared six weeks later; how a society of 200 persons was formed from Wednesbury and the adjoining parishes of Tipton, Darlaston, West Bromwich, &c.; how they proposed to erect a "Tabernacle" how insults to the Methodists were followed by riots and open violence, and damage to the extent of £500 in Wednesbury; how they appealed to the magistrates for protection; how they conducted their meetings, held twice every day, and Wednesdays and Fridays at 5 a.m., at noon, and at 7 p.m.—these two days needing tickets of admission; how there were classes of twelve, each with a leader; and how they were further organised with stewards and preachers. Then we are gravely told that these mobs from Darlaston and the neighbourhood, who raided

Wednesbury, were "enemies of his Majesty, and Friends of the Pretender"; and that when plundering, and "about seizing some malt, the property of a Methodist, as soon as they were told that that malt was seized for his Majesty's use for nonpayment of duty, the mob immediately cried out 'God bless his Majesty,' and repeating what they had said before about the Methodists favouring Popish Pretensions they accordingly left the malt untouched." And then we are informed how Mr. Whitfield's converts at Wednesbury had "been raised into unaccountable extacies," but that since the Wednesbury Riots there had been no public preachings in Birmingham in the Bull Ring or at Gosta Green.

From *Wesley's Journal* we extract the following:—

"1743. June 18. I received a full account of the terrible riots which have been in Staffordshire. I was not surprised at all, neither should I have wondered if, after the advice they had so often received from the pulpit as well as from the Episcopal chair, the zealous High Churchman had rose and cut all the Methodists to pieces.

"June 20th. Resolving to assist them as far as I could I set out early in the morning.

"June 21st. We road to Birmingham and in the morning of the 22nd to Francis Wards at Wednesbury. Although I knew all that had been done was as contrary to law as it was to justice and mercy, yet I knew not how to advise my poor sufferers or to procure them any redress."

When John Wesley had visited Wednesbury in the January of that year (1743) he had been well received by the Vicar, the Rev. Edward Egginton. Since then, however, the success and growing popularity of the Methodists had embittered the Vicar, and feeling ran very high against the new sect. Things went on however, until October, when occurred the great riot at Wednesbury, when John Wesley was dragged off to Bentley; and as Squire Lane refused to hear the case, the prisoner was taken on to Walsall, where Justice Persehouse also declined to give his countenance to these lawless proceedings. Strange to say, though, these very two magistrates issued a very extraordinary warrant, addressed more "particularly to the constable of Tipton." Squire Lane was the grandson of Colonel Lane, who had sheltered Charles II., and died in 1748, when his estate was purchased by the Ansons. William Persehouse, of Reynold's Hall, Walsall, belonged to the Parkes or Persehouse family of Parkes House, Sedgley, and of Willingsworth Hall, Wednesbury. When his family became extinct in 1771 their property passed to John Walhouse, of Hatherton, near Cannock.

The warrant, issued at Walsall, may have been addressed to the Tipton authorities, because Wesley already possessed so many sympathisers and supporters there. The Wednesbury mob had certainly been very unceremonious in their dealings with the great preacher; but for a legal document, nothing could be more remarkable than this magisterial warrant, the text of which ran—

"To all High Constables, Petty Constables, and others of His Majesty's Peace Officers, within the said County, and particularly to the Constable of Tipton (near Walsall).

"Whereas we, His Majesty's Justices of the Peace for the said County of Stafford, have received information that several disorderly persons, styling themselves Methodist Preachers, go about raising routs and riots to the great damage of his Majesty's liege people, and against the peace of our Sovereign Lord, the King.

"These are, in his Majesty's name, to command you, and every one of you, within your respective districts, to make diligent search after the said Methodist Preachers, and to bring him or them before some of us, his Majesty's justices of the peace to be examined concerning their unlawful doings.

"Given under our hands and seals this day of October, 1743

"J. LANE."

"W. PERSEHOUSE,"

Quietness was not readily resumed. Charles Wesley had certainly preached to a quiet congregation at Wednesbury on February 1st following (1744), but the more violent of the malcontents had made an oath to start to plunder the Methodists on Shrove Tuesday; and rioting broke out again.

On February 7th Wesley writes:—"On Friday afternoon I went from Birmingham to Tipton Green, but finding the mob still raging up and down I returned to Birmingham."

The next extract from *Wesley's Journals* brings us to Sunday, 5th April, 1745. He had been received in Wednesbury "without noise or hindrance," nearly all active hostility having by that time subsided. He says, "The number of people even at 5 a.m. obliged me to preach abroad. About one I preached at Tipton Green and about four at Wednesbury. A few persons at first threw some clods, but they were quickly glad to retreat, so that there was no interruption." In another year matters improved wonderfully.

"1745. November 10th, Sunday. I preached at five and eight o'clock at Wednesbury, and about one at Tipton Green; and at four in the afternoon to well nigh the whole town, high and low, as at the beginning."

The next entry referring to Tipton (vol ii., p. 225) is significant. Wesley finds opposition from the Nonconformists now, as he has hitherto from the Churchmen. "April 3rd, 1751. Wednesday. At one I preached at Tipton Green, where the Baptists also have been making havoc of the flock, which constrained me in speaking on those words, 'Arise, and be baptised, and wash away thy sins,' and to spend near *ten minutes* in controversy, which is more than I had done in public for many months, perhaps years before." As Christ began with his poor fishermen disciples, so Wesley's ministration were first addressed to such as the poor miners of Staffordshire, and other colliery districts, whose impulses were easily swayed. "1752. March 22nd Sunday. At one I preached at Tipton Green to a large congregation, though the wind was ready to cut us in two; and at five to a much larger at Wednesbury"

From this date we hear lees of Wesley being in Tipton, but of his being more frequently at West Bromwich Heath. And it is about this period that a small chapel or preaching house was built in Tipton and given to Mr. Wesley by a Mr. James Jones, one of his flock, who resided near West Bromwich Old Church. John Wesley held this in his own right until he settled it upon trustees in 1786.

From time to time smouldering animosities against the new sect broke out in various parts of this district. For instance, again in 1763 constant disturbance was made during the preaching of the Methodists, who were not without dread sometimes of being actually murdered. Says one Alexander Mather, a famous Methodist preacher of those days, " No magistrate could quell the rioters, or rather I should say none would. But at length Mr. Wortley Birch took them in hand; he laid some of the rioters in the dungeon, and left them there a night or two to cool. He fined the rest according to law, obliged them to pay the money down, and gave it to the poor. "This rigorous magistrate, so conspicuous amongst his weaker brethren on the bench, was the lord of Tipton manor—Wyrley Birch.

The references to West Bromwich are—

"1768. March 20. About one I preached on West Bromwich Heath, in the evening near the preaching house in Wednesbury. The north wind cut like a razor."

"1770. March 18, Sunday. At half an hour after one I was to preach at Bromwich Heath, but the house would scarce contain one-fourth of the congregation; so I made a virtue of necessity and preached in a ground where there was room for all that came. In the evening I preached in the house, at Wednesbury, a funeral sermon for Elizabeth Longmore, I think the first witness of Christian perfection whom God raised up in these parts. ... March 19. I rode to Cradley; here also the multitude of people obliged me to stand abroad, although the north wind whistled round my head. About one I took the field again at Stourbridge, many of the hearers were as wild as colts untamed, but the bridle was in their mouths. At six I began at Dudley. ... March 21. I took my leave of Wednesbury about five; preached about ten at Bilston."

"1774. March 19. At noon I preached at Bromwich Heath and, the room being far too small, stood in Mr. Wiley's courtyard, notwithstanding the keen north-east wind. At Wednesbury, likewise, I was constrained by the multitude to preach abroad in the evening."

It must be borne in mind that in those times Wednesbury and similar small towns possessed no large buildings (beyond the church) where a great gathering of people could assemble.

The references to Dudley made in *Wesley's Journals* are:—

"1749, October 24. About noon we came to Dudley. At once I went to the Market Place and proclaimed the name of the Lord to a huge, unwieldly, noisy multitude ... until some of Satan's servants pressed in raging and blaspheming and throwing whatever came to hand. I then retired to the house from which I came. The multitude poured after and covered over with dirt many that were near me, but I had only a few specks. I preached in Wednesbury at 4 to a nobler people, and was greatly comforted among them.

"1751, April 1. I rode [from Wednesbury] to Dudley. The dismal screaming wherewith we were welcomed into the town gave us reason to expect the same kind of reception as I had when I was there before. I began preaching immediately in a yard not far from the main road. Some at first seemed inclined to interrupt.

"1764, March 23. I rode to Dudley, formerly a den of lions. ... They had just finished their preaching house, which was thoroughly filled. March 24. We came once more to our old flock at Wednesbury.

"1776, March 27. I preached at Dudley in the midst of Antinomians and backsliders. In the evening I preached to our old flock at Wednesbury, and the old spirit was among them."

This Protestant sect of Antinomians had been first encountered by Wesley at Wednesbury, in March 1746. They had originated in the first instance in Germany, as far back as 1535, being the followers of John Agricola, a townsman of Luther's, and obtained their name from two Greek words, signifying "against law"; because they taught that the moral law (of Moses) was not binding upon Christians under the "law of grace"—they claimed as the perfection of Christian liberty to be left to the guidance of the Gospel and the constraint of Christian love.

The first chapel was established in Tipton by John Wesley himself, and was on the ground in Tipton Green, now occupied by the Park Lane Wesleyan Chapel. The building used by him was called a preaching house. The deed, a valuable relic bearing John Wesley's own signature, is still preserved in the iron safe belonging to the chapel; it is dated July 11th, 1786, being a conveyance by John Wesley, of the city of London, clerk, to

Stephen Hipkins, R. Laughton, Samuel Mills, Samuel Aston, Joseph Webb, of Tipton; William Southall and Aaron Timmins, of Dudley; John Walker, of Birmingham, and W. Smith, of Wolverhampton, of "all that house or tenement, with vestry and garden thereto adjoining, commonly called the Methodist preaching house situate at Tipton Green, in the parish of Tipton, or otherwise Tippington, in the county of Stafford." This conveyance was made by Wesley five years before he died. The "preaching house" being found too small it was pulled down, and a new chapel was built on the site, which was opened on the 3rd of December, 1809, by the Rev James Wood, of Birmingham, as the cause increased, and this chapel became also too small, it was enlarged considerably at a cost of £1,249 0s. 2d, and re-opened by the Revs. Robert Newton, Jácob Stanley, and Theophilus Lessey, on September the 23rd, 1827, and Wesley's Tipton steward, Stephen Hipkins, whose descendants are still actively connected with Tipton Methodism, lived to see this enlargement, and his name again appears at the head of the list of trustees of the enlarged chapel, and opposite his name is written a note stating that he died on January 11th, 1830. The list of trustees at that time, and immediately following, contain many well-known Tipton names, such as John Taylor, Boaz Bloomer, Samuel Round, Edward Aston, Samuel Rowley, Thomas Cox, William Crannage, Thomas Powell, Thomas Cope, David Jeavons, Joseph Hall, Thomas Morris, Jonathan E Howl, John Twist, Thomas Cox, jun., Edward Hipkins, William Hipkins, and Thomas Round.

The name of another local champion of Methodism stands revealed in that of the Rev. Jacob Stanley. Some pamphlets were printed in 1812 and in 1818 showing further local struggles between Dissent and the Church. One has the sub-title, "Religion Run Wild," to which there is added a letter on "Why do some of the clergy insinuate that Methodists and Dissenters are Knaves and Fools?" and

A Speech
Delivered at the
Formation of the Dudley Auxiliary Bible Society,
April 12th, 1812
By Jacob Stanley.
Second Edition.

Wednesbury:
Printed and Sold by T. Booth.
Sold by Maurice, Dudley; Denman, Wolverhampton,"
&c.,&c.

In 1846 it was decided to place an organ in the chapel, but this innovation seems to have caused a considerable stir, for at the next meeting of the trustees several resigned and were replaced by others. But still the alarm had not subsided, for several resolutions were passed restricting the power of the organist and guarding the funds from any charge at all on account of the organ. Evidently some of the good people were imbued with the Scotch prejudice against the box of whistles, and did not believe it right to worship God by machinery.

The chapel was licensed for the solemnisation of marriage in 1848. The room now known as Tipton Hall School, which was then the Wesleyan Sunday School, being found too small to accommodate the large number of scholars, several purchases of land and buildings were made adjoining the chapel by the trustees, and the present school building was erected in 1848, and in addition to the Sunday School the present Day School was opened, which has proved ever since such an important factor in the educational work of Tipton.

Soon after this it became apparent that owing to age and the effect of mining operations in the vicinity, the chapel was becoming unsafe and seriously dilapidated. Several purchases of land and mines were made with a view to enlargement, and after a few years, during which the subsidence caused by the mines settled down, it was considered safe to re-build and a scheme was set on foot which was warmly supported by the late Mr J. E. Howl and Messrs. Thomas Round, William Hipkins, Edward Hipkins, J. Twist, and others eager to carry out the above object. The plans of Mr. George Bidlake, architect, of Wolverhampton, were accepted, and the contract was let to Messrs. Trow and Sons, of Wednesbury.

The memorial stone of the present handsome building was laid by Thomas Davis, Esq., J.P., of Hill Top, on 7th of August, 1865. The cost of the errection was £5,874 3s. The work was completed, and the chapel was opened on the 25th of September 1866, by the Rev. William Arthur, President of the Wesleyan Conference. The building is in the Gothic style, of red bricks with stone dressings. It is not often that the local historian troubles to describe the fabric of a dissenting place of worship: first, because few have such age as to present any distinctive style; and secondly, because Dissenters have generally treated the noble art of architecture with such utter contempt and disregard. Perhaps churches, even of modern date demand a fuller description by reason of the fact that certain details of locality are common to all, and make it absolutely necessary to note how these have been attended to; and also because the provision of the customary churchyard requires that the building should be presentable to the eye from every point of view. With chapels this last-named was never an absolute necessity; and so long as a passable facade was presented the sides and back of the building might be as plain as those of a factory. In Tipton and Wednesbury and the surrounding district this is nearly always so. But at Park Lane it was sought to remove this slur upon the artistic taste of the Wesleyans at any rate. A noble front, with a large traceried window, and flanked by a staircase turret on one side, and a massive square buttressed tower on the other, approached the ecclesiastical style in some degree and; when the entrance doors were approached by large flights of steps, and the tower was gapped by a stone spire, the architecture certainly deserved full recognition. The two sides, however, scarcely carried out the idea as fully as could have been wished, between their buttresses no long Gothic windows matched the traceried one of the front elevation, for the exigencies of putting in the necessary galleries round the interior, broke into two halves what otherwise might have been noble looking windows. Still, the building is undoubtedly an ornament to the town. The ground surrounding it, used as a playground for the school children is very extensive. In addition to the usual vestries for minister and choir on the ground floor, there is a large range of rooms in the basement, consisting of a preaching room and extensive class rooms (used for Bible classes and similar work), a caretaker's residence, and everything replete for carrying on a great work. The cost of maintenance for so large an establishment must be very considerable, and speaks much for the enterprise of the Wesleyan body in Tipton, and does credit to the mother chapel established by the founder of the demonination in this parish.

In 1867 the present organ was built by Messrs Bishop and Starr, of London, at a cost of £425. Other important improvements, including pallisades, paving in front, boundary wall, &c., followed.

For some years a heavy debt, as the result of the above works, pressed somewhat heavily on the congregation, but after many and continued efforts the whole of the debt was paid off, the last vestige disappearing in the early part of the present year. Thus, in Wesley's centenary year the Wesleyan Methodist Trust Property, established by Wesley himself, in Tipton, was free from all debt, a fitting centenary memorial of the great man.

There is no burial ground, but two memorial tabets are placed on the walls of the interior. One is to the memory of Thomas Cox and the other to the memory of Jonathan E. Howl who died March 21st, 1875, aged 60 years, and whose fellow trustees and friends testify that the chapel was

"A FITTING SPOT FOR THE RECORD OF HIS VIRTUES."

Registers of baptisms are duly kept, and the whole institution is admirably organised. Wesleyan Methodism in Great Bridge has had a chapel upon the present site since 1811. Previous to that time services were held in various preaching rooms, one of which was in premises at the corner of Horseley Road, where Mr Powers' furniture establishment now is, and another in a cottage on a vacant piece of ground opposite Mill Street, belonging to Mr. W. Bedworth, C.C. The latter was a very low building, and mischievous men and lads were wont to climb upon the roof, and cover up the chimney with the purpose of smoking out the worshippers. In 1811, for the sum of £75, part of the site was purchased and conveyed to trustees, and the first chapel was erected. Great Bridge at that time was one of the places in Wednesbury Circuit which covered the ground now occupied by the Walsall (Wesley), Walsall (Centenary), Willenhall, Wednesbury, and West Bromwich (Hill Top) Circuits. The ministers of the circuit were the Revs. George Morley, who became President of the Conference in 1830, William Hill, and John Rigg. This chapel underwent alteration at various times, and in its later years was a long narrow building, distinctly remembered by several friends still connected with its cause. It suffered some injury from contiguous mines, for which, in accordance with a clause in the deeds of the land, compensation was paid in 1837. With the money thus obtained (£25) and some additional subscriptions, the vestry was enlarged to double its size and the chapel was thoroughly repaired and painted. At the same time the trust deed of the property was renewed. Deaths, removals, and other circumstances had reduced the number of the local trustees, and so for the right management of the estate and in accordance with the provisions of the deed several new trustees were appointed. Of the Trust then constituted only one member now survives, Mr Thomas Cocks, who for more than half a century has thus been in a responsible position in connection with Great Bridge Methodism. The chapel renovated in 1837 did not, however long serve the needs of the society, for in January, 1839, the trustees gave instructions to certain gentlemen "to make enquiries in reference to an eligible site for another chapel." Several pieces of ground were suggested, but the negotiations fell through, and eventually some cottages on the adjoining land were purchased, thus enlarging the site, and it was determined to build the new chapel on the enlarged site, using up as far as possible the old materials. These arrangements were made under the guidance of the resident minister, the Rev. James E. Moulton, father of the Rev. W. F. Moulton, M.A., D.D., the present justly honoured and esteemed President of the Conference, who was then a child a few years old, Some delay ensued in getting possession of the cottages, and the work could not be undertaken until the following spring, and Mr Moulton in the meanwhile having completed his term of residence at Great Bridge was succeeded by the Rev. Nehemiah Curnock. Tenders were taken for the work under the designs and specifications of Mr. Edge, architect, of Birmingham, and a contract was let to Mr. John Danks at the sum of £1,317, he agreeing to allow £500 for the material of the old chapel. The old chapel was used for the last time on March 1st, 1840, on the occasion of the anniversary sermons. On March 30th the the foundation stone of the new chapel was laid by Dr. Underhill, father of Dr. Thomas Underhill, J.P., alderman of West Bromwich, and grandfather of Dr. A. S. Underhill, of Great Bridge. An interesting incident occurred in connection with the ceremony on the day. Whilst the proceedings were in progress a messenger came to Mr. Curnock announcing that a son had been born to him. The boy born that day was named Nehemiah, and like his father entered the Wesleyan ministry, and at the present time is the able editor of the *Methodist Recorder*.

The new chapel was opened on June 28th, 1840, the preachers being the Rev. Thomas Jackson, the ex-president of the Conference, and the well-known Yorkshire farmer, William Dawson, of Barnbow, one of the most eloquent and powerful lay-preachers Methodism has ever produced.

The main building of the chapel remains to-day substantially as it was erected, but very large alterations and improvements have been made from time to time. In 1853, the Rev Joseph Heaton being the minister, an organ was erected by Bishop of London, under the supervision of Mr. Samuel Adams, at a cost of £240, also new orchestra and vestries, the total outlay being about £650. In 1864-5 the body of the chapel was re-opened and the rostrum and portice erected at a cost of £400. In 1875 the gallery pews were altered and the chapel thoroughly renovated at an outlay of £650. Other alterations have been of a minor character. The silver Sacramental service was presented by the late Mr. Thomas Bagnall, the ironmaster.

There are two memorial tablets in the chapel, one in remembrance of the wife of the Rev Joseph Heaton, who died February 18th, 1852, the other in memory of Rev. Charles Lawton, who died September 9th, 1864, whilst stationed at Great Bridge, in the 39th year of his age, and the 13th year of his ministry.

The Wesleyan Methodist Trust Property at Great Bridge includes a minister's house, situated in Sheepwash Lane, and erected in 1876, at a cost of £1,300; and also Day and Sunday School premises, situated in Fisher Street, of which the memorial stone was laid October 31st, 1859, by Miss Davis, of Hill Top.

Great Bridge belongs to the West Bromwich (Hill Top) Circuit, of which the present ministers are Rev Jabez Marratt, of Hill Top, Rev J. Conder Nattrass, Great Bridge; and Rev F. Stuart Kirkness, Ocker Hill. Day schools are connected with this chapel ...

Of Dudley Port Wesleyan Chapel the records are meagre. It was opened in 1829, and it is now contemplated to erect a new fabric as soon as a suitable site can be secured, with all the mines thereunder properly reserved. During the past few years a debt of £400 has been cleared off, There is one tradition of this chapel which serves to indicate how "old times have changed, old manners gone," in the methods of conducting Wesleyan services. It would appear that about the year 1840, in arranging for certain charity sermons two choirs were inadvertently invited to assist, one from Oldbury, and the other from Bloomfield Wesleyan Chapel. Both choirs duly put in an appearance, and both took part in the service. After it was all over the choristers were hospitably taken to the Royal Oak Inn, although it was Sunday; and, notwithstanding that only one choir had been catered for, a sumptuous dinner, and a bountiful one, too was heartily enjoyed. Public opinion has changed since then.

CHAPTER XXXIII.—TIPTON WESLEYANISM CONTINUED: GOSPEL OAK CHAPEL: OCKER HILL CHAPEL: BLOOMFIELD CHAPEL: MISSIONS: AND LOCAL WESLEYAN BIBLIOGRAPHY.

What more fitting as the name of a place wherein to erect a Christian chapel than Gospel Oak? This place-name carries us back to the time when it was the custom of the Church during Rogation Days ("asking days," because God was asked or supplicated) —at that critical period for the growing crops, namely, three days before Ascension Day, or about a fortnight before Whitsuntide—to pray for the produce of the earth. Fields were perambulated and blessed, and the boundaries of the parish were "beaten," while stoppages were made at certain landmarks to read the Gospel – hence Gospel Oak. The boundary here was evidently that of Wednesbury parish, because of the other tree in the group being designated Wednesbury Oak. Boundaries have no doubt been much changed and disputed since those times; as the boundary of Sedgley parish now meets that of Tipton, where once this group of boundary oaks marked off Wednesbury on the west and Tipton on the east, In the year (1811) when the first chapel was erected the Gospel Oak Inn was kept by a William Turner, and his sign represented a clergyman in full vestments reading the Gospel beneath the shade of an oak. The road was then lined with hawthorns, and measured by tall poplars at regular lengths apart.

The history of the Wesleyan Society here may be traced back to the year 1800, when meetings were held at the house of a Mr. Pasfield in Bradley Lane at the top of Princes End. A Mr. John Skidmore from Netherton, employed at the Moat Colliery, then joined, and with the co-operation of another Netherton man named John Williams, it was found possible to erect a small chapel in Bradley Lane. Such was the prosperity of the society that in 1811 it was decided to build a larger chapel at Gospel Oak, which was done at a cost of £1,226. The deed, dated April, 1811, contains, among other names of interest and noteworthiness, those of Philip Williams, John Bagnall, Thomas Pasfield, John Skidmore, Edward Fisher, &c. For the opening services, on Sunday, September 15th, 1811, and conducted by the Rev. Joseph Taylor, of Bristol, a four-paged set of hymns was printed (by Booth, of Walsall) to be sung by a special choir from Birmingham, and a copy, yellow and faded with age, is still preserved by Mr. S. L. Millington. In 1814 schools were built to the chapel. In 1828 Mr. Thomas Millington and his son, Mr Isaiah Millington, previously attached to the Ocker Hill Society, joined the Gospel Oak Society; the latter had been a local preacher since 1822. He filled many offices connected with the chapel, for which he laboured incessantly and ever with fervid zeal; and when he expired in September, 1835, it is said the last words upon his lips were "All is well." See also "Wesleyan Methodist Magazine," September 13th, 1835. Immediately upon his decease his brother, William Millington (and uncle of the present Mr. Samuel Lees Millington), of Summerhill, began to take an active part in the work of the society and endeavoured to fill the great void caused by his brother's death. At that time the debt on the chapel was actually £1,700—more than its original cost in building. But by both his exertions and his great liberality donations of £1,400 were raised, and only a balance of £300 remained when he removed from the neighbourhood.

The old chapel contained sittings for 400 people, and in 1850 was fitted with an orchestra containing an organ. By 1876 only £100 indebtedness remained on the old building, and then it was found necessary to replace it by a more modern structure, which was put up a few yards nearer Princes End. The new chapel was from the designs of Loxton Brothers, of Wednesbury, built by John Trow, contractor, of the same town. It is 57ft. by 42ft, and contains sittings for 525 persons. It is provided with galleries, and an orchestra is over the vestry. The site, valued at £400, was given by the late William Millington, and the total cost of the chapel was £4,780. At the stonelaying ceremony on August 28th, 1876,a sum of £2,081 15s 1d was raised. Mr. S. L. Millington, who laid the first stone, gave £262 10s, Mrs S. L. Millington laid the second, and gave a like sum of £262 10s, Mr Benjamin Lewis, for Mr Henry Lewis, gave £105; Mr Edward W. Lewis, £105; Miss L. H. Millington, £107 10s; and Mr T. Davis, £150. Six silver trowels were presented on this occasion, and the six stones contained, among other things, a parchment on which was written a history of Methodism, as connected with Gospel Oak. In the chapel are five memorial tablets, all to members of the Millington family, who have been its chief benefactors. At present the old chapel is closed and falling into decay, but it is now proposed to convert it to a school at an outlay of £700, towards which £100 is already in hand. The present schools, vestry, &c., will be replaced by a new suite of rooms to make the chapel more convenient.

Ocker Hill Wesleyan Chapel was established in 1813, or two years after Gospel Oak Chapel. At first it was but an unpretentious place, seating 250 persons, put up under the auspices of the head of the circuit, Spring Head Chapel. In 1835 the chapel was enlarged so as to afford accommodation for 450 worshippers. At this time the society was in a very flourishing state, numbering among its members such ardent supporters as Mr John Stokes, Mr Mills (father of the late Henry Mills), Mr Barnett, and Mr William Hunt. With such sources of strength the congregation gradually outgrew the accommodation of the chapel, till in 1874 additional land had to be acquired in order to re-erect a new chapel on a much larger scale. Services were held in the schools during the period of re-building and on August 3rd 1874, memorial stones were laid by Mr Edwin Hunt (in place of Mr Alexr. Brodgen, M.P, unavoidably absent), Mr William Hunt, of Castleford; Mr. Thomas Davis, J.P., and Mr William Mills and Mr. Henry Mills. The contractors were Messrs. Trow and Sons, of Wednesbury, and the total cost about £2,500. The opening services in the autumn of the following year, were conducted by the Rev Gervoise Smith, President of Conference, when, with a donation of £100 from Mr. Zach. Mills of Bradley, the collections amounted to £402. For several weeks, on Sundays and other days, special collections were made, realizing respectively £102, £96, £27, £70, £186, and £65, till the total was £948. Further subscriptions, of friends and supporters, of £1,300 brought up the grand total to £2,248. The balance has since been paid off, and a new organ bought at a cost of nearly £300. The old Sunday schools and class rooms adjacent to the chapel, were erected in 1844. Last year (1890) these were taken down, and new and handsome buildings in substitution have just been opened free from debt.

In 1817 a schoolmaster in Barfield Road, Bloomfield named Marshall, commenced, in the schoolroom of his day school a Sunday school.

In 1828 a chapel was built by the Kilhamites (of whom more will be said in the succeeding chapter), and was afterwards, in 1830, purchased by the Wesleyan Methodists, and the Sunday school commenced by Mr. Marshall was connected with this chapel. A very flourishing career was maintained, so much so that the chapel was eventually found too small, and the trustees and other friends resolved to build a larger one. The following names were connected with this scheme, which was inaugurated in 1850:— Messrs B. Nicklin, James

Crofts, Joseph Hall (partner in the Bloomfield Ironworks), Joseph Stanton, William Roberts, Edward Hipkins, Richard Nicklin, W. Tyler, Thomas Nicklin, Joseph Hall, Elijah Nicklin, and James Hughes—all these are among its benefactors and supporters.

The present chapel was built at a cost of £1,838 2s; and opened in 1851. At the opening services the collections amounted to £422 17s. 11d. A short time afterwards the present school was erected at the back of the chapel at a cost of £790 12s. 3d., thus making the total cost of chapel and schools £2,628 14s. 3d., which was eventually paid off to the last farthing. It is contemplated to re-pew the chapel and to generally renovate it at an outlay of £400.

An interesting eight-page pamphlet, printed by T. Higgins, Dudley, in 1845, is the "Rules and Regulations" for managers and teachers of the Bloomfield Sunday Schools. There are 20 rules, and fines seemed to have been imposed for all sorts of small offences; for instance, teachers found talking together in school hours were mulet one penny, being late cost threepence, and absence was punished by the imposition of twice that fine. The meetings were long, so much so as to have been absolutely tedious for young children, viz, from 9 to 12 in the morning, and half~past 1 to 4 in the afternoon.

Connected with Bloomfield Chapel is a Home Mission Room in Brown Lion Street, erected in 1868 and enlarged the following year, to accommodate 200 Sunday scholars. It was the embodiment of an idea of Mr Edward Hipkins, whose name has been connected with the Wesleyan cause in Tipton for so many years, to get at the poorest class of children; in fact to be a ragged school in all but name. Its success has been deservedly great. The room, equipped with an organ, &c, cost nearly £200, and is used also for public worship, Bible classes, mothers' meetings, a funeral society, and other social and religious purposes.

In connection with the Park Lane leadership a Wesleyan Mission—"Forward Movement"-has been in active work for some years in Coppice Street, in a region where there is ample room and scope enough for religious philanthropy. This movement began here when the place was known variously by the names of China Buildings, Old Cross Street, or Pudding Bag Street, the active spirit being Mr. W. S. Stanton. Beginning in 1868 with the teaching of the little children to sing simple hymns, and the gathering of the older people together in open air meetings, the first settlement under the shelter of a roof (in 1871) was but a very humble affair – a dilapidated house in No. 4 Court, Old Cross Street, taken at a weekly rental of one shilling, becoming the home and habitation of the little mission. Still growing, the next step was to build a suitable mission hall. The corner stones of this building were laid in December,

1875, Edmund Howl, Esq, presiding. The cost was about £280, and the hall accommodates about 150 adults and 200 children. It was opened in March, 1876, Mr. S. L. Millington taking the chair at the meeting after the inaugural service. In 1886 the addition of class rooms and further extensions were made, and under the active management of Messrs. Stanton, Dodd. Binns and others, countenanced and supported by the late Miss Sudgen, Miss Bishop, Rev. J. S. Shrewsbury and Daniel Hipkins, Esq., the work has steadily grown till the present accommodation is found absolutely inadequate to its requirements.

In the possession of Mr. S. L. Millington are interesting copies of some old Wednesbury circuit plans which, of course, include the Tipton chapels. The earliest is for the year 1822, printed by Booth, Wednesbury, and the list of preachers begins with the well-known name of Waddy, and ends with that of Millington, "on trial." The table fixes the "quarter days at Wednesbury. June 24th and September 23rd," and a footnote states that "preachers meet at 10 o'clock"; this was to get the business over in good time to enjoy a substantial and bountiful dinner that was always provided in those days. Another plan is for 1832, and a third one for 1835, both printed by Booth; and among the meeting places occur those of Moxley, Wood Green, and Wednesbury Field. A fourth for 1840-1, printed in Birmingham, spells the place name "Hocker Hill."

A plan of the Dudley Circuit for 1845 names the following places:—Dudley (King Street), Tipton, Oldbury, Bloomfield, Dudley Port, Darby Hand, Dudley Wood, Woodside, Gornal, Gornal Wood, Coseley, Mamble Square, Pensnett, Tividale, Church Bridge, Fullers End, The Dock, Strait's Green, and Kate's Hill; also Factory Bridge, Tipton; Sawny Bridge, Tipton; Day School, Tipton (Thursdays).

At the present time there are six large Wesleyan Chapels in Tipton, viz, Park Lane, Dudley Port and Bloomfield in the Tipton Circuit, and Great Bridge, Ocker Hill, and Gospel Oak in the Hill Top Circuit. Toll End Chapel is in the latter circuit also.

The preachers' circuits in this locality have altered from time to time as the growth of the denomination, the erection of new chapels, and other causes demanded. Wednesbury Circuit was formed from that of Birmingham in 1801. Then from this the Walsall Circuit was established in 1835. In 1862 the Wednesbury Wesley (as distinguished from the Wednesbury Spring Head Circuit) was instituted, but is now called the Hill Top (West Bromwich) Circuit. The Dudley Circuit was formed from the Wolverhampton Circuit (1787-1793), and from the Dudley Circuit the Oldbury and Tipton Circuit was set up in 1859.

A bibliography of local Wesleyan Methodism of an exceedingly interesting character might almost be made from books and documents in the possession of Mr. Samuel Lees Millington. Some of these have already been mentioned and quoted. Among others may be noted:—

(1) *Black Country Methodism*, by Alfred Camden Pratt (London, Charles H. Kelly, 1891). This is a neatly got up work of 174 pages, in which local incidents in the religious life of Tipton, Wednesbury Darlaston, Bilston, and the surrounding district, are graphically portrayed; it lacks an index. In the last chapter a worthy character connected with Bilston Methodism is mentioned, her name was Peggy Taylor and strange to say Mr Millington is in actual possession of this woman's class tickets, dated 1794. In fact his collection of tickets, beginning at this date with that of "Margaret Taylor," runs on to 1821, the others bearing the name of "Mr. Hickman."

(2) *Memoir of David Skidmore* (Brierley Hill, George Ford, 1839). Sixteen pages deal with this worthy who died at Old Hill, aged 45, June 5th, 1839 and whose connection with Ocker Hill Methodist Society is duly set forth.

(3) *Memoir of John Marson* (Dudley, S. Mills 1870). In this pamphlet of 16 pages is an interesting allusion to a well-known character of former years, on page 11 we read how on one occasion Mr. Isaiah Millington unexpectedly occupied the pulpit in the place of a preacher, Mr. Griffiths, better known as "Dickybird."

(4) *An Obituary* on the death of William Millington ironmaster, of Tipton, April 22nd, 1876. Extracts from the *London Iron Trade Exchange* and the *Wolverhampton Chronicle*.

CHAPTER XXXIV.—THE OFFSHOOTS OF WESLEYANISM: THE HISTORY OF DISSENT IN TIPTON CONCLUDED.

The first split in Wesleyanism occurred in 1797, and arose upon the question of the rights of the laity as opposed to the pastoral and official prerogatives of the ministers. Alexander Kilham led the opposition, and as Conference expelled him, he established the Methodist New Connexion, at first called Kilhamites. In this body the lay delegates have an equal voice with the preachers, both in Conference and in all business meetings.

The leading place of worship belonging to this denomination in Tipton is St Paul's Chapel, Dudley Port. It was built in 1872 and opened in September of that year, replacing an older fabric dating from 1836, which at last was so dilapidated that the sparrows fled in and out while the minister was preaching. The cost was nearly £3,000, which the organ and various appointments had increased by a sum of £450. Of this £1,100 is still an outstanding liability. It will accommodate 560 persons, and is licensed for the performance of marriages. The present minister is the Rev. John Benson. Two memorial tablets record the deaths of prominent members of the congregation, one to Mrs. Hannah George, who died July 2nd, 1859, aged 30 years, and the other to Elizabeth Jesson, who died suddenly whilst engaged in prayer in the lecture room beneath the chapel, June 13th, 1873, aged 63 years. It is not a common thing to find a dissenting chapel dedicated to a saint; and in this instance it signifies nothing more than that the congregation of this chapel desire to express admiration for and to emulate the spirit of the great apostle, St. Paul.

The New Road Chapel, Great Bridge, was erected in 1864, Mrs. Sylvester laying the foundation stone, and the gross cost amounting to upwards of £1,400. It contains about 800 seats. In September, 1873, the schoolroom adjoining was commenced at an outlay of £550, memorial stones being laid by Mrs. Edwin Danks and Mrs. Josiah Guest. A third stone records the opening by Miss Hannah Jordan on December 15th, 1873. The original chapel of this congregation was situated in Eagle Street; and it is said that the old building was at one time used on alternate Sundays by the Baptists and by the Roman Catholics until it fell into the hands of the New Connexion Methodists.

The New Connexion Chapel in Canal Street was built in 1836, and the first trustees were more or less connected with the Bloomfield Ironworks, as managers, or in some other prominent position there. The chief among them as an earnest worker was Mr. D. Dudley. This old chapel had become so unsafe from mining operations in 1869 that it was determined to take some steps towards providing a new one. First a debt of £800 upon the building had to be liquidated. By 1871 the present airy and commodious chapel had been erected at a cost of £1,500, and with a seating capacity for 500. A donation of £50 given by the late Mr. Henry Fletcher, of the Factory Ironworks, covered by a similar sum from Mr. W. Foster, of Woodsetton, initiated a movement whereby the debt of £1,500 was reduced to about £200, at which figure it now stands. Among others who have been friends of this chapel may be mentioned Messrs. B. Bayley and T. Rudge. Mr. D. Dudley, already mentioned for his generosity, was also most successful in Sunday school work. The Young Men's Improvement Society connected with this institution was a flourishing body in the comparatively early days of 1866.

The Tabernacle in Regent Street, Princes End, belongs to this denomination, and is really an off-shoot of the Canal Street Chapel. Its architecture is somewhat pretentious, the polygonal formation of its glazed roof giving it an interior in the form of an amphitheatre. It is doubtful whether, in the interests of economy, such a construction is suitable to the Black Country. The original cost was £1,300, but only £100 remains unpaid. Mr. Herbert Hipkins and Mr. C. Groves are among its chief supporters.

A Mission Room at Conygre is maintained in the New Connexion interest; and they have a chapel at Tividale, but as this lies in Rowley Regis parish it does not come within the scope of this history. Mr W. Hessey is one of the best known supporters of the denomination in the parish.

* * * * * *

Primitive Methodism was the second schism which rent the Wesleyan body; it commenced in this county in the year 1810. The name "Primitive" is claimed by the sect because their mode of worship is affirmed to be analagous to that of the immediate followers of Wesley; and is not in the deteriorated, cold, and unfeeling forms of the Original Connexion. They have acquired the name of "Ranters" for their ejaculations in public worship. In belief, discipline, and government this body differs little from the New Connexion; camp meetings are sanctioned, and females are allowed to preach, however.

In Tipton the Primitive Methodists are strongly represented, and well organised. Their chapel in Bell Street was erected in 1823 at a cost of £440, and enlarged in 1861 at a further cost of £1,426: a debt of £900 still remains upon it. The accommodation is for 700, and the average attendance of worshippers is 550: the members in society number 110, and there are 350 Sunday scholars, and 50 teachers. The organisation includes beyond this—Open Air Missions, Adult Bible Class, Society and Prayer Meetings, Adult and Juvenile Templar Lodges, Week Day Services, Burial Club, and other machinery for carrying on a great religious work.

Toll End Chapel was built in 1842 for £409, and since that date improvements have swallowed another sum of £626 6s. 6d, although the remaining debt is only about £200. Sittings are provided for 487, and about 350 persons regularly attend. The Society numbers 77, Sunday scholars, 330; and teachers, 47. There is a Burial and Dividend Club in connection.

Railway Street Chapel, in Horsley Heath was the next erected. This was in 1859. The original outlay was £431, and since then £357 have been expended of which £350 is still owing. It will seat 380, and the chief services are attended by about 250. Members in the Society number 28, Sunday scholars, 180; and teachers, 27.

Princes End School Chapel, built in 1873 cost £1,200, and has had £580 expended upon it since, a debt of £280 remaining at the present time. Some 450 attend regularly, but it will seat 555. Its society has 90 members, and its Sunday school about 300 scholars.

At Summerhill a small mission room is rented for Sunday school work and the use of a small Society.

Lea Brook Chapel is in the parish of Wednesbury. It was built in 1850 at an expenditure of £808, and another £800 has since been spent, of which £550 is still unpaid. It has a small residence at the rear. Seating accommodation is provided for 442, and its chief services are attended by 350 worshippers. The society numbers 86, Sunday scholars 335, and teachers 60. There is the usual burial and dividend club established in connection. Great alterations have recently been effected in the fabric of the building, and it is altogether a flourishing chapel, in which Mr. W. Aucott and Mr. David Bagnall take a great interest. The latter is steward to the Tipton Circuit, of which the Rev. James Tristram is the chief minister. The whole organisation is admirably planned and energetically worked throughout the Tipton district.

* * * * * *

The last, and perhaps greatest disruption of the Wesleyan body resulted in the formation of the Methodist Free Church. It really commenced in 1827, over the introduction of an organ into a Leeds chapel, but culminated some years later when an agitation was started against the official appointments to the Wesleyan Theological Institution. This blow to the main body occurred in 1834, when great dissensions arose and secessions were numbered to upwards of a hundred thousand. The earliest in the parish of Tipton was King Street Methodist Free Church, established in 1852, and opened the second Sunday in May, 1853, by the Rev Mr. Chipchase. The original promoters and subscribers included the names of John Heath, John Lewis (father of Mr. Harry and Mr Edward Lewis, ironmasters, and of the late Mrs J. L Thomas), Benjamin Turley, Wm. Dangerfield (ironmaster of West Bromwich), Samuel Hemmings, J. Whitehouse, Isaiah Whitehouse, Robert Price, John Hyde, and Jacob Traloe. A debt of £200 which remained on the chapel was cleared off, mainly through the instrumentality of Mrs W. Dangerfield, the late Mrs. J. Heath, and Mrs T. L. Thomas. All these founders who originally established the Society seceded from the original Wesleyan Conexion during the aforementioned Reform Agitation, and at first met in an old store room situated in High Street. When this got too small the present site was acquired and the chapel built. Mr. T. L Thomas still continues an active and earnest supporter; the Rev. B Crosby of the Wednesbury Free Church is the minister, the chapel being in the Wednesbury and Darlaston Circuit, which also includes Tipton, Bradley, and Bloxwich.

* * * * * *

Yet another offshoot of Wesleyanism is represented in Tipton in the Waterloo Street Refuge Chapel. This belongs to the Wesleyan Reformers, a body formed between 1849 and 1851, when the Reformers exposed certain supposed Methodistic abuses.

The Christadelphians hold meetings in the small room known as Odd Fellows Hall, Great Bridge.

This is possibly the first time that any succinct account of the progress and development of religious thought in Tipton has been ushered into print, and on the face of it confession must be made that within the last three-quarters of a century the parish has become a stronghold of Nonconformity and Dissent.

CHAPTER XXXV.—PROGRESS OF EDUCATION AND THE PROVISION OF SCHOOLS IN TIPTON.

From the Church to the School is an easy transition having finished the history of religious life in Tipton we pass naturally to the consideration of its educational institutions. Of such institutions nothing higher than a public elementary school will engage our attention; and Tipton is not overburdoned with a supply of these. The older ones are, of course, the voluntary schools; the modern Board schools belonging to the newer order. No doubt, the few voluntary schools originated earlier in the century as Sunday schools; carrying on their work in the buildings attached to the various churches and chapels. While many of these remained private schools the few larger and better ones placed themselves under Government inspection, and so became recognised public elementary schools. Among these St. Martin's School and Ocker Hill (St. Mark's) School rank among the earlier National Schools, while the Wesleyans claim the Park Lane and Great Bridge Schools. The last named began its rudimentary work as a day school in 1841, and carried on this work in the Sunday school rooms at the foot of Fisher Street till new premises were erected, and it so grew to its present dimensions. And this development is no doubt typical of the growth of the other voluntary schools.

In 1851 the following was reported as to the school accommodation in Tipton:—"The Solomon Woodall legacy, with £100 left in 1804 by Isaac Hawkins, was invested in the purchase of £1,102 18s. 9d. three per cent. consols. The interest of this stock has been combined with other funds, consisting of £100 old South Sea annuities left by Miss Catherine Nickens and of subscriptions and collections after sermons; with which three schools have been supported during the past 35 years on the Madras system. These National Schools are situated at Tipton Green, Ocker Hill, and Horseley Heath, and are now attended by about 500 children. They are each in two departments for boys and girls; and they are now in a very delapidated state. There are two large Wesleyan day schools also."

How long this voluntary system would have sufficed to provide school places for an overgrown and ever-increasing population it would be difficult to surmise.

Tipton School Board was formed in 1871, and at an early meeting of that body the following were reported to be the private adventure schools existing within the Board's jurisdiction:—

Zion School, Princes End;

St. Paul's New Connexion School, Dudley Port;

Mr. Beasley's Wesleyan School, Dudley Port;

Primitive Methodist School, Burnt Tree;

Bloomfield Wesleyan School;

Gospel Oak Wesleyan School;

Ragged School, Brown Lion Street, Bloomfield;

Summerhill Wesleyan School;

The Tabernacle School, Princes End;

Ocker Hill Wesleyan School;

Ebenezer Independent School, Union Street;

Primitive Methodist School, Bloomfield;

Primitive Methodist School, Great Bridge;

Ragged School, Horseley Heath.

Tipton at this time was evidently a capital field for the private enterprise of the scholastic profession.

The established public elementary schools, duly inspected by the Government inspector, and in actual receipt of Government grants, were at that time as follows:—

	Accommodation
St. Martin's National Schools, Lower Church Lane	560
St. Mark's National Schools, Ocker Hill	366
St. John's National Schools, Princes End	276
Park Lane Wesleyan	398
Tipton Hall (Mixed)	168
Waterloo Street (Infants)	175
	1943

The population of Tipton in 1871 was 29,445, so that the school accommodation was not nearly half of what was required. The average attendance at those schools was then only 1,146; it has now risen to 2,154 under the exercise of the Board's powers, and, of course, to meet this increased attendance proper provision of school places has been duly made.

The first School Board, elected in the March of 1871, consisted of the following members:—Rev. W. Ker, Rev. S. T. Tozer, Messrs. Wm. Hipkins, Wm. Bristow, James Brown, Wm. Roberts, Jos. Cox, Saml. L. Millington, and Wm. Foster. The first meeting was held on Thursday, April 6th, at the Local Board Offices, in Lower Church Lane, when Mr. Wm. Hipkins was appointed chairman and Mr. Millington vice-chairman for the ensuing three years. No clerk was appointed, economy being the order of the day, and the Rev. S. T. Tozer having volunteered to fill that office. At the meeting held on July 5th the reverend gentleman was duly installed as honorary clerk to the Board; while Mr. G. Wilkinson, of Lloyd's Bank, Dudley, was appointed treasurer.

For some years the Board rented temporary school buildings at Dudley Port, Toll End, Tipton Green, and Burnt Tree, but these have since been replaced by permanent and more suitable structures erected by the aid of loans borrowed from the Public Works Loan Commissioners. The new schools were erected in the following order:—Great Bridge (New Road), Dudley Port (1877), Burnt Tree (1880), and Tipton Green (1880); and at the present time a new school is in course of completion at Bloomfield, and which is to take the place of an iron structure long condemned by Her Majesty's inspector of schools. It will be opened on Monday, the 25th of the present month (May, 1891). Nearly all the schools erected by the Board have been enlarged to overtake the increasing demands upon their accommodation, which now stands—

	Accommodation	
Dudley Port (boys, girls, and infants)	718	places
Burnt Tree (mixed and infants)	535	,,
Tipton Green (boys, girls, and infants)	788	,,
Great Bridge ,, ,, ...	862	,,
Bloomfield (infants)	250	,,
Total	3,153	

(This last is the new school about to be opened)

In 1886 the accommodation of the Board's twelve departments was 3,032, and in 1883 it was only 2,992. The average attendance in these Board schools is 2,681 and with an average of 2,154 in the voluntary schools the total average attendance for the parish now stands at 4,835.

A full account of Woodhall's Charity, and its application to the establishment of Tipton National Schools in the year 1818, and the progress of the said schools up to the year 1823, will be found duly set forth in chapter xxvii. The present income from the charity is £42 12s. yearly. In a poor parish like Tipton this useful bequest has been most welcome to the National Voluntary Schools, in the earlier days of public elementary education it could scarcely help being their most reliable source of income, and in these later days, with the competition of rate-aided Board schools there is ever an increasing difficulty in raising voluntary subscriptions in support of schools.

Two well arranged "Triennial Reports" of the Tipton School Board have been published (by R. Elton, Owen Street), the one dealing with the years 1880-1883, and the other 1883-1886, both bearing the signature of William Bedworth, as chairman. From these we glean the following figures relating to the finances of the Board:—

Year	Rate in £.	Amount of precept.
1880	8¼d.	£2,700
1881	9d.	£3,000
1882	6¾d.	£2,150
1883	9d	£3,600
1884	6d	£2,400
1885	5d	£2,400

Strange to say no published report seems to have been forthcoming since that date, but the courteous clerk of the Board, Mr. Edward Richards, supplies the following as being the subsequent rates, calculated on the rateable value of the parish, viz.—

1886	6d in £
1887	8¼d. ,,
1888	9d. ,,
1889	8¼d ,,
1890	8d. ,,

As great economy was found necessary the Board made the most of its income to be derived from school fees. In 1881 they collected from this source £669 13s. 7d., equivalent to 5s. 6¼d per head on the average attendance, in 1882 they raised the amount to £848 15s 4d., or 7s. 3¼d. per head. By 1885 this had again fallen to 6s. 5¼d. per head. In the same year a Tipton child cost the rates 7s. 8d. for its education, against an average of 16s 3d. per child for the whole country and the gross cost was £1 10s 11¼d, as against £2 1s. 8½d. for the whole country.

The fluctuation of all these various figures indicates the great difficulty of the struggle to combine efficiency with economy, while endeavouring to overtake the neglected arrears of educational work among a dense population of the poorest class of ratepayers.

Little or no provision exists in the parish for higher or for intermediate education; and since the days of the Rev. John Howells, who maintained a capital middle class school near the church, Tipton seems to have been mostly dependent upon other places for higher grade education.

CHAPTER XXXVI.—LOCAL ADMINISTRATION OF JUSTICE.

The detection and the punishment of crime are among the gravest duties devolving upon a civilised community. How these duties have been performed in Tipton will be our first consideration in dealing with the local government of the place. Law Courts never figured very largely in the history of Tipton—the old Manorial Court, like the present Police Court, being as frequently as not held in a strange place. Singular to state, the first recorded case of a Tipton crime is found among the Plea Rolls of Henry III, in the year 1248, for the hundred of Humilford (? Hemlingford, Warwickshire).

The jury of the hundred presented that William the Sumpter [Provisioner], of Tipton, killed a certain, woman, Ivetta de Brereley by name, in the wood of Lovershull, and fled and was outlawed. He had no chattels, but was in the manupastu of Geoffrey Fitz Warin (that is, he was one of the family or household), in the county of Stafford. Geoffrey is, therefore, *in misericordia* (in fine) for not producing him.

From the local jurisdiction of the Manorial Court, the next step was the gradual acquisition of various powers, administrative and executive, by the Parish Vestry. The powers and functions of the vestry dating from the times when the domination of the State Church was undisputed, lingered on in this parish till almost recent times.

On November 22nd, 1814, the Parish Vestry offered A reward of £50 for the discovery of the murderer of George Law, and ordered the same to be advertised in *Aris's Gazette*.

On August 4th, 1819, four special constables were appointed, one for S.E. division of the parish, one for N.E., one for N.W., and one for S.W. division.

For the apprehension of Henry Proctor, who apparently had fraudulently absconded, a fee of £2 12s. 2d. was paid by the vestry to John Horton, constable, June 24,1814. There are but a few instances of the vestry exercising their powers in the local administration of justice.

Till very recently as many as six "parish constables" were annually elected at the vestry meeting. Since the Police Act their jurisdiction has become obsolete, but their services are sometimes called into requisition to serve summonses for unpaid rates.

In December, 1835, we find the vestry appointing "four Sunday constables" at 2s 6d. each per day

But in 1839 we had the modern Police Act brought into existence for the provinces, as it had previously existed for some 10 years in London. As this Act was an idea of Sir Robert Peel's, the newly established constable was nicknamed a "Bobby" or a "Peeler," to distinguish him from the parish constable.

Until the present Central Station was built there were three small police stations in the parish, namely at Tipton Green, at Dudley Port, and at Toll End. The last named was afterwards moved to Horseley Heath—two small houses converted into one. The new Central Police Station in Church Lane was opened on May 22nd, 1867, and the first case heard was dismissed by the magistrates, who were the Rev. W. Ker, Mr. Job Haines, and Mr. Richard Bagnall. Formerly there were no Petty Sessions held at Tipton, the cases of this parish being generally tried at Wednesbury, Sedgley, or West Bromwich. Then an inspector and seven constables were deemed sufficient police protection for this dense mining district. But Tipton is now a sub-division of the Wednesbury police division. At the Central Station are located an inspector, one sergeant, and nine men; at Tipton Green are one sergeant and three men; at Princes End is stationed one man and at Ocker Hill two more men are supplied from the Wednesbury centre. Eighteen is, therefore the total strength of the police force within the parish to protect so large an industrial population, and to preserve the peace among thirty thousand inhabitants. Petty Sessions are held at the Central Police Court every Monday by the local justices. The South Staffordshire stipendiary magistrate does not sit at Tipton, therefore such cases arising within Tipton as the unpaid magistracy may not try (as those under the Employers Act) have to be taken elsewhere (generally to Wednesbury) to be tried before the stipendiary who sits on alternate Mondays at Sedgley or at West Bromwich; alternate Tuesdays at Wednesbury or Bilston; on Wednesdays and Fridays at Wolverhampton, and on Thursdays at Brierley Hill. As the local justices sit only once a week, and the population is so large, many cases naturally are taken from Tipton to be tried outside the parish. The chairman of the Tipton rota of magistrates is Dr. W. L. Underhill who is the only lay justice of the peace residing within the confines of this extensive and populous parish—the Rev. A. A. Cory, like his predecessor in the living, having been made a magistrate.

* * * * * *

Coming next to debtors' courts we find that Tipton was formerly included with the parishes of Halesowen, Rowley Regis, West Bromwich, and Harborne, and with the Manor of Bradley (under an Act passed 47 Geo. III) under the jurisdiction of a Court of Requests, for the recovery of small debts not exceeding £5 These "Courts of Conscience" were really established in early Tudor times, but their jurisdiction was not so clearly defined till this Act of 1808. There was a similar Court of Requests for the "townships of Bilston and Willenhall, and the parishes of Wednesbury and Darlaston in the county of Stafford, excepting the Manor of Bradley." These Courts for the recovery of debts were superseded in 1846 by our modern County Courts for the recovery of debts up to £20, and in 1850 extended to sums of £50. Tipton with two other Staffordshire parishes of Sedgley and Rowley Regis is included in the jurisdiction of Dudley County Court, which forms part of Circuit No. 23, England being divided into 60 such circuits.

CHAPTER XXXVII.—POOR LAW ADMINISTRATION.

A parish is a place (literally) where people dwell together—where dwellings cluster round a church and its pastor. The earliest record of a church at Tipton is 1288.

It is a matter of fact that the parochial system of England was nearly the same in the reign of Edward I as it is now.

The boundaries of parishes were not settled, however, with any great amount of exactness until the introduction of the Poor Laws, when it became a matter of some consequence that the limits of each should be precisely defined. The north side of Wednesbury boundary was a subject of dispute with the Darlaston authorities, and there is every probability that the boundaries now existing between Wednesbury and Tipton are not the ancient lines of division.

In olden times (1348) while none might give alms to a beggar able to work, it was the common law that the poor were to be sustained by "parsons, rectors of the church, and parishioners, so that none should die for default of sustenance"; and by statue 15 Rich. II. impropriators were obliged to distribute a yearly sum to the poor. This was the connecting link between the tithes and the relief of the poor. Still no compulsory poor law really existed till 27 Hen. VIII., 1535 After the suppression of the monasteries Poor Laws became absolutely necessary, and our present system may be referred to 43 Eiiz. 1600. The non~residence of the clergy and their neglect of hospitality occasioned violent protestations from the House of Commons and may be accounted as one of the causes leading up to the Reformation. With the convents hospitality was a religious duty, for the Order of St. John of Jerusalem the first of duties. As this Order had establishments all over England, the poor traveller in the middle ages sought shelter in them as in modern times the tramp ward of the workhouse is made the objective point of a day's tramping. To rich as well as to the poor these knights hospitallers kept no closed door, and the expenditure of the knight~monks always showed heavy charges on account of *supervenientibus* (strangers). Only people of high rank, however, were admitted into the monastery itself. The bulk of wayfarers, pilgrims, and others were housed and fed in the Guest House. This was a building provided to receive passers-by; it stood by itself, sometimes outside the the precincts of the monastery. It would consist of a hall, with doors opening on each side into sleeping rooms, and when these were full guests slept in the hall itself. The religious houses nearest to Tipton were Sandwell Priory, Dudley Priory, and Halesowen Abbey.

When the Poor Laws were systematised in the seventeenth century, we find allusions made to the Overseers of the Poor of the Parish of Tipton in 1646, and 1653. (See Chapters xvii. and xix.)

With the Overseer was generally associated the churchwarden, because of the close connection between Church and State in the performance of the duties of local government.

Judicious administration of the Poor Laws has always been a difficult task for unpaid and untrained local rulers, the maintenance of the balance and equipoise between ratepayer and pauper testing the ability of the keenest business man who ever entered public life, The Vestry, in 1515, asked for tenders for farming the medical attendance upon the poor of the parish. The tender of Mr Thomas Underhill, at 18 guineas, was accepted in preference to that of another surgeon, Mr Moore, at £20. Soon after an inquiry was held into the expenditure upon poor relief, estimated at £120 per month, but said to be increasing, and with a debt already in existence of £460. To cope with this state of things a re-valuation of the rateable value of the parish was made in 1819, when Michael Tony, of Wednesbury, was engaged, at a fee of £100, to assess the machinery, &c; and George Boulton, of West Bromwich, was paid 50 guineas to value the land. In 1825 a survey of the parish was ordered to be made by a Mr J. P. Smith, of Birmingham, and to be completed by Lady-day, 1826, at a cost of 100 guineas, but the plans ultimately cost £142 14s. 6d, with the extras allowed. In the meantime the question of medical attendance upon the poor had passed through another phase. In 1824 Mr. Underhill took the eastern division of the parish, while the western was left to Mr. Leonard Ledbrook, each surgeon taking 10 guineas a year, exclusive of midwifery cases. By 1828 it was found necessary to treat with a third doctor (Mr. Henry Scofield), and each held office in turn for a year, at an increased fee of £30.

Tipton is now in the Dudley Union, as it also is in the district of Dudley County Court.

The Dudley Poor Law Union comprises the same four parishes of Dudley, Rowley Regis, Sedgley, and Tipton, which extend over an area of 26 sq. miles, and in 1851 had over 100,000 inhabitants. The Board Room and principal workhouse was then in Dudley (in the county of Worcester), while the two old workhouses at Sedgley and at Tipton were utilised by the union, the latter being appropriated for the reception of children. This old public building still stands in Church Lane—a quaint half-timbered fabric which was once surrounded by beautiful scenery—but is not now used for the housing of the poor. As in mediæval times the poor of Tipton find shelter in the neighbouring town of Dudley.

The Act to amend the Poor Laws, so as to save the excessive cost of management in small parochial establishments, by uniting several contiguous parishes in one Union," was passed in 1834.

The first meeting of the newly constituted joint Board of Guardians was held in the old Town Hall, Dudley, October 15th, 1836.

Tipton is represented by six members on this body, Dudley has ten members, with one extra for the Castle Hill (which is in Staffordshire, while the bulk of the parish is in Worcestershire), Sedgley has eight members, and Rowley Regis four.

The first Guardians of the poor for Tipton parish, elected October 14, 1836, were—

Philip Williams,
John York,
Richard Haines,
Richard Nicklin,
Simeon Round,
Thomas Morris.

On March 13th of the following year, a notice appeared in *Aris's Gazette* of the election of Guardians at Tipton. With local relieving officers in each parish the present system works very well to this day.

CHAPTER XXXVIII.—PROGRESS OF LOCAL GOVERNMENT: PARISH VESTRY: HIGHWAY SURVEYORS: BOARD OF HEALTH.

Local Government by the Parish Vestry was, as may be imagined, more ecclesiastical than civil in many of its functions. For instance, among the payments made we find £24 10s to Samuel Ferriday for surveying the parish for church rate assessments (16 July, 1799), and £53 6s for the fees for the consecration of the new Edifice, while in July, 1803, Edward Jesson was paid £5 6s 1d for selling the materials of the old church, "half the King's duty," &c. This same Samuel Ferriday had previously been an assessor with Edward Jessop (who was of Dudley) and with William Underhill in the year 1794.

Tipton affords a good example of local government by Parish Vestry. The parish and the township are practically identical; and formerly all the public business that was not manorial was despatched in vestry meetings. Although originally the vestry was primarily concerned in transacting church business, in course of time it acquired wide powers of parish government, for instance, as representing the inhabitants, it actually held land, the churchwardens and overseers being in effect a quasi-corporation.

The procedure in vestry meeting may be briefly set forth. (1) A meeting could be summoned by the churchwardens with the consent of the minister, and they also fixed time for such meeting. Overseers might call a meeting for purely civil purposes. (2) Three days notice of place, hour, and special purpose must be given; the place need not be in church or the vestry attached, but rather in some convenient place within the parish. (3) Voters in vestry may be ratepayers of either sex, resident in or out of the parish; not owners who pay rates instead of the occupiers. (4) Inhabitants refusing to pay rates, and being three months in arrear, may not vote. (5) The chairman of vestry meeting held in church or in the vestry is generally the incumbent, especially for ecclesiastical business, although in the absence of the minister the inhabitants may elect a chairman by show of hands. (6) Votes may be taken by show of hands, and if demanded a division or a poll must afterwards be taken, no ratepayer recording more than six votes (one for each £25 rateable value). The chairman may adjourn for taking a poll, but not for procrastinating business.

Such was the method by which the parish of Tipton was governed for a very long period of years—for centuries in fact.

Effectiveness by such government was certain and assured in all matters ecclesiastical; but sometimes the machinery of the vestry was found totally inadequate to cope with many of the civil requirements of a large area like the Tipton district. Take the matter of highways. In the year 1819 Richard Haines was nominated as surveyor by the vestry. On August 11th of the following year resolutions were passed in vestry meeting for the widening of Watery Lane. The jurisdiction of the same authority is exemplified again in 1828, when on September 10th propositions were made for the widening of a bridge over an arm of the canal leading to Tibbington Colliery, and when the state of the road from the Workhouse to Princes End—which road seems not to possess a distinctive name—was seriously complained of. Resolutions passed in vestry meeting, without proper and sufficient means for carrying out such intentions, were found cumbersome and unsatisfactory. To meet these difficulties the Highways Act was passed in 1835, which Tipton eventually adopted, and by which Tipton was governed till the formation of the present Board of Health 36 years ago.

By 5 and 6 William IV., c. 50, every parish maintained its own highways, and at the vestry meeting for nominating overseers of the poor, one or more persons were to be chosen to act as surveyors in the said parish for the year ensuing. Where the parish did not meet to elect overseers, inhabitants contributing to a highway rate had to meet to elect surveyors; and if they neglected to do so the justices might make the appointment. Such surveyor had power to assess and levy a rate for highway purposes, to appoint collectors and keep accounts, to contract for road materials, hire teams, &c, but could not sell materials or let out teams without a license from two justices in special sessions assembled.

But the special function of a local authority is the care of the public health. As we have seen, previous to the constitution of the present Local Board of Health, the mere repair of the highways was carried out by surveyors appointed under the said Highway Acts. But it was in consequence of the cholera visitation that a Sanitary Committee was formed, consisting of the principal inhabitants of the parish, to adopt measures for improving the sanitary condition of the people and their dwellings.

The minutes in the Vestry Book contain a reference on August 3rd, 1832, to a "Board of Health for Tipton," and £300 was placed at the disposal of the same. On the 22nd of the same month extraordinary expenses are recorded. On September 14th a public subscription in aid of the sufferers is mentioned and the following committee of management was appointed:—

William Johnson	–	–	Gospel Oak.
G. R Hickman	–	–	Moat Colliery.
Isaac Shepherd	–	–	Toll End Ironworks.
Thomas Horton	–	–	Toll End Furnaces.
William Holland	–	–	Sheepwash Lane.
Robert Sylvester	–	–	Eagle Furnace.
Thomas Shorthouse	–	–	Church Lane.
Charles Birch	–	–	Burnt Tree.
Edward Cresswell	–	–	Parker's Work.

It was in Tipton in the June of 1832 that the cholera scourge was first reported to have appeared within this Midland district. This parish, with a population of 14,951, had 1,452 cases and sustained 404 deaths before the plague disappeared. From a national relief fund of about £15,500 the parish of Tipton had £929 distributed among its sufferers. This was in addition to neighbourly help from the richer inhabitants, and the relief from greatly enhanced poor's rates. The last case of cholera was reported at Dudley on November 29th. Tipton mortality was only exceeded by that of Bilston, her 404 deaths occurring within the space of a few weeks.

The 1848 visitation (in fifteen months from October 1848, to December, 1849) of the same disease carried away 113 inhabitants of Tipton, while in Dudley there were only 84 deaths, and at West Bromwich as few as 21. On the other hand Sedgley lost 203 and Wednesbury 212. Bilston headed the list with 605 deaths, and Oldbury brought up the rear with 16.

The Sanitary Committee was in due time superseded by a Local Board of Health, which was elected under the Public Health Act, 1848, which Act was put in force in the parish by an Order of Her Majesty in Council, dated the 21st May, 1855. The Rev. William Ker, M A., vicar of Tipton, was appointed by such Order to be the returning officer for conducting such election.

The first meeting of the Board was held on the 10th September, 1855, and the following gentlemen were the first members:—Rev. William Ker, vicar of Tipton (chairman); Rev. E. H. A. Gwynne, vicar of St. Paul's, Messrs. Richard Haines, Job Haines, William Millington, T. L. Nicklin, J. D Jackson, Thomas Round, T. E. Ward, W. L. Underhill, Thomas Jones, W. P. Greenway, George Davies, William Howells, J. E. Howl, Thomas Morris, James Aston, William Finch, John Hyde, Edward Hipkins, John Twist, George Smith, James Solly, and William Hopkins.

The following were the officers then appointed:—

George M. Waring	–	–	Clerk
(who still holds the appointment).			
David Peacock	–	–	Surveyor.
Jesse Baxter	–	–	Inspector of Nuisances.
John Davies	–	–	Medical Officer.
Jeavon Parker	–	–	Collector.

Meetings were held at the Old Workhouse, Church Lane, for some time.

The memorial stone of the present Public Offices in Owen Street was laid by James Whitehouse, Esq., chairman of the Board, on December 13th, 1876, on which occasion a banquet was given by him at the Navigation Hotel.

The meetings, held on the last Tuesday evening of each month, now take place at these Public Offices, which cost £4,000 to erect. A few years ago (February, 1878), for the better and more direct representation of the different portions of so straggling an area, the parish was divided into six electoral districts or wards. Tipton Ward is represented by six members, Tibbington Ward by three, Ocker Hill Ward three, Toll End Ward three, Horseley Heath Ward six, and Dudley Port Ward by three. Should a District Council be substituted by a future piece of legislation, one great advantage will result in the method of electing representatives, the present unsatisfactory voting papers no doubt being superseded by the ballot box. The Chairman of the present Board is Mr. Daniel Hipkins. There are six permanent committees, viz, (1) Finance, (2) Highway, Sewerage, and General Purposes, (3) Cemetery and Hospital, (4) Gas and Stores, (5) Fire Appliances, and (6) Free Library. The nomenclature of these Committees is not a very happy one, the Fire Appliances Committee being presumably the committee controlling appliances to prevent the spread of fire; there is also a grim suggestiveness in associating the hospital with the cemetery, while the Board, which is primarily a sanitary authority, would seem to have no exclusively Sanitary Committee. Still in the practical work of local government the Board seems to have been eminently successful. The roads, streets, and highways are in good condition considering the exceptionally heavy traffic of a district engaged so exclusively in the coal and iron trades; many of these roads have been widened, as well as some of the canal bridges which previously caused partial obstructions, the town is partially sewered, sewage works having just been constructed for the most populous parts. With regard to sewering there was a proposal in 1883 to make a united drainage area for Wednesbury, Tipton, and Darlaston, and part of Coseley. A Government inquiry was held at Wednesbury on the 14th, 15th, and 16th of March, before J. T. Harrison, Esq., an inspector of the Local Government Board. The draft scheme proposed by Wednesbury was to form a joint Board (called the Wednesbury Union Drainage Board) of 15 members; 4 *ex-officio* members, being the chairmen of the four respective Urban Sanitary Anthorities; and 11 elective members, namely, 5 for Tipton, 4 for Wednesbury, and 2 for Darlaston. The cost was to be borne on a basis of relative populations. It was calculated that Tipton, consisting of 2,697 acres, had only 487 built over, the remaining 2,210 acres being mining (or agricultural land. Even the population of this urban area was scattered, as thus—

	Place.	Area built over. Acres	Pop.
1	Tipton	116	9,220
2	Dudley Port; Horaseley Heath; and Great Bridge	160	12,310
3	Tibbington and Princes End	109	3,130
4	Ocker Hill, Lea Brook, and Toll End	102	5,340
		487	30,000

Within the parish there was no land fit for treating sewage by means of irrigation; all the streams were damaged by mining operations; and in the same proportion as these streams cost the Mines Drainage Commissioners (who maintain 10,000 yards of such surface streams) it would have cost £650 per annum to keep 6,500 yards of main sewers with mineral support left under them, and for the repair of those running along roads and undermined lands. These sewers would have carried the sewage to an intercepting sewer on the confines of the parish, by which the matter would have been carried on through Wednesbury towards a proposed outfall works at Newton. Mr. Henry J. Martin, M.I.C.E., advised the Tipton authorities that as the configuration of their parish would not admit of treating sewage at a concentrating sewage farm, to treat their sewage refuse by means of subsiding tanks. He grouped the parish into three principal and two subsidiary drainage areas—

		Population.
1	Tipton proper, Tibbington, and part of Princes End	11,000
2	Great Bridge, Burnt Tree, Dudley Port, Horseley Heath, Toll End	14,000
3	Ocker Hill Drainage District	1,500
4	Lea Brook Drainage District	2,000
5	Princes End Drainage district	1,500
		30,000

Calculating 25 gallons of sewage per head to be discharged, the land needed for tanks would have been—

No.		Gallons per day.		Acres.
1	Drainage District with	275,000	equals	$1\frac{1}{2}$
2	,, ,, ,,	350,000	equals	$1\frac{3}{4}$
3	,, ,, ,,	37,500	equals	$\frac{1}{2}$
4	,, ,, ,,	50,000	equals	$\frac{1}{2}$
5	,, ,, ,,	37,500	equals	$\frac{1}{2}$
				$4\frac{3}{4}$

The "united" scheme fell through, each of the three parishes deciding since to adopt separate schemes [See "Proceedings," published by Kirby and Bytheway, Wednesbury, with map, 1883.]

The Tipton Church Act contained provision for extending the cemetery or churchyard. In 1825, the burial ground being still found too small for the increasing needs of the parish, the vestry appointed a committee to deal with the matter. In April of the following year it was decided to purchase about two acres adjoining "the present churchyard," for enlargmg the same. The sum stated in the minute book under date of April 12th 1830, was £822 11s. (inclusive of rent and interest), which was paid to the representatives of the late Thomas Fletcher, for an area of 2 acres 2 roods. The present Public Cemetery controlled by the local authority as a Burial Board, had the church portion consecrated by Dr. Selwyn, Bishop of Lichfield, on July 25, 1873; it cost the ratepayers about £8,000. The whole of the sanitary improvements effected by the Local Board has reduced the death-rate very considerably, and Tipton now compares favourably with surrounding towns.

Since the beginning of the century the population of Tipton has increased rapidly and consistently till the recent decline in the volume of the inland iron trade.

In	1801	the population was	4,288
,,	1811	,,	8,407
,,	1821	,,	11,546
,,	1831	,,	14,951
,,	1841 (or 1844)	,,	18,891
,,	1851	,,	24,853
,,	1861	,,	28,870
,,	1871	,,	29,445
,,	1881	,,	30,013
,,	1891	,,	29,316

In 1851 there were 12,827 males to 12,026 females, a very fair balance between the sexes; it was said to be in favour of the male sex in 1811, who largely outnumbered the females, as 4 to 3. In 1798 there were but 800 houses in the parish, mostly inhabited by poor people; by 1851 there were 4,705 occupied houses 176 unoccupied, and 23 in process of erection. By 1871 there were 5,858 houses, though soon after this the local prosperity and communal increase reached its zenith. There are more houses in existence now, however, the last census giving the number as 6,418—so evidently there is less overcrowding.

Generally a better state of things exists all round ,The Free Libraries Act was adopted on March 24th, 1883, but was not put into operation till December 9th, 1890, when two public Reading Rooms were opened by the Hon. Philip Stanhope, M P., one at Horseley Heath, and one at Toll End. Towards this £250 was appropriated from the the profits of the gas undertaking.

When the Birmingham Corporation secured Parliamentary powers in 1875 to purchase and to work the undertaking of the Birmingham and Staffordshire Gas Company, acting for its own parochial area, Tipton with commendable enterprise, secured the right to buy the mains within its own jurisdiction, and has since put up as neat and compact a gasmaking establishment as any in the country. The construction of these gas works cost upwards of £70,000, but it was about six years before they were ready to make and supply gas. So far as a small gas producing concern can do, it has been fairly successful in a financial sense, the present year being the first in which an actual loss has been sustained by the trading.

Tipton is supplied with water by the South Staffordshire Water Works Company.

CHAPTER XXXIX.—PARLIAMENTARY AND COUNTY REPRESENTATION: CONTRIBUTION TO NATIONAL DEFENCE.

For centuries Tipton had to share with Staffordshire in that modicum of Parliamentary representation which was comprised in the return of two knights of the shire. Other members representing the county were two for Lichfield, two for Stafford, and two for Newcastle, with two more for Tamworth. With the Reform Bill of 1832, Wolverhampton obtained two representatives, while Walsall and Stoke secured one member each. Sedgley, Bilston, and Willenhall were included in Wolverhampton. At the same time the county was divided into Northern Division and Southern Division, with two members each. Tipton was with Wednesbury, Darlaston, &c, &c., included in the South Staffordshire Division. At the election for a member for South Staffordshire, February, 1854, the candidates were Lord Paget (Whig) and Lord Ingestre (Tory). One of the election songs on that occasion began—

> "March! March! West Bromwich and Wednesbury,
> Handsworth and Smethwick march forward in order;
> Tipton and Rowley, Kingswinford and Sedgley,
> Drive the young Tory Lord over the border."

The final close of the poll on Saturday, February 11th, resulted as follows:—

Paget	4,325
Ingestre	2,757

At Wednesbury the votes recorded were 355 and 191 respectively; at Walsall, 223 and 194; at Tipton, 183 and 84. Other polling stations were at Bilston, Brewood, Handsworth, Kingswinford, Lichfield, Penkridge, Rugeley, Tamworth, Sedgley, West Bromwich, and Wolverhampton—truly an ample constituency, wide in area and thick in population!

At this election Lord Ward, although generally understood to be a Tory, threw all his influence on the side of the Liberal candidate, which in some measure accounts for Lord Paget's majority of 1,568. When Wednesbury was created a Parliamentary borough in the next Reform Bill, Tipton, with West Bromwich and Darlaston, was included in it. The first borough election took place in November, 1868. On Monday, the 16th, the nominations were made at a hustings in Wednesbury Market Place, the candidates being A. Brogden (Liberal), T. E. Walker (Tory), and Dr. Kenealy (Independent). The last named found many supporters in Tipton, and they marched in procession to the nomination. Rioting took place at

Great Bridge and other places, notwithstanding the presence of many police and the swearing in of 200 special constables. Next day (Tuesday) was the polling, by open voting, the ballot not then having been introduced. The result of the polling was known every hour, from 9 till 4. The four parishes voted as follows:—

	Brogden.	Walker.	Kenealy.
Wednesbury	1,288	1,251	30
Tipton	1,335	714	862
Darlaston	1,195	721	59
West Bromwich	2,383	1,123	24

Brogden thus secured a clear majority of 2,392, and out of 15,000 voters 10,995 actually voted. At this time Tipton was replaced in the eastern (new) division of Staffordshire as regards freehold voters, while the borough of Wednesbury, in which were its household voters, was the largest constituency in England represented by one member, the population of Wednesbury borough being no less than 116,809.

In 1885 a new Re-distribution Bill took West Bromwich out of Wednesbury borough, and erected it into a separate borough by itself. At the same time Tipton became part (with Wednesbury, Walsall, &c.) of the Handsworth division for the purposes of recording freeholders' votes for county representatives.

* * * * * *

Tipton was rated to the county in 1867 at £89,594, being the highest in Staffordshire, except Wolverhampton, Stoke, and West Bromwich, and was even £10,000 higher than Walsall. This arose from the large area covered by prolific mines and flourishing ironworks, as against so much residential property in the other places. In 1890 the rateable value of Tipton had fallen to £68,553. When the County Councils were established nearly three years ago, Tipton had three representatives on the Staffordshire Council allotted to it—one each for Tipton (proper), Ocker Hill, and Horsley Heath. The first Ocker Hill representative (Mr Edwin Hunt, of Wednesbury) was made an alderman, and Mr Bedworth was elected to fill his place—thus giving Tipton four members. It was suggested at this period that Wednesbury, Tipton, and Darlaston parishes should have been united in one county borough, just as it was proposed to form a number of parishes in the north of the county into a Pottery Borough. The advantages claimed for the proposed Black Country Borough were that it would have received full control of the Government "grants in aid," and have been governed for "county" purposes by a joint council for the three parishes, at the same time retaining their separate urban sanitary authorities for their respective parishes.

The substitution of this County Borough Council for that of the Staffordshire County Council, it was contended, would have been an advantage in many ways, as, for instance, police control, maintenance of highways, control of Government grants for technical education, &c., &c.

* * * * * *

In the defence of the kingdom Tipton has had to perform its proper share of military duty. Tipton men followed to battle their feudal lords, the Fitzwarren's and the Wyrleys in the middle ages, and in later times we have already recorded the part played by Tipton in the great Civil War. Coming a little later down the corridor of time, we find an entry in the Parish Register, under date, July 7th, 1695, of the following words, after a marriage record, "I received the king's pay, 2s 6d."

It would appear that in the previous year there was imposed, "for carrying on the war against France with vigour," a graduated scale of duties for five years upon all marriages, births, and burials. The tax-collectors inspected the registers, and clergymen were fined for neglecting to make entries. The tax was unpopular and allowed to lapse. Dr. Willmore (of Walsall) is of opinion that this entry in Tipton registers referring to the tax is unique. It is certainly interesting.

Our next military item will be found in *Aris's Gazette* of May, 1798, where is printed a list of voluntary contributions to the National Defence Fund during the Napoleonic scare, and among the subscribers is the name of James Smith, of Willingsworth Hall, with the amount of 10 guineas against it. And among the Staffordshire auxiliary forces of this same period we find the Tipton Infantry in existence as late as 1806, with a strength of 100, under Captain John Adams.

Next record in our military history is an entry in the vestry minute book, where we find that in March, 1826, the parish had to raise 12 men for service in the militia; and if its quota could not be made up by volunteering the whole civil parish would have to ballot for the deficiency. This force has lasted from the time of Alfred the Great to the present day; the old feudal military tenures from the days of the Fitzwarrens and the Wryleys are now involved in this national force, consolidated under various Acts since the days of Charles II (1661).

Among the earliest adherents to the present volunteer movement of 1859 may be reckoned the parish of Tipton. A company of about 100 strong is still in existence. It is attached to the Wolverhampton Battalion, and its headquarters are at a room or hall near the Navigation Inn.

A portrait of Colour-Sergeant Ford, of the Tipton Rifle Volunteers, and winner of St. George's Vase at Wimbledon shooting competition in 1888, appeared in *The Graphic* for July 28th of that year. The St. George's prize, which was one of the most favourite of the Wimbledon compositions, comprised not only the vase, but such tempting rewards as the Dragon Cup, Gold Cup, Silver Jewel, &c. But a very sad incident in connection with this Tipton triumph was the sudden death of Major Round from excitement caused by this occasion.

CHAPTER XL.—THE POSTAL HISTORY OF TIPTON.

A history of Tipton, without a glance at its postal progress, would be incomplete, because there is nothing by which the prosperity of a town can be more accurately guaged than by the rise and fall, the ebb and flow, of its correspondence; and although the correspondence of Tipton has not increased so extensively as that of other towns, which have progressed more rapidly as regards both commerce and population, it still shows a steady and substantial increase year by year. For instance,

In 1861 the average weekly number of letters, &c., passing through the office was	16,700
In 1871	26,100
In 1881	34,550
In 1891	43,700

The parcels, telegrams, &c., also show a proportionate increase, clearly proving that Tipton is not going downhill so rapidly as many people appear to imagine,

The first Tipton Post Office was about 30 yards distant from the present building at Dudley Port, and was situated at the corner of Park Lane and Horsely Heath, on the site of the house occupied by Mr. George Orton. It was kept by a Mr. Partridge, an uncle of the late postmistress (Miss Baker), and subsequently by his sister, "Old Lady Partridge," at whose decease Miss Baker was appointed in 1866.

The building in which the work is at present carried on was erected about 1840, and shortly afterwards the office was removed into it, the staff at that time consisting of the postmistress and two letter carriers. At first the post office consisted of a lobby, which is now used as the postmen's entrance, with an arrangement somewhat similar to a booking office at a railway station through which the public were attended to. The stage coach running between Worcester and Birmingham conveyed the mails, and the horses were changed at Kidderminster and at the "Swan," at Swan Village. The two letter carriers referred to used to sort the letters for delivery in an outhouse attached to the office. They were allowed to make a charge of ld. for each letter for places beyond one mile from the office—in some cases 2d. was charged—and it was no uncommon sight to see them sitting and snarling over their correspondence like a couple of dogs over a heap of bones, and it was not an unfrequent occurrence, when a difference arose as to which should deliver a particular letter, for them to adjourn to the yard, and in true Tipton style, "fight it out."

It was to assist these two worthies that George Whitehouse, the well known Great Bridge postman was first employed 42 years ago.

As the work increased it became necessary to enlarge the office, by taking in the front room of the house, and to establish the subordinate offices at Great Bridge, Tividale, Tipton Green, Princes End, Ocker Hill, and Burnt Tree. Subsequently, on the introduction of the parcel post, the office was again enlarged, and the whole of the ground floor monopolised. Since then the work has largely increased, and the Department have now decided to provide an office adapted to the requirements of the service—a building which will be worthy of the town, and the plans of which are now under the consideration of the Postmaster-General.

In June, 1888, Miss Baker resigned and Mr. John Lees Taylor was appointed postmaster. Mr. Taylor belongs to a very old Tipton family, and naturally takes a keen interest in everything that concerns the prosperity and welfare of the town, and during the time he has been postmaster many important improvements have been effected. Among others, eight additional wall boxes have been erected in various parts of the parish, and that the necessity for these existed is proved by the fact that since their erection the weekly number of letters posted shows an increase of something like 2,000. The Tividale Post Office has been opened for telegraph and postal order business. Arrangements have been made for affording Sunday relief to the postmen. The outdoor and indoor staff has been revised and augmented. The time for posting letters has been extended at Tipton Green and Great Bridge. The head office is now open for telegraph business till 9 p.m. Several additional collections and despatches have been established, and a supplementary bag is received from Birmingham at 6.25 a.m. So that whatever penalties may be attached to a residence in Tipton the want of postal facilities is certainly not one of them. In the next chapter we will proceed to notice the area of Tipton and its various integral parts needing postal accommodation.

CHAPTER XLI.—Local Topography: Place Names: Old Mansions: Roads and Maps.

The parish has an area of about 2,600 acres, but it is straggling in outline, and the urban parts are separated from each other by works and mining lands, while railways and canals further obtrude themselves in such a way as to cut off direct communication between the various centres of population within the parish. Thus Ocker Hill and Horsley Heath are separated, while Lea Brook and Dudley Port are as the poles to each other. Again, Tibbington and Bloomfield are distinct from Toll End, while Great Bridge is still further from Princes End. One part of Great Bridge is in West Bromwich parish. The central urban portion is round Tipton Green; but it is possible to walk in any direction across the parish for about two miles. But the unfortunate stranger who does stray "within the gates" of Tipton, is not only at a loss to find these various districts, but he is at a further disadvantage owing to a "plentiful lack" of street name-plates. This indefiniteness of description is exemplified even in the surviving nomenclature of the districts themselves; whole localities were formerly vaguely discribed as "Ends," and called after the names of some prominent resident therein. So we obtain *Todd's End, Princes End*, and *Toll End*—all apparently named after families.

A map of the county drawn by John Speech, in 1610, shows Tipton at the source of "Tame flud."

Published with Plot's "Staffordshire" is a map of the county, bordered with shields, charged with the heraldic bearings of the county families of that date (1682). Tipton is shown as a parish, whilst we also have marked its hamlets of *G: Bridge, Tolend* (both these having bridges across the Tame), *Tipton Green, Horseley*, and *Grit Green*. Wednesbury is shown as possessing three windmills, while *Finspoth* is between Wednesbury and Great Bridge. The mansions are also indicated by reference numbers to the arms of their residents, shown in the border aforesaid. For instance, we get *Willingsworth* with a referenoe number (201) to Hon. Ward Esq., Oakeswell Hall; (107) to William Hopkins, Bradley Hall; (105) to John Hoo, &c. Beyond this the name of Tipton scarcely occurs more than twice in Dr. Plot's history, evidently indicating that the place was little known, or considered of no importance.

The "outmost boundes" of the parish of West Bromwich are described in 1666 as "from Brandforde Bridge downwards the river of Tame doth divide that from Halesowen, Rowley, Tipton, Wednesbury, Barre and Aldrich and Hansworth," &c.

The Tame has its source within a few hundred yards of the western boundary of Tipton, and riparian rights in this locality have always been valuable.

In an indenture of sale from John Shelton to Josiah Turton, in the year 1708, there is described "a parcel of land called *Mill Closes*, divided into two parts, near the dwelling-house of the said Josiah Turton, called *The Mill*": it further mentions the lane leading from Josiah Turton's corn mill towards "*Greet Bridge.*"

Again Edward Dudley, a yeoman of considerable means, "of the Green House, in the parish of Tipton, gent.," who married Elizabeth, daughter of Richard Sheldon, of Wednesbury Hall, yeoman (23 November, 1591), and who was fined £14 for not taking the order of Knighthood at the coronation of King Charles I, says in an answer to an Exchequer Bill (sworn at Tipton 21 October, 1651) that "he now ys become very aged," and it further appears he had purchased "*Greet Bridge* meadow, with a close or moor adjoining in Tipton," &c.

There was in existence another indenture of 1635 by which William Turton gave in trust certain lands near "the King's highway leading from Birmingham towards Wolverhampton, and the lane leading from *Greete Bridge* towards *Harvell's Oak.*"

Yet another indenture belonging to the same family, and made in 1531, speaks of a pasture "near the oake called *Harvyl's Oke*. The place is now called *Harvills Hawthorn*; oaks got scarce through iron smelting by charcoal. Harvill is a corruption of Heronville, the name of the ancient lords of Wednesbury Manor. A deed of the Ryder family, dated 1632, speaks of "a lane leading from the King's Majesty's highway, called the *Portway*, towards the nether end of *Greet's Green*. These Ryders gave their name to *Ryder's Green*.

The names of William Malpas and Margerie, his wife, of Tybyngton, are mentioned in an old deed of the year 1500. See Willetts' "History of West Bromwich," p. 210. Then on p. 212 of the same work a deed of 1527 is quoted describing certain pasture lands "between the hye-way ledyng from Robert Ryders to the town of Dudley, and on the other side a closse longyng to a Chantrye of the Chirche of Walsaill * * * and at the nether end towards Dudley a water called Tame."

Further on (p. 214) is mentioned land between "the King's highway leading from *Greate Green* to the town of Duddele"; this is dated 1556, in the reign of Philip and Mary, and we note here the transition of the name from "*Greet*" to "*Great.*"

According to Shaw, in 1799 "the parish contained about 2,300 acres of land, including roads; 800 dwelling~houses. They are nearly all inhabited by poor people. The number of inhabitants are estimated at about 3,600.

The proprietors of the large works do not live in the parish, excepting Mr Amphlett, who has an excellent square house at Horsley, pleasantly situated, at a proper distance from the coal works, in which he is a principal partner, and also in a bank at Dudley."

This residence was sometimes knows as *Horsley Hall* and sometimes as *Dixon's Hall*; and the staircase of this house was generally esteemed so excellent a piece of work that it was removed bodily by "little John Fereday" to the "*Ellowes*" *Amphlett's Hall,* this same residence of the family of that name, used to stand near Toll End, and its Shrubbery which once lined both sides of the road – then a dark, narrow, and sort of cut-throat lane – still gives its name to the locality. The materials of this edifice were carted away when the place was demolished some 60 or 70 years ago by the said John Fereday, a Tipton colliery-owner, who built therewith the mansion now known as *The Ellowes*, at Gornal, the residence of Sir Horace St. Paul. This man was a celebrity in his day, and a well-known character in Tipton. He had a quaint way of expressing his own estimation of his want of size in introducing himself he had a "saying"—an apologetic formula of introduction which ran thus—"I'm little John Fereday, five foot and an inch, five score and a pound, and—such another man as me!"

Another residence, known as *Denbigh Hall*, stood at Horsley Heath, but near the West Bromwich side.

Mr. John Bagnall, the founder of the great ironmaking firm died in 1853 at the age of 66. At the beginning of this century he lived at Toll End, in a large house, sometimes known as *Tibbington Hall*, and sometimes as *Bagnall's Hall.* It was in the Elizabethan, or rather Jacobean style, and has only recently been demolished, after lying in ruins for some years. It was on the Wednesbury side of the open triangular space at the junction of three roads, and it overlooked the *Pound*, facing towards the east. It was here Mr Bagnall was once besieged by a mob of angry colliers during a strike riot, and was only saved from violence by the tact, courage, and presence of mind of his manager, Mr. Edward Naylor, who contrived to divert the attention of the rioters. Latterly a man named Bennett lived in it; formerly it was the property of Bayley Caddick, and possessed pleasant rural surroundings.

A few yards from the *Moat House* stands the ruins of a substantial residence in the Georgian period in its later style. It was sometime known as *Walker's Hall*, from the fact that its last occupant's of importance were the three bachelor brothers of that name (connected with the once well-known firm of Tipton iron-masters, J. and E. Walker), who sold the estate to Grazebrook and Aston, who are now mining it. It is a square brick building on a stone plinth, having a small stone portico with Doric pillars.

Its grounds even now indicate that its surroundings were once really charming, with its accessories of shrubbery, orchard, and fishpond.

Nearly a quarter of a mile to the east of the *Moat House* stands a far more interesting old building formerly known as *Okell's Farm*, and now as *Cotterill's Farm*. It is on the mining estate of Messrs Dixon Amphlett, and Bedford. In the first decades of this century it was divided into two tenements, occupied by James Botteley and Samuel Lees—the grandfather of the late Councillor Lees, Mayor of West Bromwich.

It is an old, large, and substantial farmhouse, somewhat in the Tudor style, the date 1638 appearing on the base of the chimney; while on a tablet in the gable over the porch is carved—

C
W M
1695.

There is presumptive evidence that the outer wall is a strong casing of much later date than the interior walls of timbered construction. The plan consists of a main block, with central projecting porch, while two wings at the rear form a kitchen courtyard or quadrangle. The barns, outbuildings, and stock yard, stand immediately to the west of the house

The kitchen is of ample dimensions, with wide ingle-nook fire-place, the windows having splayed reveals forming recessed seats. Some of the original stone paving remains in the pantry or buttery; and the whole structure stands on a base of stone-work evidently quarried in the immediate vicinity. From the centre of the roof rises a pile of six clustered chimneys, which, though now devoid of their heads, present a quaint and graceful appearance, having angular nibs, and a massive base on which appears the aforementioned date. At the extremity of the eastern wing is a boldly conceived chimney-breast, with ramped sides, and terminating in two flues, designed in harmony with the central chimney. The house is a three-storey building, and the windows have brick mullions, some of which are now cemented. An extraordinary large buttress supports the gable of the eastern wing, and seems constructed of brickwork and large brazil stones. The position occupied by this honse commands an extensive view, and it is one of the most interesting old buildings within the parish of Tipton. The family name of O'Kell occurs in the pedigree of Stanley of West Bromwich, and may possibly be the modernised form of the name of Ochull, which appears in Staffordshire history as early as the 13th century.

On the eminence upon which this house is built the local Peace rejoicings were celebrated after Wellington's victory at Waterloo. A great bonfire was lighted and an ox was roasted whole for the delectation of thousands from Tipton, Wednesbury, and West Bromwich. At this time Mr. John Bagnall, the iron-master, lived at Toll End, and he took an active part in this celebration, as did also Mr. Samuel Lees and Mr Botteley.

The *Flax Field* mentioned in Chapter XV. was more probably so called from the futile attempts once made by the Legislature to force people by law to grow certain crops, whether they were profitable or not. This particular case was an attempt made by Henry VIII. to bolster up the linen industry, and the covenant may have specified distinctly how often—or how less frequently than the usual period of fallow—such leasow was to be sown with flax.

Horsley is a somewhat common place-name, signifying "the horse field." We have it not only in the name *Horsley Heath*, but in Horsley Fields at Wolverhampton, Horsley Down, London, &c.

Conigrie is derived from two words signifying "the rabbit holes."

Cunnigree Lodge, according to Tipton Parish Register (1664) is same as *Conygre*, where was a mansion and a park in olden times.

The same name occurs at Walsall, near "Clayhanger," and at Birmingham the present street-name of Congreve Street is another survival of it. There was also a Connigrie Croft at Perry Barr.

"Ye *Bloom-smythes*" appears to denote the name of *Bloomfield*, and also of a smithy there, in 1673, according to the Parish Register.

A Bill in Chancery was exhibited by Robert Dudley, Dud's eldest brother in 1638, against Dud, Henry Addenbrooke, and Oliver Amlett, and in the joint and several answers of Amlett and Addenbrooke, dated June 8th, of that year, occurs the following allusion to place-names in the parish:—

"It is true that there are divers closes called *Parkfields* in the Bill mentioned, situated in Tibbington, alias Tipton, co. Stafford, between the lands leading from *Tipton Green* to the workway through lands called *Tipton Park*, the land late Mrs. Wryley's (divided into two parts, one called *Smythe's* and the other *Hall Fields*), and land late of Richard Whitehouse," &c., &c.

The Govermnent report on Turton's Charity, West Bromwich, 1823, speaks of a farm on the "*Pudding Lands* near Great Bridge" thus: "The farm was the property of Mr. Edward Elwell, who has lately become bankrupt, and is now in the possession of his assignees."

In a report on Birch's Charity, at Handsworth, there is reference to "pastures of land, commonly called the Sling and the *Gorstie Croft*, next unto the lane side leading from *Gold's Green* towards Tipton, and being part or parts of the lands called *Gold's Ground*, lying in West Bromwich," &c. This charity dates from 1663, and the same George Birch, of

Wolverhampton, who was of the Harborne family of that name, left other lands at "*Gold's Ground*" to Wolverhampton; the report of 1823 states that three-fourths of the last named lands "now belong to the family of Danks, of Wednesbury." The Handsworth dole, too, was received from Mr. Josiah Danks, of Wednesbury.

Field-names are always interesting reminisences of the old agricultural era, before mining and manufacturing effaced the rural aspect of the place. Even in 1801, there was an advertisement of a sale of lands close to Tipton—in fact portions of West Bromwich Common, which are described as "elevated and cheerful," and "all surrounded by the most delightful scenery of Dudley Castle and the Rowley Hills."

Blakeley Wood Colliery is on the borders of Tipton parish, adjoining close to Wednesbury *Old Field*—the district which was first mined on any extensive system and which at the end of last century was one of the causes for bringing canals into this locality in order that Birmingham manufacturers might be supplied with cheaper fuel.

Communicating with the parish of Tipton, but outside its boundary and jurisdiction, are two roads to which allusion may be made—one on one side of the parish and one on the other.

Walter Stanley, lord of the manor of West Bromwich, died in 1615, and by will left among other things, including armour, furniture &c., two gilt cups, one to his son William, and one to William's wife. This custom of making heir-looms of drinking vessels we have already noted in chapter vi. He also bequeathed a sum of money to be applied towards the completion of the *Bilston Causeway*, and the highway between Bilston and Tipton. Evidently he was a man of considerable public spirit, and it is a pity his son William afterwards became impoverished and compelled to part with the manor of West Bromwich. He parted with it in 1626 to Sir Richard Shilton, his cousin, "a solicitor-general to the King," whose nephew, John Shelton (or Shilton) succeeded him, and who purchased in 1663 the manor of Wednesbury, afterwards sold by his son John to John Hoo of Bradley about the year 1710."

In the Churchwarden's Books at West Bromwich there is a record of a meeting on October 8th, 1847, to consider the "diverting of a certain public highway situate between a certain canal bridge galled *Persehouse's Bridge*, at Gold's Green, and the Eagle Furnaces." It was resolved "that Messrs Bagnall having consented to the alteration, and proposed to make the diversion at their own expense, on the condition that they may not be called upon for a highway rate for the period of three years, that the proposition be acceeded to by this meeting." This seems to be the present *Bagnall Street*, by which Tipton is approached from the West Bromwich side.

CHAPTER XLII.—INTERCOMMUNICATION WITH TIPTON: CANALS, RAILWAYS, TRAMWAYS, &C.

Tipton has often been called the Venice of the Black Country, for, owing to the sinuosity of the Birmingham Canal, there are over 20 miles of artificial waterway within the parish boundaries. The "Old Birmingham Canal" passed from Oldbury through Tipton Green to Bilston and Wolverhampton. It was constructed by an Act of 1767, but its levels were altered about the year 1787. There is a branch of it to Wednesbury about 4½ miles long. Near Tipton Green it is connected with the Dudley Canal. In the year 1783 an Act was obtained by a new company "to extend the Wednesbury branch of the Birmingham Canal from Ryder's Green to Broadwater Engine, and to make six collateral cuts; one from Butcher's Forge Pool to Brooke's Meadow; another from near the south end of Butcher's Forge Pool to Wood's Engine Forge, a third from the head of Willingsworth Pool to near the nine-mile stone on the turnpike road leading from Ocker Hill to Wolverhampton; a fourth from the Willingsworth Pool Tail to Wednesbury Open Field; another from the last mentioned cut into another part of the same field, and a sixth from out of the last mentioned cut to a place opposite Taylor's Engine." From the mines of Tipton, Wednesbury, and Bilston a tonnage of 4d was charged into Birmingham at that time. By another Act in 1794 power was given to make a collateral cut from Broadwater in Wednesbury to Walsall, with three branches to neighbouring mines, and another branch from Bloomfield to Deepfields. This latter, which was a mile and three-quarters long necessitated 1,000 yards of tunnelling to be done, to avoid a detour of 4 miles round Tipton Hill. The Wyrley and Essington Canal anthorised in 1792, also enters this parish. This canal was afterwards annexed to the Birmingham Canal Navigations, as was the Dudley Canal, a portion of which runs through Staffordshire, with a tunnel from Dudley Woodside to Tipton Green 2,926 yards long, and several minor cuts. A canal made since 1840 from Birmingham, through Saltley, enters Staffordshire near Barr, and is continued to Gold's Hill and Tipton.

In the Canal Act of 1783 is used the expression "Broadwaters Fire Engine"—meaning a steam engine, and that the first of its kind made by the celebrated inventor, Savary, who erected it at Broadwaters in 1739. In 1784 followed an Act for extending the Dudley Canal to the Birmingham Canal at or near Tipton Green.

In 1785 came the Act for incorporating the company of proprietors of a Canal Navigation authorised by a former Act to be made from Birmingham to Bilston &c, &c.

From a book called "A Tour through Great Britain," published in three volumes in 1788, we find, under the heading of "Birmingham," the following:—

"A navigable cut was begun in April, 1768, and finished in November, 1769, to the collieries at Wednesbury, from whence the inhabitants here [i.e.. Birmingham] are supplied with exceeding good coals at a very moderate rate, which before were sold at a very exorbitant price, to the great distress and detriment of the poor."'

The first boat load of coals from the collieries at Wednesbury passed along the Birmingham Canal into Birmingham on November 6th, 1769, and coals which were sold in Birmingham from 15s to 18s per ton were immediately reduced to 7s 6d. Coals were carried thither from Tipton mines in May, and from Bilston in October of 1770.

From Ryder's Green to Broadwaters Mines the canal is $4\frac{1}{2}$ miles and 6 chains in length, with a fall of 46 feet.

About the beginning of this century an Act authorised the new cutting from Broadwaters into Walsall, and also three branches of the same, (1) from Broadwater to the township or liberty of Bradley in the parish of Wolverhampton: (2) another to terminate at David's Barn Farm: (3) and another from Bloomfield (Tipton) to Deepfield (Sedgley), as before mentioned all these numerous cuts and canals were made necessary about this time by the perfected process of smelting iron with pit-coal, after so many years of experiments and failure. And the numerous blast furnaces that were at that time erected in the vicinity of Tipton and Wednesbury absolutely demanded the provision of these waterways for the heavy freights of coal and iron travelling up and down the district.

Long before the railway era, canals had been put to greater use than that in which they are now employed. Tipton in those times was fortunate in the large extent of its canal service. In addition to the plying of the ordinary slow boats, such as are now in common use, drawn by a horse at a walking pace, and generally carrying a cargo of one single class of goods (as coal, or iron, or barrels of beer, or hay, &c.), there were fly-boats which travelled at a much quicker rate and which were dispatched with a cargo of mixed goods at certain specified times of departure. The horse of a fly-boat travelled at a good trot or hand gallop; and horses were changed at regular intervals along the canal route, just as post horses were in a chaise journey. These fly boats were timed, too, all along the line of route, just as railway trains are now-a-days. They were built almost the size of the present cabin boat, but with a sharp shiff-like bow to cut easily through the water; in fact they have been known, in coming swiftly and suddenly to an arm or basin, to have cut through some unfortunate boat projecting too far at right angles from the aforesaid arm or basin.

These fly-boats, however, were forbidden to carry passengers, although there is on record the tale of a local tragedy, in which two of Pickford's boatmen having consented to carry a young girl, ravished and murdered her on the journey, for which crime they were in due course arrested and hanged. In course of time an attempt was successfully made to cultivate a passenger traffic, by lines of "Swift Packets," the boats being generally of Scotch build and their accommodation somewhat similar in capacity to the inside of our modern tram cars. A local pioneer in this method of passenger locomotion was a Tipton man named Monk, he was a canal boat builder, and his first Swift Packet, plied between Birmingham and Wolverhampton some 60 or 70 years ago. It was named the Euphrates, and its "Captain" was another Tipton man named John Jevon. In 1851 we find these Swift Packets carrying passengers from Wolverhampton to Birmingham in 2 hours 10 minutes for a fare of one shilling

While on the one hand, Tipton had been favoured with a multiplicity of canal accommodation, Dudley, on the other hand, was for a long time inaccessible by these inland water navigations. The approach to Dudley from Birmingham and the South Staffordshire and East Worcestershire hardware districts, over which so much mineral and other heavy traffic was necessary for the industrial prosperity of the Dudley and Black Country districts, was barred by the Castle Hill and other heights equally formidable to the navvy and his master, the contractor. The difficulties of the cutting the canal tunnel—of course certain water levels have always to be respected by the engineer—which was eventually made through the limestone rocks, are too well-known. But Dudley traffic had not been lost or neglected in the meantime by the canal companies. Large warehouses were established on the side of Tipton nearest to Dudley, for the receiving and forwarding of Dudley merchandise. As the business of this water carrying increased and developed, and as the trade was so largely connected with Dudley, the place in time not unnaturally acquired the name of Dudley "Port."

The Tipton carriers who developed this system of intercommunication were the local firms of Bissell and of Whitehouse, together with the well-known national carriers Pickford & Company and Crowley & Compacy. The firm of Fellows, Morton, and Company was originally established in a small way by a carrier named Turley.

At Ocker Hill, the Birmingham Canal Company have an extensive pumping station, where five powerful engines lift the water from the lower level to the higher level of their canals, a gross height of 66 feet. This is necessary to keep the Tipton higher level canals in working order. Recently the resident engineer there, was Mr Timothy Hackworth, a grandson of his celebrated name-sake, the rival inventor with George Stephenson.

In 1835 we find the canal traffic of Tipton thus set forth in a directory:—

(1) To London, Liverpool, Manchester, Birmingham, and all parts of the kingdom, fly boats from Pickford and Company and Crowley and Company's Wharf, Tipton Green daily.

(2) To London, Liverpool, Manchester, Bristol, Worcester, Birmingham, and Shrewsbury, fly boats from John Whitehouse and Son's Wharf, Tipton Green, every day.

(3) To London, Liverpool, Manchester, Shardlow, Hull, and Gainsborough, from Job Bissell's Wharf, Tipton Green, three times a week.

(4) To London, Liverpool, Manchester, Worcester, &c, from Tildasley and Sturlands Wharf, Tipton Green, three times a week.

(5) To Birmingham in two hours, Thomas Monk's packet for goods and passengers from The Bush Factory Bridge, and Fountains, Owen Street, every Tuesday, Thursday, and Saturday morning at ½ past 8, return same evening.

* * * * * *

The South Staffordshire Railway from Walsall and Wednesbury runs through the parish of Tipton to Dudley, and was incorporated by an Act of 1846. On May 1st, 1850, it was opened for the length between Alrewas and Dudley. In 1851 a new Act authorised the construction of a branch to Tipton, a junction with the Stour Valley Line, and the making of working arrangements with the London and North Western Railway Company. Another extension from Wednesbury, has since entered the parish, *via* Ocker Hill and Princes End towards Wolverhampton. The chief line in the parish is the Stour Valley section of the London and North-Western system. Running from Birmingham to Wolverhampton it passes through Tipton, but its principal station is Dudley Port, at which most of its express trains stop for the South Staffordshire traffic, which is of considerable magnitude and importance. Dudley is connected with the main line system also by junctions. The Stonr Valley line has been leased in perpetuity to the London and North-Western Railway Company since 1847.

From Wednesbury Station the two branches were out about 25 or 30 years ago, one to Darlaston and the other through Ocker Hill and Princes End to join the London and North-Western Railway main line for Wolverhampton. Neither of these seem to have paid for running passenger traffic, and Sunday trains were scarcely ever tried. The Darlaston Branch was closed more than three years ago, and the branch through Princes End was closed in November last (1890). This great railway company have never properly catered for the convenience of the travelling public on their Black Country local lines.

The Midland Railway Company have their principal depot for Sonth Staffordshire at Great Bridge, and within Tipton parish; from which point they cover the district by canal boat as far as Stourbridge in one direction and Soho in the other, and also from Walsall to Bilston, including of course Tipton itself. In addition their horse teams cover not only Tipton parish, but a considerable distance beyond.

The Midland Company have powers extending over the London and North-Western Company's line from Wichnor, near Burton, to Dudley, such being originally the property of the South Staffordshire Railway, of which the London and North-Western Company became possessed (about the year 1859) subject to such running powers being retained by the Midland Company, but as a matter of fact the latter company now only utilise the line from Walsall, they having opened an independent route, connecting with their main line at Water Orton.

The Midland Company own a considerable quantity of land at Dudley Port, and this will be, no doubt, eventually opened cut as an important goods depot, and enable them to increase their facilities for covering the whole of the busy South Staffordshire district.

The Great Western Railway passes through Tipton parish by its Birmingham and Dudley section. A new length was cut from Swan Village, through Great Bridge, and joining the South Staffordshire section of the London and North-Western Railway, near Dudley Port. This Birmingham and Dudley Branch was opened November 2nd 1874.

* * * * * *

Before the railway era, local traffic was almost as insignificant as intercommunication with more distant places. Our forefathers certainly walked more than we do now-a-days. Coaching was an expensive method of travelling, and omnibus fares were not arranged in penny stages like modern tram-ways.

By Pigot's Directory for 1835 we are informed that coach or omnibus to and from Birmingham Dudley &c, passed through Great Bridge and Dudley Port every hour; while Tipton monopolised the services of a van for both goods and passengers, starting from Joseph Lyndon's, Union Street, every Tuesday, Thursday, and Saturday at 8.30 a.m.

A new class of traffic has been created by our street tramways during this last seven or eight years.

The South Staffordshire Steam Tramways run through Tipton parish from the boundary at the brook near Great Bridge, Market Place, to the boundary at Burnt Tree, the mileage of route being 1m. 5fur. 140yds. The cars passing to and fro for the accommodation of the public gave a service of upwards of 10,000 yearly, and have been worked so far without a fatal accident, although the street is the chief playground of numerous children. The engines by which these cars are worked weigh, when fully coked and with tank full, between ten and eleven tons. A great and increasing number of people travel annually to and from Birmingham, taking through tickets available on both steam and cable cars, and a large parcel traffic is now done locally with Dudley, Walsall, Handsworth, and other parts of the system, the rates being much cheaper and transit much more expeditious than by the railways. Workmen, too, living at Dudley and West Bromwich avail themselves daily of the cars for conveyance to and from Tipton and many have their mid-day dinners forwarded to them daily at a special charge of 1d per time.

During the summer months the clergy and school managers employ the cars to take their school children for an outing, and several times a year there may be seen strings of eight and nine special cars (two attached to each engine) carrying these crowds of juvenile excursionists.

The tramways also work through Tipton parish from Wednesbury to Dudley, the mileage of route on this section being 3m. 1fur. 161yds., carrying very much the same class of traffic, though here the company get a weekly element upon certain days when coursing and dog-racing is going on in the vicinity of Lea Brook. Crowds of men literally besiege the car several of each lot has his own dog carefully clothed in woollen, which he takes on the top of the car with him, leaving a box of rabbits under the car stairs. This class of passenger usually hails from Tipton (Five Ways), and they are found by conductors very awkward to deal with, the men naturally rough in themselves being assisted by the dogs upon the slightest provocation. Monday is the principal day for this class of passenger. On Sundays, and indeed other days, the pigeon flyer with his birds is found upon this route more than any other, and puts up his homers at different points on the journey. The Tipton Fair is usually a source of attraction from parts so far distant as Darlaston, although it is held in Tipton proper, while the nearest point to which the cars run is the Five Ways. At Princes End which is in the Tipton parish for a short distance of about five chains, the tramway runs through Coseley parish, as it here crosses the line; but it is calculated in the mileage of this route as just given.

The section between Hill Top and Dudley was opened January 14th, 1884; the Wednesbury and Dudley section was opened January 25th of the same year. Previously to this a horse tram system between Hockley Hill, Birmingham, and Dudley Port had been opened on May 20th, 1872, but after a few years it was abandoned as unprofitable.

CHAPTER XLIII.—JAMES KEIR'S CONNECTION WITH TIPTON: HIS CHEMICAL "FACTORY."

Connected with Tipton by business ties was one of the most remarkable men among those local worthies who adorned the society of this vicinity at the close of last and the beginning of the present century. This was James Keir, whose residence was within the limits of West Bromwich parish, although its situation was nearer the centre of population in Wednesbury, he resided; in fact, in that outlying portion of West Bromwich now known as Hill Top, but in mediæval times called by the name of Finchpath—probably because in a still earlier period a bridle-path led over a wooded hill and then steeply descended to the ford at Wednesbury Brook.

Shaw, vol. ii., p. 134, writing of West Bromwich says:—"A number of small houses extend in a line south from the church to the turnpike road, and along that westward by the side of a large common called Bromwich Heath at the extremity of which, near Wednesbury, is a large street of them with several good gentlemen's houses, one of which, with pleasant gardens and grounds backwards, commanding rich and fertile prospects, is the residence of the ingenious chemist, James Keir, Esq, whose excellent essay upon the mineralogy of this part of the county is printed in vol. i., and whose curious manufactory of soap, white lead, &c., in the adjoining parish of Tipton, has afforded me with his valuable aid some more valuable matter in the following pages." James Keir, F.R.S., lived at "The Woodlands," Hill Top, afterwards occupied by Mr John Bagnall. He was head of the firm of Keir, Blair, and Playfair, who had collieries at Tividale. Mr Keir was a colonel of militia, and a friend of Boulton, Watt, and Priestley, The Blair family was the same which included the author of "Family Sermons." The Soap Works at Tipton, called "The Factory," were afterwards carried on by a family named Stevenson. Mr Keir is said to have lost valuable papers by a fire at his house in 1807. He died 11th October, 1820, and was buried at All Saints' Church, West Bromwich. Particularly interesting at this juncture is the fact that exactly a century ago Keir took a prominent part in the public dinner which led to the Birmingham "Church and King" Riots of July, 1791.

Relating to the philosopher's family are the following entries in the West Bromwich Church Registers:—

1801.—May 19th, John Lewis Moilliet, of Birmingham, merchant, married Amelia Keir.

1802.—November 25th, Mrs Keir, wife of James Keir, Esq, buried.

1820.—October 11, James Keir died, aged 85.

Shaw, writing under the head of "Tipton" in 1801, says—

"Besides the various ironworks which, from the abundance of coal and iron-ore in this neighbourhood seem to be the natural trades of the country, there is in this parish one extensive manufactory of a different species, which was established here by the present proprietors, under the firm of James Keir and Company, about 18 years ago, on account of the cheapness of fuel, and of the convenience of the canal by which the goods are brought from and sent to Hull, Liverpool, Bristol, London, and many other parts of the kingdom. It consists of several articles:—

"(1) A manufacture of Alkali, which is an article similar to that of which various kinds are annually imported from abroad, under the names of barilla, pot-ash, pearl-ash, &c. This alkali is made by a process invented by the proprietors from various neutral salts, and residuums of chemical operations, such as those left in the distillation of aqua fortis, and making of oil of vitriol; all which residuums were before the establishment of this manufacture, generally thrown away as useless; but are now converted into a valuable article of commerce. The alkali here made is not sold, but employed in the second branch of this undertaking; namely—

"(2) Soap-making; which business was entered into merely as an advantageous mode of employing the above-mentioned alkali, by means of which it is carried to such an extent that it yields to the revenue of excise about £10,000 annually.

"*White-lead*—This article is here manufactured by a new process, invented by the proprietors, and differing from the common mode in this respect, that vinegar is not employed. The white-lead here is principally used by the potters for glazing their wares.

"(4) *Red-lead* is made here in considerable quantities in the usual manner, and is principally consumed in the manufacture of flint-glass, which is carried on to a great extent in Dudley, the neighbourhood of Stourbridge, and in Birmingham.

"(5) *Metal Sashes for Windows.*—This elegant improvement in architecture, by which the greatest lightness is combined with the greatest strength is executed here in mouldings made either of a peculiar golden-coloured metal, or of wrought iron, which is afterwards to be painted or japanned. The yellow metal is a compound of copper, zinc, and iron invented by the proprietors, and possesses singular properties which make it fit for this purpose. It is as strong as iron, and like iron may be forged or rolled when red-hot. Bars of this metal or of iron are rolled hot between steel rollers, in which concavities are so cut and turned that they give corresponding convex mouldings to the bars as they pass through them. Windows of this manufacture are in Windsor Castle, Carleton House, and in many principal houses in the kingdom.

"This manufactory of alkali, soap, white-lead, red-lead, and metal-sashes occupies a space of several acres adjoining to the Birmingham Canal receives the power requisite for its various operations from two water-wheels and two fire-engines, and gives employment to a number of people; among whom, it may be added as a singularity there is not a single person, from the proprietors downwards, who are now employed in these manufactures, who had been bred to them. In the businesses of red-lead and soap, which differ little from those in other places, workmen have been sometimes employed. The other manufactures, being quite new, could not receive this assistance, and are carried on by labourers."

Such is the testimony of Shaw as to the connection of the philosophic Keir with the parish of Tipton; indeed it is probable that Keir contributed this technical portion of the history himself, so that no doubt as to the scientific accuracy of the statements is perhaps admissible. Comments upon these statements must necessarily be few in a history of this kind. First, with regard to the window-sashes, it may be surmised that they were something of the nature of gun-metal. Some of the windows at Christ Church West Bromwich, are said to be of a similar material. As regards the soap made at Tipton, it must have been manufactured in large quantities if the £10,000 relates to the duty paid from this parish alone. Historically it may be noted that soap was but imperfectly known to the ancients, while during the middle ages washing of clothes was generally accomplished by rubbing and stamping on them and by repeated rinsing. The better classes indeed tried to overcome the want of cleanliness in their persons and their clothing by the plentiful use of scents and essences. The manufacture of soap began in London in 1524, before which time it had been supplied by Bristol at one penny per pound, The duty on soap set down by the Chancellor of the Exchequer (Mr Gladstone) as yielding a yearly revenue of £1,126,000 was totally abolished in the session of 1853. Since then no tax on cleanliness has been in existence!

No chemical works now exist in Tipton, the nearest to that parish at present being those of William Hunt and Sons, Lea Brook, Wednesbury.

Dr. Plot, writing in 1686, on p. 122 of his "History of Staffordshire," says—"Other potters-clays for the more common wares, there are at many other places, particularly at Horseley Heath, in the parish of Tipton; in Monway-field above mention'd, where there are two sorts gotten, one of a yellowish colour mixt with white, the other blewish (*sic*); the former stiff and weighty, the other more friable and light; which mixt together work better than apart: of these they make divers sorts of vessels at Wednesbury, which they paint with slip made of a reddish sort of earth gotten at Tipton."

In a work called "Magna Britannia," published in 1730, this statement is repeated in different terms: "In this Parish, upon Horsley Heath, there is dug Potters Clay for Common Ware: and in other places a reddish Sort of Earth which they call Slip, with which they paint their Vessels of divers Sorts made at Wednesbury." Common brown stone-ware (as gallon bottles, pans, &c.) is still made at Lea Brook—the last remnant of the local pottery industry.

The soil of Tipton is clayey, and the subsoil is clay, and it has been a famous place in recent times for brick-making. There are still several firms in the parish; the Tibbington Collieries and Brick Works Co., Ld., at Princes End, make glazed stoneware, sanitary pipes, terra cotta chimney-pots, vitrified blue bricks, red facing bricks, fire-bricks, &c.

An equivalent of the Wenlock limestone is found at Dudley Port where, as formerly it was at Wednesbury is got by shaft and not by open-work. It was largely used as flux in iron-smelting when there were more blast furnaces in the vicinity than are now left.

Peldon stone, from the new mine measures, is found extensively used throughout Tipton and Wednesbury in old walls, and in foundations of houses. In some cases in Tipton, foundations will be found to be even largely made up of massive blocks of brazil coal.

But the glory of Tipton trading has been its wonderful resources in coal and iron. Casually much has already been said in this history of the vast mineral wealth of this parish: and only a few more points remain to be gathered up under the heading of this chapter.

In 1849 there was a fearful accident on June 26th at the "Blue Fly Pit" of Messrs. Morris, near Dudley Port Railway Station, by which no less than 16 men and boys lost their lives.

In 1851 a large piece of coal was sent from Tipton to the Great Exhibition in London. It weighed about six tons, was cut into a cylindrical shape, six feet across and six feet high, and its surface was polished quite smooth till it was almost bright as jet. It was prepared at Round's Colliery, Tividale. (Another version says it was a mass of 13 tons, raised by Messrs R. Haines and Sons, at their Denbigh Colliery, from a depth of 495 feet.)

Illustrative of the value of mining lands in Tipton it may be mentioned that in 1835 land was rented at £1,000 per acre per annum for mining purposes.

So recently as March, 1890, the Mines Drainage Commissioners took steps to obtain from various colliery owners throughout the district returns as to the quantities of minerals not yet worked. The returns that had so far been received showed a total of 43,000,000 tons of workable coal and ironstone in the Tipton district alone There were other returns yet to come in, and the complete statistics would no doubt show a very much larger amount even than this, but the quantity at present ascertained was sufficient to enable them to show that they, as a Commission had a most valuable coalfield still to be worked and still worth draining.

By "Tipton district" was meant the whole mining area that runs from Dudley to Wolverhampton, over which the Commissioners have their Parliamentary powers, and in which the area under water was considerably larger than the area then workable.

(Previous to 1875 all mine owners in this district drained their pits as best they could; many maintaining large pumping engines at great cost, and others reaping the benefit of their neighbours' pumping operations without any outlay on their own behalf. Again, while the pits at one level were relieved, those at another were flooded beyond remedy; for those who pumped their own pits dry cared little where they sent the water so long as it ran safely over the surface of their own mining lands. To rectify these inequalities the South Staffordshire Mines Drainage Commission was constituted (Acts 1875-1882) empowered to erect pumping stations, to make good the beds of streams, &c., for the common good of a mining area of 50 square miles, and to levy rates of 9d. per ton on coal, slack, and ironstone, and 3d. per ton on fireclay and limestone).

At the same time, and at the same meeting of the Commissioners already alluded to, it was suggested that a large pump should be put down at Wednesbury. A plan of the Wednesbury mines showed that the Patent Shaft Company alone had 1,500,000 tons of coal available on their property, and in the whole of the Wednesbury district there was a coal-producing area with 11,552,000 tons.

At the commencement of the long-continued trade depression (1875) out of a total of 30 collieries in Tipton, 12 were standing idle. Even in 1890 the deep mines of Tipton produced only half the output of the year 1874, and £75,000 was stated to be the sum required to drain them completely so as to bring them into use again.

Although the introduction of canals may have been the means of bringing one or two industries in the parish, the great fact remains that Tipton owes its commercial prosperity to the coal and iron trades. To the iron manufactures, therefore, we at once proceed in the due and direct course of our local chronicles.

CHAPTER XLIV.—THE GRADUAL DEVELOPMENT OF THE TIPTON IRON TRADE.

The iron trade of Tipton began, as in most other Black Country towns, with the production of the smaller wares; and then as the capacity of the blast furnaces increased the production of larger goods, of merchant iron, and of pigs gradually took the place of nails, edge-tools, screws, &c. Shaw, writing about the year 1800, speaks of furnaces producing less than a tenth of their present capacity, and of mills specially making nail-rods for immediate local consumption, thus—

"Messrs George Parker and Co. (or brothers) have—

"Two furnaces, which are estimated to make 20 or 25 tons of pig-iron per week.

"One rolling and slitting mill, where they sometimes roll boiler plates.

"Three forge-hammers.

Messrs Zachary Parkes and Co, near Dudley Port— One furnace, estimated at 20 or 25 tons per week.

"One forge.

"One slitting mill.

"Messrs. Read, Banks, and Dumaresq—

"One furnace, estimated at 25 tons per week or more.

Forge.

"Richard Hawkes and Co.—

One furnace, lately erected about 20 tons per week

"Branches of the iron trade are manufactures of hinges, viz., Edward Fisher, James Fisher, and James Bate, who employ about 100 pair of hands. The nail trade is of the first consequence (and employs about one fourth of the number of people in the parish), as it gives employment to young and old men, women and children, which begin at six years of age. It is supposed that nearly one-half of the inhabitants are nailers by trade; but since the nail trade has been so bad a great number have gone to other businesses, which are chiefly the best workmen. Others are thrown out of work in consequence of their not being able to make good nails. These are chiefly children and old people, which is found to be very hurtful to the poor.

"Taylor's foundry, at Toll End where they cast chiefly heavy goods for engines, whimseys and millwork.

"Daniel Moore, formerly Price Thomas's forge. One slitting-mill, worked by water, with two under-shot wheels; to which is now added a steam engine; and one of the water wheels is a substitute for a fly-wheel and does very well.

"The different sorts of nails made are very numerous; from 2oz tack, which is 1,200 nails to weigh 2oz (some having been made as small as $1\frac{1}{4}$-oz for curiosity) up to large spikes. Considerable quantities of horse-nails are made likewise here, and some few ox-nails. The place is reckoned rather famous for making horse-nails.

"There are several shops that make shovels and tongs, which may employ about 40 pair of hands.

"Auger and edge tool makers is another branch that employs a considerable number of hands,

"There are several wood-screw makers, and one or two awl-blade makers.

"The fender trade was another branch, but is now removed to other places, or declined, all but one watermill, which is employed in grinding fenders. There were two, and each did more than is now done."

All these smaller trades spoken of by Shaw have now left the parish, although some of them still flourish at Dudley and other places not very far removed.

At the beginning of this century when the country was impoverished by the prolonged Napoleonic struggle, and Tipton was still engaged in the production of such small wares as hinges and nails, the distress was so great that it eventually led to bread riots. On Monday morning, April 28th, 1800, a Dudley mob sought to enlist the Tipton colliers on their side in an attack on the bakers' shops, but were dissuaded by Mr Amphlett and other local magistrates from immediately carrying out their purpose. In the afternoon, however they found their way to Nine Locks, Brierley Hill, and there took possession of two canal boats laden with grain for Birmingham. When the Dudley Volunteer Cavalry put in an appearance they were assailed with bricks, stones, sticks, bull-dogs, &c. Then the Riot Act was read, and the Infantry Association and some regular Dragoons coming to the assistance of the local cavalry, the tumult was quelled after one rioter had been killed and many wounded. The next day, Tuesday, the remnant of this riot was suppressed at Bilston by the same Dragoons and the Bilston Loyal Volunteers, under the Rev. Mr. Haden, vicar of Wednesbury, a magistrate of the county (see *Aris's Birmingham Gazette* for May 5th, 1800).

By 1831 the industrial progress of Tipton had not been so very marked—that is, as compared with the next quarter of a century. Lewis's Topographical Dictionary for that year speaks only of nine forges, and of its blast furnaces producing "more than 70 tons of pig-iron per week, consuming 600 tons of coal." This is evidently an error—probably the figures of a return made some years previously—as the same work gives the industries of Tipton as "Nails, hinges, fenders, fireirons, boilers for steam-engines, manufactures of tinned plates, soap, muriatic polish, and red-lead."

In 1857 Mr Joseph Hall, of the Bloomfield Ironworks published a book (London: Hamilton, Adams and Co.) entitled, "The Iron Question." It was illustrated by folding diagrams; one showing a specimen of $2\frac{1}{4}$in. round iron tied into a knot, cold, the original of which was sent to the Geological Museum, Jermyn Street, London, in 1851, another shows his patent horse-shoe nail, made of his toughest Staffordshire iron. The book described Mr Hall's process of puddling this iron, and as it is somewhat technical it may be as well to give a condensed description of it in the words of another expert—Mr Samuel Griffiths, in his "Guide to the Iron Trade":

"About the year 1825, sand-bottom puddling furnaces began to be abandoned in favour of what were then galled 'iron bottoms.' Various silicates and oxides of iron were melted on the plates to make the bottoms and for fettling. This plan was adopted for some years; and to distinguish it from what we must call Mr. Joseph Hall's invention, we shall call this the wet or water process. At a certain point of the heat, while the 'fore-hand' was puddling after the iron was melted, the 'under-hand,' with a dish properly constructed for the purpose, threw water, *via* the 'stopper hole,' upon the molten iron—about three half-pints at once, the 'fore-hand' puddler frequently calling out,' Water, water,' as he thought it was required. What was called the drying process now commenced. The damper was dropped, and with the 'paddle' the puddler turned and re-turned the iron over in all parts of the furnace for some time until the whole was disintegrated into a kind of powder, and was moved about until it became something like rough sand, though not so fine. Then the damper was pulled up, the word 'fire' was given by the puddler to the 'under-hand,' the calorific power was increased rapidly, the iron become bright in the furnace and as its malleability and adhesiveness were gradually established, the puddler separated the iron, rolled it up into 'balls,' and with his tongs gaily dragged it to the helve. This was the old process. The present boiling process is too well known to require a lengthened description here. It was discovered and invented by the late Mr Joseph Hall, one of the partners at the great Bloomfield Works at Tipton, and from that day to this has been universally adopted, not only in tho United Kingdom, but in all parts of Europe and America. Briefly, Mr. Hall's process consists of *boiling* the iron not *roasting* it. Under the old plan the pigs lying on the bottom of the furnace were subjected to the action of the cutting flame passing over them more on the top part than the bottom of the charge of pig metal. On this account the upper portion of the pigs, particularly the very highest part, became melted before the bottom; and as the action of the caloric was more intense upon this portion of the iron by the passing flame, *ab initio*, the puddler had to watch the process, and, by means of his paddle, remove the more extreme incandescent portions, or turn the pigs over, in order that, by the uniform application of the accumulating caloric, the whole mass by these mechanical means might be rendered uniformly incandescent, and finally thoroughly melted. But during this irregular action of the fire on the metal, one portion of the iron became liquid before the other was thoroughly melted, and, as the heat was constantly increasing, great waste occurred by evaporation before the whole was properly melted, notwithstanding the great care on the part of the puddler. Mr. Hall's process. however, introduced boiling in silica. – Here the iron is protected by the molten bath of silica which covers it, and although more intense heat can be applied to the iron through this molten sea of silica which envelopes it, the cutting flame which continually passes over the furnace spends itself *upon* and is absorbed *in* the cinder and iron without burning or damaging the iron. While the iron is in this boiling state it is the duty of the puddler to agitate and puddle it, and, by all the means in his power, to facilitate the elimination of the carbon, the exit of which is seen plainly enough by the globules constantly rising on the top of the molton cinder until the iron comes into 'nature.' This is, we believe, a correct though short description of Mr, Joseph Hall's boiling process."

Staffordshire puddled iron was then in the hey-day of its glory, and this Tipton firm was one of the most famous producers of it. Even now, when the era of mild steel has set in so completely, Tipton can still hold its own, as we shall proceed to demonstrate.

The invention of the steam engine gave a great impetus to the local iron trade. In 1796 blast furnaces were at work at Dudley Port, Gospel Oak, and other parts of Tipton. By 1800 additional furnaces were in operation at Bloomfield, Wednesbury, and other parts of the Black Country (as it was just then beginning to be called), in fact, in these four years the number of furnaces in the South Staffordshire district increased from 18 to 30. In 1875 the following statistics were made relative to iron mills and forges in the *immediate* locality:—

	Place	Works.	Puddling Furnaces.	Rolling Mills.
1	Bilston	19	261	49
2	Darlaston	2	44	8
3	West Bromwich	21	329	43
4	Wednesbury	11	211	22
5	Tipton	11	208	30
6	Oldbury	3	28	6
7	Dudley	7	172	18
8	Great Bridge	2	36	4
	Totals for *all* the county	129	2,507	482

In a list of Puddling Furnaces published in 1872, in addition to those at Lea Brook, of John Bagnall and Sons, and of the Chillington Iron Company, there were then in the

TIPTON DISTRICT:

	No. of Puddling Furnaces.	No. of Mills & Forges.
Bloomfield, *Factory, *Tipton Green (W. Barrows and Son)	100	10
Globe and Tividale (J. P Haynes)	9	2
*Groveland (G Hickman)..	24	3
Great Bridge (Great Bridge Iron and Steel Co., Limited)	20	2
Gospel Oak (Gospel Oak Iron Co.)	24	5
*Sheepwash Lane (Stonehewer and Co.).......................	16	2
Summer Hill (W. Millington and Co.)............................	16	4
Church Lane District Steel and Iron Co.)	10	2
Hope Iron Co...	6	2
Toll End (E and T. Bayley	7	2
Wednesbury Oak (P. Williams and Sons)	32	5
Dudley Port (Wilkinson)	8	1
(Plant and Fisher)...	20	3
Portfield (James Holcroft)	18	3

*Since closed down.

CHAPTER XLV.—BARROWS AND SON, BLOOMFIELD IRONWORKS.

It will be necessary to take up the thread of our history by dealing first with the firm to which allusion has been compelled by the fact of its connection with the development of the trade. The Bloomfield Ironworks were commenced in the year 1830 by Mr Joseph Hall, who at that date started three puddling furnaces. He was early joined by Mr. Bradley and soon after by Mr. Welch. After a short connection the last-named partner withdrew, and Mr. William Barrows took his place (1834). Soon after the firm made rapid additions to the works, and its productive power was considerably augmented. Eventually Mr Bradley retired and was succeeded by Mr Bramah, of Kingswinford. At Mr Bramah's death, about 1846, Messrs. Barrows and Hall constituted the firm (holding equal shares), and when the latter died, 18th January, 1862, Mr Barrows was left sole proprietor. He, however, did not long survive, dying suddenly at Stafford on December 10th, 1863, after which the works were carried on by his sons under the style and title of Messrs Barrows and Sons. In 1867 the firm employed about 800 men producing some 800 tons per week of sheets, plates, bars, &c, from their 58 puddling furnaces and eight mills (and supplemented by a foundry). At the present time the number of furnaces is about 70, and the proprietor of the works is Mr. Joseph Barrows, of Himley.

Quoting again from Griffiths' "Guide" (1873) which gives three illustrations, consisting of capital views of these extensive works, we read: – "W. Barrows and Sons, proprietors of the Bloomfield Factory and Tipton Ironworks, have one hundred puddling furnaces, quite the largest number of any ironworks in South Staffordshire, and produce 1,000 tons of finished iron per week. The brand is B.B.H., taken after the names of the originators of the firm, Bradley, Barrows, and Hall, and is known and appreciated, not only in this country and the colonies,but its world-wide fame has caused it to be eagerly sought after in all parts of the world, being preferred in Australia and other colonies before all others. It has for many years deservedly been the most favourite English brand imported into Holland and the Low Countries, the excellency and uniformity of its quality having created a living faith in the B.B.H. brand which *no other iron made can boast of to the same extent*, in the number of its customers, or degree of implicit faith willingly reposed in the quality of the article itself. The Bloomfield Works were erected by the above-named gentlemen a little later than 1826, having from time to time been amplified to their present dimensions. The brand remains unchanged, the quality, amid the changes of fifty years, has remained the same, unattenuated, unadulterated, always uniform B.B.H. in quality. All the old partners have been long since dead and gone to rest, still Mr Hall's original plan is carried out, both in the kind of pigs used, the boiling process which he invented, the best workmen engaged. and perhaps better pigs and coals used than anywhere else, with good managers on the ground day and night. This large concern belongs to the late Mr. William Barrows's sons, Colonel Barrows and Mr Joseph Barrows being the managing partners, and follow their father's footsteps in attending daily at the works. The superior quality of the Earl of Dudley's pig iron is well known in Staffordshire, in fact, it is quite the best. The name and fame of Earl Granville's Lilleshall is equally celebrated. W. Barrows and Sons purchase and use more than half the quantity of Earl Dudley's pig disposed of in Staffordshire, and quite half the whole quantity of Shropshire pig sent into Staffordshire is consumed by this firm. They still adhere to their father's plan of buying none but the very best, it is, therefore rigid attention to this rule, which enables this firm to make such very uniform and matchless iron in quality which is seldom equalled, and never surpassed by any other house. In fact, the uniformity of the quality of B.B.H, Iron is not equalled by any other house, and their quality remains unrivalled."

So valuable was the property in the right to use this B.B.H. mark that when the two families severed their connection with each other, it is not surprising to find that litigation ensued over the matter. It had been adopted in 1836, and continued through every change of partnership. The case of Hall v. Barrows was the first of the kind tried in the iron trade, and the decision of the Lord Chancellor was that the trade mark must be included in the capital of the partnership to be valued. It would seem that when the senior partner (Mr. Joseph Hall) died, in 1862, the articles of partnership had run out, and were said not to have been renewed. Consequently the works came into the hands of the surviving partner, Mr. Wm. Barrows, who died the next year (1863). And to this day the works, with full and exclusive use of the world famous brand for their "marked iron," are carried on by the Barrows family, as already stated. The Tipton Green Works, however, are demolished and the Factory Works have been abandoned. The latter are the property of the late Sir Horace St. Paul, and till recently were occupied by a manufacturer named Stevens. They are now closed, But the original works at Bloomfield still flourish as Wm. Barrows and Sons.

CHAPTER XLVI.—JOHN BAGNALL AND SONS, THE GREAT IRONMASTERS, OF TIPTON, WEDNESBURY AND, WEST BROMWICH.

Not only by residence at Toll End, but by prosecuting their industrial enterprises in various parts of the parish, are the Bagnall family connected with the commercial history of Tipton. At the present time however, their connection with the place is limited to the working of that part of the old establishment situate at Lea Brook. It was in Tipton that the founder of the family commenced his commercial operations. At the close of the last century John Bagnall, who had for a number of years been a ground bailiff, commenced business for himself as a coalmaster, by taking some mines at Toll End, the Coppice, and at Lea Brook, where he worked the thick coal for a period of years. His next venture was to start as an ironmaster, which he did by taking the adjacent blast furnace, which had been erected by Michael Tony. To this he attached a foundry, and placed his son William in the management of the place, where he produced both raw pigs and finished castings, with ever-increasing profit to himself. With his augmented capital he built the Gold's Green furnaces, at West Bromwich, at the same time taking his sons, John, William, Thomas, Samuel, and James into partnership, thereby establishing the famous firm of John Bagnall and Sons. The next acquisition of the firm was the Toll End Iron Works, which had been standing idle for some years, and which were purchased from the Birmingham Coal Company, by whom they had been erected. A few years afterwards they bought the Lea Brook Ironworks from Messrs Bate and Robins, bankers, of Stourbridge, and which had previously been worked by John Hartland of Tipton.

Leaving the commercial aspect aside it will not be at all uninteresting to go more deeply into the personal family history of these magnates of our local coal and iron industries.

The first of the Bagnall family of whom we have any record was one John Bagnall, supposed to have been a kind of mining engineer, who came from the County of Salop to these parts, with the great ironmaster John Wilkinson. He married his wife Margaret on 2nd December, 1753; he was buried at Darlaston Church, 1800. It was his son John who was the founder of the firm of John Bagnall and Sons of Gold's Hill, Lea Brook, Toll End, and Imperial Works, Wednesbury; whose celebrated "I.B.-Bagnall" (with a crown surmounting the two initials) was justly known for its excellencies throughout the manufacturing world. This "John Bagnall, Esquire," was married at Wednesbury Church, on the 13th May, 1792, to Mary, daughter of J. Royle, Esq, also of that town. This was his second marriage; the issue of his first wife being a son Edward, who died unmarried, and two daughters, one of whom was married to Mr. Thomas Davis, Gold's Hill; and the other to Mr. Richard Ashmore, of Wednesbury.

The second wife died 22nd January, 1826, but he survived till 23rd November, 1829. By this second marriage there were eight sons, most of these were born at Toll End Hall, Tipton. Mr. Bagnall resided there during the great riots of a colliers' strike at the beginning of this century, and even then, such was the standing and influence of the firm, that the Bagnalls were accused by the ignorant colliers of being the sole cause of the reduction in wages; and the Hall was besieged by an angry mob, who conspicuously displayed a stout rope, with which they threatened to hang the head of the firm.

The sons of this second alliance were:—

(1.) John, born 11 Sep., 1794; married twice, first to a Miss Jesson, and secondly to a Miss Robins: worked very hard in the establishment of the firm.

(2.) William, born 4 April, 1797; married twice, first to Miss Sherwood (daughter of Captain and Mrs. Sherwood, the latter an anchoress of some note); and secondly to Miss Smith, a sister of Mr. Fisher Smith, of Dudley, and the late Mr. Joseph Smith, of the Crown Tube, Wednesbury. When this Mr. William Bagnall died (at Hamstead Hall, Aug. 12, 1863) his brother James became the sole proprietor of the Works.

(3.) Thomas, born 15 April, 1799; this gentleman is treated by *Burke*, in his *Landed Gentry*, as head of the family, concerning whom more will be found further on.

(4.) The Rev. Henry Bagnall married Miss Adams.

(5.) Samuel, who died unmarried.

(6.) James, of Meyrick House, Hill Top was born 31 Dec, 1804. This son, and his brother William already mentioned, became sole proprietors of the firm after the first dissolution of partnership in 1856. James was a J.P., and D.L. of this county; he married the only daughter of Mr. Joseph Hately, solicitor, died 1872, without issue, leaving the Works, Collieries, &c, to his brother Richard.

(7.) George, born 12 Feb., 1806, married a Miss Williams, of Wednesbury Oak, and practised as a physician at Cheltenham.

(8.) Richard, born 18 Nov., 1809, married a Miss Gordon, and resided some time at Cliff, near Tamworth, and afterwards at Bescot Hall. He was a magistrate of this County; and died a few years back at Severn Stoke, Worc. He did not carry on the business of the firm when it was bequeathed to him by his brother James, as will be explained further on.

To revert to the "head of the family," as per *Burke*. "Thomas Bagnall, Esquire, of Newberries Park, Watford, Herts," was married twice. On 1 June, 1825, he married his first wife, Mary Keen, only child of John Nock, Esquire. The issue of this union have been three sons, John Nock, Charles, and Thomas.

(1.) The eldest was John Nock Bagnall, Esquire, of Shenstone Moss, Staffordshire, J,P., Deputy-Lieutenant of Staffordshire, Lieut.-Col. of the Fourth Battalion of the Staffordshire Rifle Volunteers, &c., &c, In 1875 he was High Sheriff of the County. He married in 1848 Mary Ann, eldest daughter of William Ward Esquire, of Wolverhampton, by whom he had issue, *inter alios* (1) John Ward Bagnall born 1854, is the eldest child: (2) a daughter, married to Rev F. Willett, late vicar of West Bromwich, and who has published a *History of West Bromwich*. Col. J. N. Bagnall, who is the author of THE HISTORY OF WEDNESBURY, interested himself greatly in the ecclesiastical affairs of the town, particularly of St. James's Parish where he was formerly churchwarden in conjunction with Mr. Wm. S. Nayler. The patronage of this living has since been bought by the late Col. Bagnall.

2.) The second son of this marriage is Charles Bagnall, Esq., of Sneaton Castle, Whitby, Yorkshire. He was born at West Bromwich in 1827. In 1860 he married Harriett Curtis, second daughter of the late John Chapman, Esq, of Whitby. He was educated at King's College, London, he is a magistrate of Staffordshire and the North Riding of Yorkshire. He was elected member of Parliament for Whitby in the Conservative interest in 1865, and sat till 1868; he had previously unsuccessfully contested Walsall.

(3.) The third son is Thomas Bagnall, Esq., of The Hall, Milton Ernest, Bedfordshire. In partnership with his brother Charles, he became proprietor of the Grosmont Furnaces, Cleveland.

For his second wife, "Thomas Bagnall, Esquire, of Newberries," married Caroline, daughter of Lancelot Haslope, Esquire, by whom he has had further issue. Henry Haslope Bagnall, Esquire, M.A., is the only son of the second marriage. This Thomas Bagnall, Esq, died about three years ago; in 1863 he was High Sheriff of this county of Stafford.

Having given the chief connections of this extensive family, a few words may now be devoted to the great industry with which that have identified themselves for three quarters of a century. As stated at the outset the fame of the Bagnall brand of iron was world-wide. Their smelting operations at Gold's Green and Capponfields at one time could scarcely keep pace with the requirements of their various mills and forges. The collieries were equally extensive and equally productive. When several colossal fortunes had been amassed, and when nearly every branch of the family (either directly or indirectly) had been enriched, no wonder the concern was eagerly bought up when at last it came to be put into the market. After the death of James Bagnall in 1872, Richard, his residuary legatee, declined to carry on the great ironworks and collieries of the old firm. A limited company was readily formed, and there was almost literally a struggle to obtain shares. In Wednesbury alone a vast amount of capital was readily forthcoming; but to nearly every application for allotment a courteous and formal reply was received stating that the application was too late. The few in the town who considered themselves lucky at the time in obtaining shares, soon had cause to rue their confidence in an old name. The Bagnall family having cleared out, the London speculators who got hold of the concern soon came to grief. To float the company an enormous commission had been paid to Baron Albert Grant, a great part of which legal proceedings afterwards compelled him to disgorge. Then bad trade set in. This date seemed about the turning point in the condition of our Black Country iron trade. Anyway the concern collapsed. Its very site at the principal department—Gold's Hill—knows it no more. However, under careful management the remnant at the Lea Brook and Imperial Works, Wednesbury, is now making a good profit.

Great interest is now being taken in the management of what still remains of the old works (Lea Brook and Imperial Ironworks) by Mr William Gordon Bagnall, a son of the late Mr Richard Bagnall, and chairman of the present limited liability company bearing the family name. He is to be congratulated on the resuscitation of the firm's former prestige, for, true to the traditions of his family, he has made the concern pay.

The Lea Brook works (of John Bagnall & Sons, Ld.), to which our attention must now be exclusively confined, at present employ about 250 men. It consists of 25 puddling and one ball furnaces; and one mill (16-inch) for the production of all kinds of strip, as best boiler, gas, hinge, lock, nail, and tube strip, from 0 to 15 wg. thick, and $1\frac{1}{4}$ inch to $12\frac{1}{8}$ inch wide The responsible manager of this thriving strip-making concern is Mr. Michael J. Whitehouse.

CHAPTER XLVII.—PHILIP WILLIAMS AND SONS, OF WEDNESBURY OAK IRONWORKS.

The firm of Philip Williams and Sons, of Wednesbury Oak Ironworks, is a very old-established concern, with a world-wide reputation as makers of the Mitre Brand of iron, and of the hot and cold blast pig-iron of the very finest quality. The personal history of the family is very much involved in the industrial and commercial development of this part of the Black Country.

Walter Williams, the first of the family, migrated from Salop about the year 1776, being an expert in the art of iron-making as then practised by the use of the Chaffery Furnace in the Wyre Forest, near Ludlow. After a time came his only son Philip, the founder of the firm of Philip Williams and Sons, about the year 1800. He commenced at a very early age to contract for work, and after attaining his majority never returned to manual labour himself. He joined in several small undertakings in the iron trade, but his first large venture was made in joining the firm of Gibbons, Whitehouse, and Williams, who built their first furnace at Wednesbury in 1814. His partners soon severed themselves, after the "Peace," when banking troubles affected one of his partners, the other one left him to start an independent concern. In 1818 he bought the whole of the foundation timbers for a forge and mill from the Government authorities at Woolwich, where before the fall of Napoleon they were preparing to enlarge the output of Government war appliances. In 1820 the forges and mills at Wednesbury Oak were built, and then was commenced the manufacture of the celebrated "Mitre Brand." In 1847 additional plant was put down. Those works and furnaces have continued with improvements to the present day; the furnaces of their kind (after being rebuilt and modernised in 1876 and 1880 are as fine a plant as any existing for the production of sold blast pig-iron. Philip Williams had a large family, all of whom were connected with the iron trade. They built the Union Furnaces at West Bromwich in 1829. They also took and worked the Albion Works, the Union Works at Smethwick, the Birchills Collieries and Furnaces, the Mabbs Bank and the Bunker's Hill Collieries, and in the years between 1846 to 1860 employed over 5,000 men. Philip, the third son of Philip, never married; he became a banker, and was elected chairman of the Iron Trade in succession to Mr Richard Grazebrooke. He served as sheriff in 1858, was a J.P. And D.L. for the county, and served on the police and other county committees. Most of his brothers were on the commission of the peace, and were directors of large companies, like the London and North-

Western Railway, the Birmingham Canal Navigations, &c. The only surviving grandsons of Philip Williams were the sons of Walter (his eldest) and one son of Henry (his youngest). The three former, after his death, in 1864, continued the old business at Wednesbury Oak. The names of those nephews who took up the affairs of the firm were Messrs Philip A Williams, Walter Williams, and Joseph W. Williams.

The present Walter Williams acted as honorary secretary to a scheme for inducing ironworkers and colliers to keep their children at school in the days before School Boards were established, and for a number of years he managed the funds of this scheme most admirably. At the same time he wrote a good deal on the value of education to the labouring classes—but always anonymously. He also held the office of honorary secretary to the Iron Trade; and that of chairman and president of the Mining Association of Great Britain—for all of which no man could have been more fitting. He has also been chairman of the local Mines Drainage Commission, and chairman of the Birmingham, Dudley, and District Bank, on the Board of which he served about 19 years. In the Yeomanry Mr Walter Williams served a long period of 29 years. In the county of Stafford he was a J.P. and D.L, filling the office of sheriff in 1880-81. Most of the members of this well-known and much respected family have found sepulture at Wednesbury, West Bromwich, or Handsworth old churches.

From the earliest days of the firm to the present the chief member in authority has usually resided opposite the works at Wednesbury Oak—a quaint, old-fashioned residence where traces still linger of the time when Tipton possessed rural attractions, and when employers of labour made a practice of living close at hand to keep a watchful eye on the works in which their interests were so largely bound up. For the last 15 years Mr George MacPherson has taken the active management of the works, furnaces, and collieries, and about a year ago was admitted into the firm as a partner. The present members of the firm are Messrs Philip A. Williams, Walter Williams, Joseph W. Williams, and George MacPherson. In addition to the blast furnaces, forges, mills, and the extensive collieries, there are saw-mills, carpenters and pattern makers' shops, shopping for moulders, mill-wrights, engine fitters, and blacksmiths; boiler makers' sheds, &c—all giving employment to a large number of men. The finished products consist of bar iron, angle iron, strips, nail rods, sheets, &c., &c.

CHAPTER XLVIII.—WILLIAM MILLINGTON AND CO., OF SUMMER HILL IRON WORKS.

The Summer Hill Iron Works of Messrs. W. Millington and Co. were established about 70 years ago. The firm has always been personal to the Millington family, although it has passed through various phases of style and title. In the first instance it was established as Thomas Millington, then as Thomas Millington and Son, afterwards as T. Millington and Sons; again as William and Isaiah Millington, and lastly as W. Millington and Co., of which Mr Samuel Lees Millington is the present and sole proprietor in succession to his uncle Mr Samuel Millington. Quoting from Griffith's "Guide to the Iron Trade" (1873), which gives a large view of these works at Summer Hill, we read:—

"These works are more useful than ornamental in their external aspect. The works, however, themselves, the steam engines, rolls, and machinery are abreast with the progress of to-day, the boiler plates and other kinds of iron made by this firm are known and appreciated in the market. W. Millington and Co's boiler plates were honourably mentioned at the Paris Exhibition, with Earl Granville, Shelton Bar, Barrows and Hall (the B.B.H.) and the British Iron Company's, and from that day to this the iron of this firm has maintained a high position in all markets, care being taken here to select good pig iron, and Mr. William Millington who from the first was a thoroughly practical man, having constantly paid personal attention to the construction of his works, and the quality of his brand."

The establishment consists of 16 puddling, five mill, and one annealing furnace"; four mills, forge (two trains), and one helve. The productive capacity is 200 tons per week consisting of merchant bar iron, plates, strips, angle iron, shoe tip iron, horse shoe and rivet iron, cable and chain iron, &c., of nearly every size, shape, and variety. Some 150 men are employed. The growth, development, and history of the firm are of considerable local interest. The founder of the firm had been a boiler maker on the same site. The late Mr. W. Millington was also identified with the industrial interests of this neighbourhood from the close of the last century, and some fugitive memoranda of his preserve to us some quaint old-time memories. Among his stray jottings we find the following:—

1792. Gospel Oak Works: Captain Dumaresq began the furnace.
1794. He began the forge.
1784. Hocker Hill Engine (first) started.
1793. ,, ,, ,, (second) ditto.
1800. ,, ,, ,, (third) ditto.

1798 (about). Hawkes Furnaces, Toll End.
1799. Moat Colliery No 5 was sinking.
1803 (about). Lea Works, by Michael Tony.
1804 Attwood's Works. Wednesbury Field.

In June, 1851, some severe tests were made at the cable manufactory of H. P. Parkes, of Dudley, to demonstrate the tensile strength and fibrous toughness of the iron used in the fabrication of chains. At that time public attention had been drawn to the loss of life frequently caused by the breaking of a single link in a chain, whether used on board ship, or as part of lifting or engineering tackle, or elsewhere. The iron that stood the severest test on this occasion was that supplied by the firm of Millington and Co. An exhibit of these chains was made and placed among the ship models at the first Great Exhibition (1851) or Crystal Palace, as it was called. Again in 1855 this firm took a prize medal at the first great French Exhibition—as already mentioned.

In the year 1861, during the first great struggle for supremacy between armour plates and penetrating shot, this firm again came to the front in the production of tough-fibred iron. On the invitation of the Government they manufactured a 3 inch plate to be tested at Shoeburyness, which was done on October 15th of that year. The plate received a blow from a 40-pound shot, fired at a distance of one hundred yards: the plate was not pierced, but merely indented with a hole the size of a teacup, and, of course, bulged on the opposite side in a corresponding degree; not a fibre had given way. In fact this character for strength and tenacity of fibre has been cultivated from the first and maintained to the present day.

CHAPTER XLIX—THE HORSLEY WORKS.

The original Horsley Works stood on the opposite side of the Horsley Road leading from Horsley Heath to Toll End. Its founders were first known as the Horsley Coal and Iron Company, who commenced business some 60 or 70 years ago near the site of the present Cemetery. Here there were some blast furnaces, which, however, were let off to John Hartland, who relinquished them in turn to John Colbourn and Sons. Evidently successful in working, this firm erected two other furnaces, which have been dismantled only a year or two ago.

The traditions of the old Horsley Works are rich in early engineering triumphs. One of the first locomotive engines built in the Midlands was constructed here, and at a period when results were so extremely doubtful that a pair of temporary rails, the length of the shedding, had to be laid down to try the novelty and test its travelling capabilities. But even earlier than this these works produced a marine engine when that engineering invention was in its experimental stages of development; this attempt was secured a trial by bolting together two canalboats and revolving a pair of paddle wheels in a convenient stretch of the canal. In foundry products the Horsley Works took a leading position. The fine iron bridge, called the Galton Bridge (or Summit Bridge), at Smethwick was cast here. Somewhat elementary must have been the method of designing if, as asserted, the segments were struck out in an adjoining field with a long wooden trammel.

About 1846, certain losses having been sustained, the concern passed through some rapid changes and vicissitudes. It is said to have fallen into the hands of the Stratford Bank, when three gentlemen of considerable eminence in the local iron trade came to the rescue. These were Mr J. J. Bramah, Mr Deeley, and Mr Cochrane. In succession to these proprietors came Messrs Broad and Tierney, about 1849 or 1850. These partners worked the place most successfully till 1865, when Mr Broad wished to launch out further in the business, while Mr Tierney seemed somewhat reluctant to do so. A new site of several acres was acquired on the opposite side of the road where the new Horsley Works were erected, a process which occupied some 12 months, as may be guessed by the most casual observer who glances at the substantial buildings comprising them, and which would be considered an ornament in any industrial neighbourhood. No expense was spared to make them replete with every accommodation, including elegantly fitted offices, draughtsmen's rooms, dining rooms, &c. The pattern shop and the foundry were well laid out, too, and castings from one pound to several tons in weight are of daily production. The fitting shop was provided with newest machinery of every kind for drilling, slotting, planing, boring, screwing, turning, or any other process of mechanical manipulation.

There was a period of transition in 1866, lasting some 12 months, during which part of the work was conducted at the old place, and part on the new premises. In May, 1867, Mr Tierney died, and Mr Broad conducted the new works on his sole responsibility till January, 1874, when, by a strange coincidence, he died on the same day that the present limited liability company came into possession. In 1878 the works of Mr. P. D. Bennett, of Spon Lane, were amalgamated with this concern, and Mr Bennett became managing director, this position he held till his accidental death in November, 1885—a tragic incident connected with the banquet given to the Prince of Wales on his visit to Birmingham on that occasion.

The present Horsley Company, Limited, is as successful as any concern can be, which is dependent upon the fluctuations of the coal and iron trade. As engineers, ironfounders, and manufacturers of structural iron and steel work they hold a high reputation. As makers of roofs, piers, and gasholders they are well-known throughout the trade, while as builders of every kind and variety of bridge they can direct attention in all quarters of the globe to specimens reflecting the highest credit upon their name. They employ some 600 men, and have recently paid a dividend of 6 per cent. to their shareholders.

CHAPTER L.—OCKER HILL PUMPING STATION, AND THE BIRMINGHAM CANAL NAVIGATIONS.

Acts had been obtained in 1766 for canals from the Trent to the Mersey, with a branch to the Severn. Birmingham determined not to be behindhand, and in 1768 obtained the Act to join the system by a canal to Autherley. This was completed so far as Bilston in 1770, and the whole course in 1772. It was connected to the system leading to London at Fazeley, in 1783. The local canals were made by the well-known engineer, Brindley, and, in the fashion of that day, were taken at a level (or contour line) to avoid locks; and thus - in the words of Brindley himself—to "keep the giant water always on the flat of his back." But the lines on plan look tortuous as they wind round all the ravines and hills to avoid cost of aqueduct or outline: and as they had been hastily and very inefficiently constructed and equipped to carry on the unexpected traffic, they had become so dilapidated in 1824 as to be described as being "little better than a crooked ditch, with scarcely the appearance of a haling-path, horses frequently sliding or staggering into the water the haling-lines sweeping the gravel into the canal, and the entanglement at the meeting of boats incessant, while at the locks at each end of the short summit crowds of boatmen were always quarrelling, or offering premiums for a preference of passages, and the mine-owners injured by the delays were loud in just complaints.

It was to remedy this state of things that Thomas Telford, the famous engineer, re-arranged the canals in 1824, and made for seven miles a nearly straight course, 40 feet wide, with towing path on both sides. from Birmingham to Smethwick, involving some important works, such as a cutting 70 feet deep at Smethwick, and the reduction of the length from Birmingham to Autherley from 22 miles to 14 miles. The remains of the obsolete curvatures are sometimes seen in the numerous basins and arms still used at various works in the district. The engineer received great encouragement from such men as James Watt, and much help from Mr John Freeth, for many years in the service of the Canal Company. It was thus that Birmingham become a great "centre of inland navigation." Rotten Park Reservoir, with its specially contrived feeders and carriers, was constructed at this time, previous to which the canal had been supplied chiefly from a reservoir at Oldbury, and from various mine-pumping engines. In the years 1835-6, 1840, 1844, and 1846, the Acts were consolidated, and the various canal undertakings were combined into one, known now as the Birmingham Canal Navigations. Certain traffic arrangements were also made with the London and North-Western Railway Co., and a fine gathering reservoir was constructed on Cannock Chase.

At Smethwick a group of large engineering works may be seen, which form a distinctive feature of the locality. There may be admired in close proximity— (1) the Wolverhampton or high level canal, in a deep cutting; (2) nearly adjoining it, the Birmingham or lower level canal in a deeper cutting; (3) the Stour Valley Railway running along side it; (4) also a cutting for the Great Western Railway running over both the canals and the other railway, while just beyond the famous iron Galton Road Bridge tops them all.

For many years there was only the Dudley tunnel through the limestone rocks to connect the canals on the east and west sides of the coalfield. Though interesting, this canal is highly inconvenient for traffic; for not only have boats to be taken in locks on one side and lowered on the other, but they have to be propelled through its narrow length by the process known to the boatmen as "legging it." To avoid this the fine Netherton tunnel was constructed by James Walker, the engineer, in 1850, it connects the lower or Birmingham level, and is wide enough for tow paths on each side. Its gas-lit depths reveal the fact that the coal measures are connected beneath the Rowley Hills, the well known "Rowley rag" being shown to be merely an overflow of lava from some other outburst, and not an outburst through the coal at that spot, as was once supposed.

At Ocker Hill is the chief of the pumping stations of the Birmingham Canals, for lifting water from one level to another, or from the bottom to the top of flights of locks. At Ocker Hill the highest and the lowest levels meet, and at this station six large engines are gathered under one roof. Some of these are of an ancient design and construction, but "are none the less interesting on that account." To quote Mr. E. B. Marten's words—"There are six engines under one roof, and they give examples of the styles of engines most approved as experience grew or the exigences of the work increased; much as a cathedral often displays the same thing in the different styles of architecture found best adapted to the times by the monks, who were the engineers of past ages."

Around Tipton the mining operations had once caused the surface to sink as much as 30 feet, and there was much injury consequently caused to the canals. During the time of the present engineer to the Birmingham Canal Navigations, Mr Jebb, the chief anxiety has been to repair this vast amount of damage done by the mining throughout the district. This, with many improvements in the pumping machinery, has placed the local canal system in a higher state of efficiency than it has ever attained before. With concerted action on the leaky streams by the Mines Drainage Commissioners gigantic efforts have been made during the last few years to free our water-logged mines.

CHAPTER LI.—THE TIPTON DISTRICT OF THE MINES DRAINAGE AREA.

So early as November 6th, 1865, Mr. E. B. Marten, C.E., read a prophetic paper on the drainage of the South Staffordshire Coalfield before the Dudley Geological Society, advocating some concerted plan of action for the whole area rather than placing continued reliance on the individual pumping in the numerous sectional areas of the various mine-owners. Parliamentary powers were foreshadowed as the only economical system on which to do this; and allusion was casually made to an abortive attempt to introduce into Parliament a Bill seeking similar powers for the drainage of the Tyne coalfield in 1860.

The area then proposed to be drained contains about 125 square miles, and being situated on some of the highest table-land in England, no water can be brought on to its surface by natural streams from other districts: its only source of supply beyond the small quantity introduced by waterwork companies being the usual rainfall, which is given at an average of about 22 inches per annum. This area is divided into two parts by a ridge running diagonally across in a south-easterly direction from Wolverhampton, Sedgley, and Dudley to join the Rowley Hills. This gives two natural basins, viz.—;

I. The Stour (or South) Basin containing—

Halesowen,
Lye,
Cradley,
Brierley Hill,

Netherton,
Gornal.

II. The Tame (or North) Basin containing—
Oldbury,
Tipton,
Bilston,
Darlaston,
Willenhall,
Wednesfield,
Walsall,
Wednesbury.

On the extreme north was another area of this coal-field, viz.,

Church Bridge		Saredon Brook.
Norton		Bentley Brook.
Cannock Chase	drained by	Bilston Brook.
Hednesford		How Brook.
Brereton		Crane Brook.

Alterations and modifications to these natural drainage areas had by this time been made by *artificial* railway cuttings and embankments, and again by canals absorbing the flow for some 25 miles; but notwthstanding all the water from mines pumped to the surface by some 139 pumping engines, the quantity flowing off the district in its streams was then no greater than it had been before mining was commenced. What then became of the 220,000 tons, or 50 million gallons of water raised by the 5,000 horse power of these engines every 24 hours? It could only be accounted for by the supposition that it must have once more penetrated the surface and fallen to lower levels than formerly. Of the 50 million gallon's pumped, 37 millions fed the canals, and only 13 millions ran into the streams. But while it was to the interest of the canal company to keep their canals water-tight, the streams on the other hand were neglected; their water ran into swags, catch~water pits between spoil~banks, and other ready receptacles whence it percolated again to the depths below. So that great waste of effective work existed under such a method of drainage as then prevailed The engines, too, were most varied in description, unequal in results as compared with fuel consumed, and very often they were affected by the corrosive nature of the water dealt with—which in amount was equal to ten times the coal raised in the same time, and the cost of raising which added $3\frac{3}{4}$d. per ton to the cost of that coal.

In 1872 Messrs, Fowler and Underhill, solicitors, took up the matter as one of urgent public necessity, called a meeting (in Wolverhampton) of mine-owners and others interested, and formed a strong committee, of which Mr. George Barker was made chairman and Mr. Henry Smith secretary. Mr. Marten was appointed to prepare evidence as to the surface drainage, and Mr. Peacock and Mr. Johnson were appointed to deal with the underground work. Application to Parliament resulted in the passing of the South Staffordshire Mines Drainage Act in 1873, which was afterwards amended in 1878 and in 1882.

The magnitude of the work may be gauged by the fact that the area was not only traversed by 100 miles of canal but also possessed 500 miles of streams, all more or less injured by mining, and some 11 square miles of surface had been so sunk as to be absolutely below their nearest available outlet (by natural watercourse drainage) and had to be dealt with by surface pumps.

Mr. Henry Lee, M.I.M.E., addressing the local Institute of Mining Engineers in March 3rd, 1890, on the engineering operations of the Commissioners, gave the dimensions of the area dealt with, as follows:—

I. *Surface Works*. 72 square miles, being 12 N. to S. and an average of 6 E. to W., and extending from the Great Bentley Fault on the N. to near the Clent Hill on the S.

II. *Underground Works*. The whole of the aforesaid area, excepting the districts of Oldbury on the E. and Kingswinford on the W.

He described the basin or bed beneath the coal as having an uneven bottom, but with a tendency to get deeper from north to south; for instance, while the thick coal crops out at the surface just north of Bilston it falls away at Halesowen near the southern boundary of the Mines Drainage Area to a depth of 1,000 feet below the surface, or 600 feet below sea-level. As the shallower measures had been worked first, the great difficulties with the water-logging of the mines had occurred in that portion of the area while in the Tipton district the removal of the ten-yard coal had (as before mentioned) worked great havoc with the surface also. Hence the Commissioners had been compelled to drain swags, stop leaky canals and amend natural streams by raising, widening, puddling, and making them of uniform section—indeed, often removing old boundary lines by actually straightening their curves. Then having stopped access to the workings, the Commissioners' pumps, by raising 17 million gallons per day instead of 50 millions, brought to the surface all the "come" of water in the various "pounds" in which it accumulated—and all the pounds were tapped by the driving of levels in various directions to do so—and at the same time they claimed to be gradually reducing the level of the water in these pounds throughout the whole district. Describing these underground levels, the speaker thus illustrated the aspect of them in the Tipton District:

"Conceive a large shallow tank, having a number of buckets placed within it, and resting upon its bottom. Let the tank and the buckets be assumed to be full of water. Fix a pump whose suction-pipe shall reach the bottom of the tank. Proceed to pump out the water. You may be able to empty the tank, but the individual buckets will remain full of water, and the only way to empty them as they stand will be either to put a pump into each, which will be too expensive, or to approach each one from the level of the bottom of the tank, and bore a hole into it to allow its contents to find their way to the pump. I have no doubt that eventually the question of emptying the buckets will be satisfactorily solved, and that then the district will become completely unwatered, and its valuable stores of minerals will become generally accessible."

The floor of this basin or "tank" is of Silurian limestone, and it must be remembered that the southern half is divided obliquely by that ridge (or rising of this limestone) in the line of hills from Sedgley through Dudley to Rowley. And with regard to the extreme northern half, as the Great Bentley Fault permitted no water to pass through it, the difficulties were in that district so much the less: the Bentley district was not included within the range of the Commissioners' operations.

In the transitional period, when appointed arbitrators were settling differences and arranging terms between the private firms who had been working their own pumps, and the new Commissioners who were taking up the work of pumping under the Act the greatest difficulties arose in the vicinity of Tipton. In the Bilston district the arbitrators advised four new engines, and the temporary working of 44 old ones, at a capital cost of £46,000, but this not being agreed to, the Bilston water soon overflowed into the Tipton district, and so swamped the arrangements there that the Tipton people had to work the Bilston engines to save themselves, without receiving rates for the coal raised there. In the Tipton district itself the arbitrators had suggested the erection of two new engines, and the temporary employment of 38 old ones, at a capital expenditure of £70,000. As an alternative the owners of old pumps were paid for their pumping at the rate of 6½d per lock (25,000 gallons) per 100 feet raised, equal to about £20 per annum per horse power: and this eventually resulted in the Commissioners having to take most of the pumping engines into their own hands. By 1880 these two districts were practically joined, and the arbitrators suggested a scheme for the whole (now called the Tipton district), including the renewal of Stow Heath engine, and the putting down of two large new engines at Bradley and at Moat.

Of the other districts * wide of Tipton it may be necessary to say that the Oldbury people took advantage of a clause in the Act, and exempted themselves from the underground portion of the work, under the impression that they were safe from any influx of water so long as pumping was performed in Tipton. In the Kingswinford district the mine-owners also exempted themselves in a similar way, and so prevented the Commissioners continuing the effective drainage that had there been commenced by a private owner.

It was in the Tipton district the greatest amount of work had to be accomplished, and there the most serious difficulties had to be overcome; and notwithstanding the many embarrassments caused to the Commissioners by the depression in trade which continued so many years immediately after the initiation of their undertaking—inaugurated by a large capital outlay—and the consequent shrinkage in the sources of their revenue by the diminished output of coal, they have still many valuable results to show. They have stopped most of the percolation of water from the surface, greatly reduced the number of pumping engines, and they have curtailed in a high degree the comparative annual cost of unwatering the mines in this vast area with its honeycombed measures and its disturbed surface.

CHAPTER LII.—THE CHAIN AND ANCHOR TRADES.

Shaw, writing in 1798, refers to Taylor's Foundry at Toll End as an important place for the production "of heavy cast goods for whimseys, engines, and mill work." At that time Tipton employed 100 workpeople in the production of "cast-iron hinges," 40 in making shovels and tongs, while one-fourth of the population were engaged in nail making. In 1848 Mr Hingley commenced to make heavy anchors; and since that period Tipton (together with Netherton, Rowley, and Cradley, places in the very heart of England) has supplied our ships with anchors of a size at one time unheard of, when their manufacture was an industry confined exclusively to seaport towns or places in their immediate vicinity. At first an anchor of a ton weight was considered something gigantic; but the improvement in machinery, especially the substitution of the steam-hammer for the old-fashioned sledge, now enables manufacturers to turn out more reliable

* Originally there had been six *underground* districts proposed for separate treatment, viz.—1 Bentley, 2 Bilston, 3 Tipton, 4 Oldbury, 5 Old Hill, 6 Kingswinford.

anchors in one day, and of several tons in weight, than were formerly produced in three or four days, and of much smaller proportions. Heavy machine castings are also now produced of a calibre and weight altogether undreamt of in the days of Taylor's Foundry. Reverting to the anchor trade, chain making must be associated with this industry; for Tipton not only produces pit chains for local consumption, but is also famous for its ship's cables to go along with its anchors. This chain making was established about the year 1824, and therefore is considerably older than anchor forging. At first ½ inch to 2 inch cables were among the largest produced, but after 1834 the manufacture developed very rapidly, just as in 1838 Hingley's had been content to attempt the forging of a 20-cwt. anchor, and in later years were not satisfied till a 74-cwt. anchor had been successfully turned out. But as this history concerns itself specially with Tipton, we must transfer our attention from the Netherton to the industry as developed in that parish.

Joseph Wright and Co, of the Neptune Chain and Anchor Works, had their place described in Griffiths's "Guide to the Iron Trade" in 1873, illustrated by a view, thus—"This is one of the largest chain and anchor works in England, well represented by the plate opposite. The situation is admirable, being on the banks of the coal and labour market. Mr Joseph Wright, the proprietor, is the son-in-law of Mr Theophilus Tinsley, the well-known nail factor of Dudley, and we believe the Tinsley family are still connected with these great works. Mr Wright's chains are famous not only in the London and Liverpool markets, but throughout the world; the cables made at this celebrated forge stand unrivalled. When in the Black Country the other day we were particular in our enquiries in respect to Wright's chains and cables at the Government testing and proof establishment at Tipton, and were there informed that the testing and proving of the cables and chains turned out at the Neptune forge completely justified the celebrity for quality which Mr Wright's chains have in Germany, Russia, the Levant, and other foreign markets. The anchors made here are well known throughout the world, the Neptune forge having turned out from time to time the best and largest made. We understand the excellency of the quality of the chains and cables is owing in a great measure to the use of B.B.H. and the Earl of Dudley's bars which are unsparingly consumed at this great factory, although the price paid is £1 per ton to £1 12s 6d per ton more than any other iron of this class made in Staffordshire. Messrs Wright and Co. are now engaged on large orders for the Russian and Turkish Governments"

Writing to the editor of the "Engineer" in April 1886, this firm makes public the following statement:

"We may say that some years ago we were of those who thought that very mild steel might, sooner or later, supersede iron; but after 25 years of careful observation, during which period we have no hesitation in saying that a steel chain, with welded links can never hope to be classed with anything above a third-rate quality of iron, in consequence of the difficulty in insuring a sound weld, on account of the treacherous nature of the material.

We may quote an instance which has recently come under our notice:

Since the correspondence upon "Good and Bad Chains" commenced, we have been favoured with an order from Manchester, for a quantity of wagon couplings, consisting of two links each, 13½ in. long over all, and made of 1⅜ in, exact iron A1 Special Best S. E. Crown Iron, manufactured by Wm. Millington and Co., Summerhill Ironworks.

The couplings were made in our usual way, and duly advised for delivery. Mr. Nicholas Fogg, the company's special inspector, called at our works to examine them, after which he promiscuously selected two samples from the bulk for testing purposes, and in order to compare them with other brands, he brought with him two other couplings, one in steel and one in iron, of the same size and dimensions, but made specially for high testing, by another house.

The four samples were taken to Lloyd's Public Testing Machine, at Tipton, on the 3rd instant, and tested to destruction, in the presence of Mr Fogg and Lloyd's Superintendent, with the following results:

Sample. Quality.	Breaking Strain.
No. 1.—SIEMEN'S STEEL, made purposely for testing, broke in weld	at 45 Tons.
No. 2.—BOWLING IRON, made purposely for testing, broke in iron	at 59½ Tons.
No. 3.—A1 SPECIAL BEST BEST S.H. CROWN IRON "taken promiscuously from bulk, broke in weld........	at 65¾ Tons.
No. 4.—"A1 SPECIAL BEST BEST S.E. CROWN IRON "taken promiscuously from bulk, broke in iron	at 67½ Tons.

The "Lloyd's" here mentioned, who have a testing establishment at Tipton, and another for the chainmaking district on the far side of Dudley, are the same great firm of marine insurance brokers (established in the year 1772) whose classification of ships is accepted by the Government as the standard. In the same way their test of ships' cables and other chains is now also recognised as the standard by the Board of Trade. Within recent years large hydraulic machines for this testing of chain cables have been fitted (in Tipton and at Netherton) with the weighing levers required by the Board of Trade in testing all ships' anchors, &c.

Henry P. Parkes and Co., of the Tipton Green Chain and Anchor Works, are also manufacturers in the same lines. The largest anchor ever made up to that period was produced in January, 1867, by the firm of H. P. Parkes. The founders of this establishment belong to the very old local family of Persehouse whose genealogical tree was published in the "Midland Antiquary" in 1884 (Vol. ii., pp. 133-138).

CHAPTER LIII.—ROBERTS AND CO., OF THE TIPTON GREEN FURNACES AND COLLIERY.

These furnaces were built in the year 1808, as was shown by the date remaining on them up to 1850. The furnaces and the colliery were all standing in 1846. The property belonged to Messrs Bradburn, Scott, and Foley, and when Messrs Roberts and Eberhardt acted for them they were pressed to open the colliery, which had been standing for many years. They let the furnaces to Mr. Benjamin Gibbons, jun, of Corbyn's Hall. He started them in 1847, and Mr William Roberts joined him in 1848 and became an equal partner in 1851. The furnaces which in old times had worked at cold blast and made small quantities of iron, were relined and enlarged, and hot blast stoves and winding engine added. The make of iron, which had been some 30 tons a week, was increased to 100 tons. It was commonly reported that if the make did reach 40 tons in the old days every man employed on the work had a leg of mutton given him. In the earlier period (1808), when the mines and the furnaces had probably been worked by Bradburn, Scott, and Foley, there was no winding engine. The furnaces were built on the side of a hill, and the materials were wheeled into them up a gentle incline; and this method of filling continued up to the year 1847. The owners of the estate in 1848 were Mr. Bradburn, of the New Forest; Sir Edward Scott, of Barr Hall; and Lady Emily Foley, of Stoke Edith, only the lady survives to this day. The manager of the furnaces in the earlier part of the century had been a Mr. Roberts (no relation to the present Messrs. Roberts), whose sons now constitute the well-known firm of ironfounders in West Bromwich.

At this time, 1848, there were three furnaces, square clumsy buildings, giving their name to a public-house in Wood Street, Tipton, The adjoining Tipton Green Colliery was opened by Messrs. Roberts and Eberhardt (the latter was a solicitor of Stourbridge), who required Messrs. Gibbons and Roberts to take their coal from them. In 1856 the iron trade was very good, every blast furnace was at work that could be started, and every cottage was occupied that was fit for habitation. Mr. Gibbons offered £1,000 rent for six months for an old furnace at Bilston, and not being able to get it,

Messrs. Gibbons and Roberts started to build two new furnaces, the brickwork was done in eight weeks, and the fittings finished in another eight weeks (there was no limit to hours of labour then). One furnace was blown in, but the good trade was already gone, and it only remained in blast 11 months. The other was not started at all for three years after. In 1860 two more furnaces were built, making four, the original old ones having been pulled down. In 1858 Mr. Gibbons left the firm, and in 1869 Mr. Alfred Roberts joined Mr. William Roberts, and Mr. E. A. Spurgin joined in 1882, and they have since carried the furnaces on with varying success. In 1889 Cowper stoves were added in lieu of the old iron ones and one of the furnaces was pulled down and rebuilt with all the newest improvements, The firm then, in addition to their well-known foundry iron, began to make basic iron for the steel works at Wednesbury, Bilston, and Round Oak, at which places their make seems to be much approved of. At the present time, owing to the high prices of coal and wages, only two furnaces are at work, whereas the whole four furnaces have been in blast, except in times of colliers' strikes, &c, for the last 20 or 30 years. Their capacity is 200 tons each per week, the brand is "Roberts' Tipton Green Iron."

Reverting to the colliery which was worked by Messrs Roberts and Eberhardt, we find it subsequently fell into the hands of Mr. Charles Roberts alone, and upon his death was carried on by his executors. But the expenses entailed by paying for houses damaged through getting the mines; the cost of pumping; and the extra expenditure upon labour since the nine and the eight hours movement, made the whole undertaking so expensive that the colliery had to be closed when the last margin of profit had disappeared.

The firm of Roberts and Company consists of three partners, Mr. William Roberts, Mr. Alfred Roberts, and Mr. E. A. Spurgin. Mr William Roberts in 1866 married a daughter of the Rev. John Spurgin, B.D., rector of Great Hookham, Norfolk. He built Fern Dale House, Pedmore, 1868, where he now resides. At this home of a wide-reaching hospitality the kindly disposition of the owner has provided tents, sheds (with boilers for extensive tea-making), swings, and other recreative preparations for the amusement the juvenile visitors whom Mr Roberts is in the habit of inviting. It is quite an institution for the thoughtful proprietor of all these childish delights to entertain schools and bands of hope from the surrounding districts, particularly from the murky streets and alleys of Tipton.

Mr. Alfred Roberts is a bachelor, and occupies the family residence, Field House, Clent.

Mr E. A. Spurgin, B.A., is a son of the Rev. John Spurgin, B.D. and married a daughter of Dr. William Lees Underhill, He lives within the parish of Tipton, on the Dudley Road.

Messrs. Roberts and Spurgin were instrumental, amongst work in other parishes, in building the Wood Street School, and the church and parsonage of St Matthew's. Towards the building and endowment of this church they collected about £20,000. See also Chapter XXX.

CHAPTER LIV.—VARIOUS MAKERS OF IRON; AND OTHER IRONWORKERS.

For very many years the concern now known as the Great Bridge Iron and Steel Company, Limited, was known as Solly Brothers, who were in their day amongst the largest and oldest makers of puddled steel. Mr. James Solly, J.P., resided, in the good old-fashioned style, on the site of his works nearly up to the last. (See "Wednesbury Papers," p. 94.). Perhaps it may be said that no master and magistrate lived so much beloved and respected by all his immediate neighbours as did Mr. Solly; and when at last he removed his residence to Edgbaston as he did a few years ago just before the close of his busy and well-spent life, it was the removal of a form and figure that could ill be spared at Toll End. At the present time the works are under the supervision of Mr John Woodhouse, managing director of the company. With two forges, two merchant mills, and two sheet mills the works have a productive capacity of 320 tons per week, consisting of every variety of section of all qualities of iron and steel, as well as sheets of both iron and steel.

At Toll End is the Crown Iron and Galvanizing Works of Edward Bayley, manufacturer of sheets, plates, &c. On the present site of Bayley's work was formerly a forge worked by Deeley and Motteram. There were also three blast furnaces close at hand, and one was worked by John Hartland. This ironmaster also worked the two blast furnaces of the Eagle Works, an establishment that formerly stood on the spot now occupied by Great Bridge Station (South Staffordshire Railway). The Eagle Coal and Iron Company had a capital foundry and fitting- shops here, the front facade of which was adorned with the bold figure of an eagle. The Crown Works were established in 1870, since which date two sheet mills and a large galvanizing works have been added. The full plant consists of ten puddling and three mill furnaces, with a capacity of nearly 100 tons per week and giving employment to about 200 men. This establishment is noted for the production of the best qualities of "special" black sheet iron and galvanized corrugated sheet iron.

Among the iron makers in Tipton not yet enumerated must be mentioned the three Coneygre Furnaces of the Earl of Dudley, at Dudley Port, worked with the adjacent colliery, and producing about 200 tons per week. Messrs. James and Charles Holcroft are both ironmakers and galvanizers at Portfield Works, also near Dudley Port. Nearly every size, shape, variety, and section of iron seem to be produced here. George Gadd and Company, of the Church Lane Works, with 14 puddling furnaces, two mill furnaces, and one ball furnace, have a capacity of 180 tons of bar iron and 200 tons of puddled iron per week.

The Gospel Oak Iron and Galvanised Iron and Wire Company have 24 puddling furnaces and six rolling mills. The Dudley Port Furnace Company (James Roberts and Fred Deeley, junior, partners) have a blast furnace, with a capacity of 250 tons per week, producing cinder pig, part mine pig, and basic pig. The Hope Iron, Steel, and Tinplate Company, Limited, have four mills at their works in Summerhill, producing 750 boxes per week. Plant and Fisher, at Dudley Port Works, produce 250 tons per week from 20 puddling furnaces and three mills.

Charles Lathe and Company, of the Moat Foundry, Summerhill, employ about forty pairs of hands. The concern was established in 1877. The productions chiefly consist of builders' ironwork, in which the firm has many specialities. Some of these are registered; for elegance of design, combined with utility, should ever be the highest aim of the ironfounder's art. Among the specialities produced here are cottage ranges (or oven grates), kitcheners, grates fitted with marble and enamelled chimney pieces, register grates and stoves with curbs, tiles, &c.

Beyond all these Tipton is full of workers in iron of all sorts, galvanisers, boat and boiler makers, engineers and founders, hurdle and iron fencing makers, makers of anvils, vices, and hammers; in fact, the artificers in iron are to be found within the confines of this parish in endless variety.

CHAPTER LV.—A TIPTONIAN DESCRIPTION OF THE BURNING OF DUDLEY CASTLE IN 1750.

One of the most awe-inspiring sights ever witnessed in Tipton and a spectacle ever to be remembered by those who almost breathlessly watched it for three dreadful days, was the burning of Dudley Castle. This memorable event happened in July, 1750, and so complete was the devastation of that conflagration that there is said to remain in the ruins not a single piece of its original timbers. As to the real origin of the fire much doubt exists; but as immense quantities of metal—chiefly, however, constituting the lead roofs of its numerous buildings—were so completely melted as to run down the Castle hill like the most volatile of liquids, tradition has generally pointed to the presence of coiners.

But a capital account of the last ball held in the Castle, together with some allusion to the fire, has been penned by a very delightful writer, Mrs Sherwood (see Chapter xlvi.), just as it was recounted to her by her grandmother in 1776, when the latter was 84 years of age. And these are no doubt the impressions of a Tipton woman, as she describes her native place as between West Bromwich and Dudley.

At the time of the ball she was 15 years of age, and was maid to a lady who was present at the ball. As a matter of course she had to accompany her mistress to the ball. They set out in a coach, and as it was quite dark when they reached the Castle, lamps were fixed on the trees all along the private road up to the Castle, and there were lights upon the towers, which shone as beacons far and near. The old courtyard was littered with splendid equipages, sounding with the rattling of the wheels and the voices of the coachman and the grooms, and blazing with lights from every window. The keep looked huge and gloomy as it does now, but all that part of the Castle which was now comparatively modern was at the time alive with the stir of persons bent on pleasure. The windows were filled with coloured glass, and the sounds of merry voices, harps, and viols issued from every doorway. When she got inside the Castle she was handed over to the housemaid, who said she had lived in the Castle 40 years, and spoke of her lord and lady as if there were none that could compare with them. She had seen many noble palaces since the day of the ball but never had she admired any as she did Dudley Castle, when she was led round by the faithful and antiquated housemaid. There were three large doors opening into the ballroom, and at one of these she took her place among the servants and maids. The hall was illuminated with many candles in sconces of brass hanging from the ceiling, and every corner was as bright as day. While the band kept up the spirit with harp, pipe, tabor, and violin, the floor rocked beneath the quick and measured steps of the gay company engaged in the dance. She had before her still the figures of that distinguished company, for it consisted of the nobles of the land; the ladies shone with glossy silks and jewels, and the gentlemen with gold and silver lace. The dresses were splendid, and she did not think she had ever seen faces so fair as some of those which shone that night in that old hall: But now the room in which that gay company assembled was roofless and floorless; the merry dancers had now passed away, and their names were scarcely known to their children's children. Soon after this ball the old servants dropped off one by one, the valuable movables were carried away, and the place was abandoned. Then it seemed a gang of coiners took possession of the vaults (in 1750), and there carried on their nefarious trade. No one suspected this till the gang set fire to the building, and flames burst forth from every window. It was a glorious sight; the whole summit of the hill was a mass of fire, and for three nights and days the flames raged with unabated fury. The roof, chiefly of lead, poured down fiery torrents, and when the fire smouldered away there remained a huge disfigured ruin, blackened with smoke. Ivy and other creepers had grown upon the walls as if to hide the ravages of the fire, but the glory of the complete edifice had departed, and the glory of the ruin now reigned in its stead. The key of the Castle was found 50 years ago in a hole above the gateway, by a boy who, mounted on another boy's shoulders, was groping after a jackdaw's nest.

CHAPTER LVI.—REMINISCENCES OF TIPTON HALF A CENTURY AGO.

Starting at the boundary of Tipton parish, divided from Dudley by it, is a small water-course running through a field adjoining the turnpike road near the old gate and the Trindle House. Running through the fields towards Dudley Castle this brook was used by the Fellmongers to wash their sheep-skins some 60 years ago and for some years after. These fields later on were turned into a race ground, and finally used for storing the minerals (ironstone, &c.) from the adjacent collieries belonging to the Earl of Dudley, by whom also the land was owned.

Among the prominent and more obstrusive establishments of the time were the canal wharves situated on the right hand side of the Tipton Road, a little lower down from this brook. The first was that of Messrs. J. Whitehouse and Sons, carried on by them for many years, and their head office being at the top of the Birmingham Road, at Dudley, was a great convenience to the grocers and other retail traders in Dudley, as by enquiry there they could obtain early information as to whether their goods had arrived or were on the way, and when they were likely to reach the Tipton Wharf, whence they could be carted by the company, or by the owners, to their destination. This wharf and receiving establishment passed into the hands of the Grand Junction Canal Company about the year 1850; they carried on the business there for some years and then removed it to their new premises at Dudley Port, which had been built for the purpose. The Tipton warehouses became dilapidated through mining operations till they had to be cleared off, and then the ground was worked for the minerals underneath. The next wharves and carrying establishments were those of the old firm of Pickford and Co., and then those of Crowley and Co, and some others. The carriers conveyed by canal the chief of the goods and merchandise for the grocers, drapers, and other shopkeepers from London, Liverpool, and Manchester, and also from the Potteries from Nottingham, Leicester, Northampton, and Stafford for all the retail traders in Dudley and the district. They also carried the various local products and manufactures to those centres, and all the places on the way, fifty years ago and long before any railway had penetrated or was thought of in this vicinity.

When the railways had been made, and the companies had established their usurping business with the assistance of the principal common carriers like Messrs Pickford and Co. and Crowley and Co. who became agents to the railways, the other and lesser carriers gradually withdrew their fly-boats from the canals in favour of the railways, though the Grand Junction Canal Company, who owned the canal of that name (97 miles from Braunstone to Paddington, London) carried on a large carrying business in heavy goods, to and from London, for many years afterwards and in fact until a few years ago, when they returned to their old system of revenue by charging tolls for boats plying in their waters.

At the corner of the lane called Todd's End, on the Tipton Road, leading up to the fort of the Castle Grounds, and on the side now named Castle Mill (after the extensive engineering works belonging to the Earl of Dudley) stood an old-fashioned mansion in park-like grounds, which was the residence of Mr Bradley, of the firm of Bradley, Barrows, and Hall, Bloomfield Ironworks, Tipton. Within the last 40 years it has been demolished and the land either leased or sold for building purposes, and there now stands on it a terrace or two of very respectable houses and a fine new church (St. Matthew's).

On the opposite side of the above stood a moderate sized, comfortable, homely house, occupied by the owner, one Mr. Thomas Cox, builder and timber merchant, whose workshops, stocks of timber, slates etc, at the back reached down to the canal. Near this house stood a number of old dilapidated houses which have since given way to the erection of a better class of houses, and many of which now occupy the site.

Tipton at that time, forty or fifty years ago, was the abode of many highly respectable families, the heads of which were usually iron and coal masters, or others engaged in the iron trade; there was also a middle class of respectable traders, while the working classes were chiefly ironworkers and miners.

The working men seemed at that time to be doing well, if judged by the busy Saturday night markets that flourished at Tipton and at Dudley. The popular amusements at the great annual festival of Tipton Wake included bull baiting, which took place in different parts of the parish. One well-remembered exhibition took place on a space of ground adjoining the Hen and Chickens Inn, Canal Side, Tipton Green. The bull was chained to a stake in the ground, with so many yards of free play; around him stood his tormentors, chiefly big burly men each with a large bull dog held between the knees ready to be thrown down to the bull. Sometimes the dog would alight on the bull's back and sometimes on his neck, or on the ground in front of him; while the roaring of the bull, the barking of the dogs, and the yelling of the excited men made up a scene altogether demoniacal, and one that has happily passed away for ever.

With all these degrading pursuits the religious life of the parish was not so dormant as one might suppose For instance, "White's Directory" for 1855 says: "The dissenting places of worship in Tipton are numerous. The Baptists have a chapel situated at Toll End and another at Princes End; the Independents in Union Street; the Unitarians in Waterloo Street; the Wesleyans at Dudley Port, Bloomfield, Great Bridge, Lower Gornal, and Gospel Oak; the New Connection at Horseley Heath and Canal Street; the Primitive Methodists at Upper Green, Toll End, Waterloo Street, Dudley Port, and Chapel Street; and the Welsh Independents have a chapel at Dudley Port." In 1850 there was in Dudley a Protestant Dissenters Chapel in Wolverhampton Street, which was originally built in 1701, and destroyed during the Sacheverell Riots in 1715. The second building there was re-erected at the Government expense.

CHAPTER LVII.—TIPTON BIBLIOGRAPHY.

Perhaps the earliest historical sketch of Tipton appeared in the columns of the *Birmingham Daily Post*. In the issues of this paper for January 23rd and January 30th, 1865, appeared—among other very interesting articles upon Black Country towns—some notices of Tipton and its history. Passing allusions to the neighbourhood no doubt appeared in various quarters at a much earlier period.

In the *Penny Magazine* for 1843 (p. 53) is to be found a capital description of "South Staffordshire by Night," when the whole landscape was lit up with the lurid glow of countless furnaces, a startling sight to the visitor from many other parts of England. Speaking of the wood- charcoal once so extensively used here for iron-smelting, a curious surmise is offered. It is surmised that much of the timber of Arden (signifying *Woodlands*) in Warwickshire has been from time immemorial employed to smelt the iron ores of Staffordshire. But more directly interesting is a Tipton printed account of the place. This is contained in a local Almanack for the year 1867, printed by Williams, of Horsley Heath. From this publication we take the following extracts:—

"There is a Masonic Hall adjoining the Navigation Inn, an institution which we believe receives a fair amount of public support, and which is used as a drill room by the Tipton Volunteers.

"A new Police Station has been erected in Church Lane, and we should say it is the finest in the county. The building is an ornament to the locality and now only awaits the formal opening by the Earl of Lichfield, after which the magistrates will hold their weekly meetings therein.

"The Birmingham Canal, winding in and out among the mines and ironworks, has twelve and half miles of its length in the parish, besides about four miles belonging to colliery proprietors effecting with its collateral branches communication with every line of inland navigation. The principal canal carriers are Pickford, Crowley, Fellows, Foster, and the Grand Junction Canal Company. The Electric and International Telegraph Company have eight miles of wires running through the parish, and the United Kingdom three miles.

"The town is well supplied with gas in the supply of water there is, we are reluctantly obliged to confess great complaints."

There is also an advertisement in this almanack stating that a new first-class family weekly journal entitled *The Dudley Herald*, will be published on and after 22nd December, 1866.

About half a century ago there emanated from Tipton a technical handbook which has since been used by many writers as the basis of their authority on iron trade questions. Its full title runs:—

> "The Catechism of Iron; or, The Merchant and Mechanic's New and Complete Guide to the Iron Trade: By Benjamin Legge, Many Years Practically Employed by Messrs Philip Williams and Sons, Wednesbury Oak Iron Works, Tipton, Staffordshire. Tipton: Printed By and For Thomas Danks. Price Seven Shillings."

In the form of Question and Answer we get information on the nature and properties of iron, descriptions of bar iron, rod iron, strip iron, hoop iron, boiler plates, single sheet, double sheet, lattin sheet, small rounds and squares, angle iron, half rounds, ovals, fancy iron, &c., &c. Then from p. 68 we get another hundred pages of Tables of the Weights of these various makes of iron by measure on the rule, and by numbers on the wire gauge, with the nearest proportionate number of feet equal to a ton in weight of the various sizes. The book is small post octavo size, oblong; bound at the end for convenience of use as a pocket-book of ready reference by practical iron makers and others engaged in the iron trade. From the notice of this Tipton printed book, we pass on to note a work less directly interesting, but of some importance to the local genealogist. The Jevon family were originally of Sedgley, but several important members have lived in Tipton. Their pedigree, arms, and crest may be found in *Miscellanea Genealogica*, vol iv. (new series) p. 384. An extract of Wednesbury Parish Register says:—

"Edward Best, minister of Wednesbury, and Elizabeth, ye daughter of Mr John Jevons, sen., of Tipton, were married in the parish church of Wednesbury, 20 May, 1706."

This Vicar died in 1719 and was buried in the chancel of the church. His son Edward Best became Incumbent of Bilston in 1736 and Vicar of Wednesbury in 1743. He was made a magistrate in 1771 and died in 1782. Sarah, a grand-daughter of the last-named Edward Best married James Russell, of Bescot Hall, in 1800. The arms of Russell are also given on p 18 of vol iv. above mentioned.

More strictly bibliographical is the following collection of Tipton books, specially prepared for this History by Mr. Geo T. Lawley, the eminent authority on Staffordshire Books:—

1. "Cambrian Superstitions, comprising Ghosts, Omens, Witchcraft, Traditions, &c. To which are added a concise view of the Manners and Customs of the Principality and some Fugitive Pieces. By W. Howells.

"'Fairy tales to lull the heir,
Goblins grim the maids to scare.'
Sir W. Scott.

" 'Black spirits and white, red spirits and grey.'
Tipton: Printed by Thomas Danks. 1831."

This is a scarce local production by the author of "Chidha." He was a brother of the Rev. J. Howells, vicar of Tipton.

2. "Aspects and Prospects of Humanity. By the Rev. G. Grundy. London: Partridge and Oakey. Tipton: Silas Henn.

The author of this volume was a Methodist New Connexion minister, stationed at Tipton at that time. He was a native of Sheffield, and in 1850 was stationed at Hanley, in this county.

3. "The Things which must Shortly Come to Pass."—A series of discourses on the prophecies of "The Last Days," delivered in the Parish Church of Tipton, Staffordshire, and affectionately dedicated to the members of his congregation. By the Rev William Ker, M.A., incumbent of Tipton. Author of "Popular Ideas of Immortality, Everlasting Punishment, &c." "The Bible *versus* Geologists," &c. Dudley; W. H. Laxton, High Street. 1868.

An 8vo volume of 398 pages, in which the question of "last day prophecies" is dealt with in an original and able manner. The views expressed are not in all cases orthodox, but they seem nevertheless to be more in accordance with a Christianity of love than many of the notions entertained by clerics as a body.

4. "The Popular Ideas of Immortality, Everlasting Punishment, and the State of Separate Souls, brought to the test of Scripture."—A series of discourses delivered in the Parish Church of Tipton, Staffordshire, in 1863-4, and affectionately dedicated to the members of his congregation. By the Rev William Ker, M.A., vicar of Tipton. Dudley: W. H. Laxton, High Street. 2nd Edition. 1870.

This is an original and startling contribution to the theological literature of the age.

5. "S. Henn's Journal of Christian Experience and Labours."—"Come and hear, all ye that fear God, and I will declare what he hath done for my soul," Psalm lxvi, 16 London: Partridge and Oakey. S. Henn, Printer, Tipton. 1853

6 "The Basket of Fragments, or, Broken Pieces of Bread for Hungry Souls."—By Silas Henn. Author of "Heart Yearnings," "Religion in Earnest," "Musings with Paul," "Pulpit Earnestness," &c., &c. London: G. Lamb, Primitive Methodist Book Room. 1871.

7. "Pulpit Earnestness; or, the Ministry of Earnestness and Power the Great Want of the Sacred Desk."—By Silas Henn. 4th Edition enlarged, London: Elliot Stock. 1874.

8. A series of papers on the following subjects: - 1. A Voice to the Church; or, Thoughts on the Revival of Religion. 2. Unfolding the Bud; or, the Duties of Parents. 3. The Blessed Future; or, the Second Advent of Christ. 4. The Divine Excellence of Jesus. 5. Christ at the Door.

6. Trumpet Sounds. 7. The Evils of Smoking; or, a few Words to Ministers who use Tobacco. 8. The State Church, or, the Union of Church and State Anti-Christian and Sinful. Being a reply to some of Joseph Barker's statements on the subject in the "Methodist Times."

9. A Scriptural and Moral Catechism, designed chiefly to lead the minds of the rising generation to the love and practice of mercy, and to expose the horrid nature and exceeding sinfulness of Cruelty to the Dumb Creation. Illustrated by examples, With an address to ministers of religion, parents, instructors of youth, and Christians in general. Inscribed, by permission, to Her Royal Highness the Princess Victoria. By Abraham Smith master of St. Bartholomew's National School, Birmingham. Birmingham: Richard Peart, Bull Street.

The author of this rare little volume was a school-master for many years at Tipton, where he resided when the book was printed, It contains a list of subscribers, most local, and is a very praiseworthy attempt to show the horrors and wickednesses attendant upon those brutal Black Country sports known as bull and bear baiting, cock fighting, &c. Mr Smith was author of several other similar productions.

CHAPTER LVIII.—HABITS, SPORTS, AND PASTIMES.

In common with all other specimens of humanity, the people of the Black Country possess a strong dramatic instinct. But in Tipton and the neighbourhood the ungodly tendency of such an instinct is strongly counteracted by the deep religious sentiments of the prevailing forms of Dissent. Occasionally, however, the dramatic faculty is allowed free bent by the performance of Scriptural plays in the chapels and schoolrooms. There is one Biblical play called "Joseph and His Brethren," well known in Wednesbury and Tipton, and which formed the subject of a lengthy notice in *The Graphic* of July 4th 1891. On p 4 of that number will be found six illustrations, and on p. 17 a letter-press description of a performance of this play at Coseley.

In the old days of bull baiting and dog-fighting improvidence was rampant, and not unfrequently it was accompanied by drunkenness and all its hideous concomitants. But with the progress of popular education these traits are gradually disappearing. Thrift is more extensively practised, as would be evidenced by the most cursory examination of the local Post Office Savings Bank accounts. Another form of thrift is manifested in the eager disposition to acquire small lots of land on which to build cottages; if freehold so much the better although copyhold is by no means despised (See chapter XVI). Benefit societies of all kinds are largely patronised, and among numerous lodges of all the different orders of friendly societies is one which takes its name from the locality; it is "The Wolverhampton and Tipton Juvenile Foresters," which has (or had) a membership of about 300.

Of sports and pastimes nothing new can be said of Tipton which has not been written of the immediate vicinity many times over. It seems strange, however, that no aquatic sports have ever taken root within the parish in connection with its many inviting stretches of canal. Perhaps the surroundings of these artificial waterways were too sordid to ever associate themselves with the idea of amusement. And yet some of the remains of the old iron bridges fancy palisades, and waterside architecture would seem to point to a period when the canals were not altogether devoid of ornamental features.

At the present time the genuine "Tip'on mon" being legally restrained from the pursuit of his oldtime "sport" of cock-fighting, finds an outlet for his ornithological proclivities by devoting himself to the fascinations of pigeon flying. Similarly his acquaintance with the canine race is no longer maintained through unrestrained indulgence in the savage delights of dog-fighting, but is kept up by the milder excitement of dog running and rabbit coursing.

Tipton proper has never reached a high position in the annals of the national game of cricket; probably because of the dense centres of population, or the unsuitability of its mining lands which prohibited practice of it. But on the greener and more rural looking outskirts of the parish as at Coseley and at Tividale, some famous local cricket clubs have flourished for many years past. When Association Football was revived with such a boom some seventeen years ago, Tipton was one of the few places where the game was then already found to exist in the Black Country. The Tipton club played opposite the Cemetery in the Horseley Road, but at the present time the centre of this popular game would seem to be nearer Great Bridge.

Reverting to the older sports which flourished in the parish in those bye-gone times when brutality always seemed inseparable from every form of popular amusement it can only be said that Tipton was no worse than its neighbours, notwithstanding the uncontroverted assertion of the local poetaster that

"The life blood of a hundred bulls
Has flowed on Tipton Green."

In the domain of "Sport," Tipton claims a pre-eminence in one department, namely, that of pugilism, the name of the parish having been immortalised by its connection with the professional appellation of a certain champion of the Prize Ring, known as the "Tipton Slasher." Men of lesser calibre in the same line have also hailed from Tipton, as one John Broome. But the first-named was the greater hero in the popular mind of half-a-century ago. Even novelists, from Albert Smith (in "Christopher Tadpole," chap. xl.) to Christie Murray and Walter Besant have quoted the Tipton Slasher as a typical hero of the pugilistic "fancy." Certainly no history of Tipton would be considered complete which did not make more than a passing illusion to this local worthy—perhaps the only man the parish produced who ever made its name familiar throughout the length and breadth of the land. But first may be briefly reviewed the general condition of the "noble science" in the whole of this immediate neighbourhood in the earlier part of this century.

Over half a century ago pugilism, with many other sports of an equally brutalising tendency, was rampant in every part of England. Tipton certainly was no worse in this respect than other places; as reference to *Boxiana* will soon demonstrate. This classical text-book on pugilism was written by a "professor" of the noble art of self-defence—one Owen Swift, by name, and a great fighter himself. The book was published in London in 1840, and from it we learn that recorded prize fights took place in this neighbourhood at Essington (December 7th, 1835), at Muckley Corner January 12th, 1836), and at Oldbury (December 13th 1838). Sometimes we read of two or more contests taking place in the "same ring," one after the other. It is also recorded that on November 18th, 1833, Lane beat Ball in 21 rounds £20 aside at Smithwick (Smethwick) Coming nearer home we learn that on October 22nd, 1838, David, the Collier beat Harry Kane in 19 rounds for £10 a side at Gospel Oak Corner. On December 16th, 1833, two more local worthies have their encounter chronicled thus—

"Parker beat Wednesbury Bounce,"

but neither the stakes nor the place is mentioned.

CHAPTER LIX.—THE TIPTON SLASHER, CHAMPION PRIZE FIGHTER OF ENGLAND.

William Perry, known in the popular world as "The Tipton Slasher," was born in this parish in 1819. In due course he became a boatman on the canal, and gaining some local reputation for his prowess in taking his own part in his disputes with other boatmen, he ultimately became a *protegé* of

Lord Dudley. Be it remembered that Lord Palmerston, an English Prime Minister, was not above patronising the prize ring in those days. But in the personal appearance of Perry there was little or nothing to identify him as a professional pugilist, for his face usually wore a rather kindly expression of features. The most striking characteristic about his bodily build was the shape of his legs, one of his knees being bent inwards, so that when standing in an attitude of defence, he appeared to be not only firmly set, but actually "spragged" or propped up. This was what made it so difficult for his antagonists to fell him in the ring. That he gained a high position in the profession of pugilism may be gathered from a glance at the following list of "English Champions."

According to one "official" list the Champions of England during the present century have been—

1803.—Jem Belcher.

1805.—Pearce, the Game Chicken.

1808.—Gulley (declined office).

1809.—Tom Cribb received a belt which was not transferable, and a cup which afterwards passed to Tom Sayers.

1824.—Tom Spring received four cups and resigned office.

1825.—Jem Ward, received a belt, not transferable.

1833.—Deaf Burke claimed the office.

1839.—Bendigo beat Deaf Burke claimed the championship, and received a belt from Jem Ward.

1841.—Caunt beat Nick Ward and received a belt (transferable) by subscription.

1845.—Bendigo beat Caunt and got the Belt.

1850.—Perry, the Tipton Slasher, after his fight with Paddock, claimed the office, as Bendigo declined fighting again.

1851.—Harry Broome beat Perry and succeeded to the office.

1853.—Perry, the Tipton Slasher, again claimed the office, Harry Broome having forfeited to him in a match, and retired from the ring.

1856.—The office still claimed by the Tipton Slasher, who during that year received forfeit from both Tom Paddock and Aaron Jones, but on June 16th, 1857, lost the title by being beaten by Tom Sayers. Belt presented to latter at Nat Langham's, Castle Street, Leicester Square, June 22nd, 1857, he was to retain it three years without being beaten, to fight all comers within six months of each fight, and not for less than £200 aside unless the champion thinks proper.

1860.—Tom Sayere retired after his fight with Heenan, leaving belt for competition. Sam Hurst beat Paddock for it in the month of November.

Then followed Jem Mace, Tom King, &c. &c

The wear and tear of the pugilists' life may be gathered by the observant reader as we proceed with the veracious history of this "eminent" Tiptonian, who began his fighting career in 1835.

His first great encounter was with Freeman, the American giant, in 1842. Freeman was the same age as his opponent (23), but was 6ft 10½in high, and scaled 17 stone. The result may be guessed when it is stated that the giant was quite as active as his shorter opponent. But a full description of this fight, together with a woodcut engraving of the Slasher, may be had in a penny pamphlet, "Famous Fights in the Prize Ring," No. 32. published by Charles Fox 4, Shoe Lane, E.C. It would appear that the American had arrived in England early in the year, and issued a challenge to fight anyone except his friend Caunt. No one took up the gauntlet till some English sportsmen expressed their willingness to back their countryman from Tipton, then unknown to fame except as a big, strong, rough and ready customer. After their training they met to uphold the reputation of their respective nationalities, and according to the opinion of experts it was soon seen that neither of the men really knew anything of the art of self-defence, and a poor exhibition of the fistic art could not but result. The Slasher took to the tumbling dodge and lost the match by his bad judgment. Freeman was hailed conqueror through bad tactics on the part of Perry but it was his first and last appearance, for the American had his fast life brought to an untimely end three years later.

In 1849 the Yankees were boasting of a new champion named Hyers who had beaten everybody on his own continent, and in consequence a defiance was sent over to England. The Tipton Slasher was regarded as the most formidable man in England at that time, and he was invited to repair to the states; Hyers offering to pay his expenses across, and to fight him for any sum. Perry not fancying the undertaking or being a sufferer from sea sickness, declined to accept, and it remained for a newer man to become champion in place of Perry, and to fight a newer champion from America.

The professional career of William Perry, alias the Tipton Slasher, was as follows:—

Height, 6ft. 0½in. Weight, 14 stone.

1835, November 3.—Beat Dogherty in seven rounds at Chelsea.

1836. December 27.—Beat Ben Spilsbury, £10 aside 19 rounds, at Oldbury.

1837. November 22.—Beat Jem Scunner, £25 aside 31 rounds in 60 minutes, Kingswood, near Wolverhampton.

Forfeited to Deaf Burke.

1842. December 14—Met to fight Charles Freeman the American giant, £100 aside, at Sawbridgeworth, after an interruption by the authorities commenced fighting at 3.53, and fought 70 rounds in 84 minutes, with equal advantage, when, becoming too dark, the referee interfered and adjourned till the Thursday.

1842. December 16—Went to Tuplow Heath, when police interfered; retreated to Haydon Grange, Essex, where police interfered. "No go."

1842. December 20.—Met Freeman for third time below Gravesend, and after fighting 38 rounds in 39 minutes, Freeman was declared winner Perry having gone down without a blow.

1843. December 19.—Fought Tass Parker, £100 aside, at Dartford Marshes, 67 rounds in 95 minutes when police interfered.

1844. February 27.—Beat Tass Parker £100 aside 133 rounds in 152 minutes, at Horley. Parker went down without a blow.

1846. August 4. -Beat Tass Parker, £100 aside, 23 rounds in 27 minutes, at Lindrick Common.

1849. September.—Forfeited to Con Parker.

1850. August 22—Draw with Tom Paddock, neither party ready with the deposit.

1850. December 17—Beat Tom Paddock, £100 aside 27 rounds in 42 minutes, at Woking, foul blow.

1851. September 29—Beaten by Harry Broome, £200 aside and championship, 15 rounds in 33 minutes, at Mildenhall, foul blow.

1853. August—Received £25 forfeit from Harry Broome.

1856. Received £70 forfeit from Aaron Jones.

1856. October 2.—Received £80 forfeit from Tom Paddock.

1857. June 16.—Beaten by Tom Sayers, £400 and the championship 10 rounds in one hour 42 minutes, on the Isle of Grain, River Medway.

It was in 1850 that Perry aspired to become Champion of England. For this proud position he announced that he would fight all comers for £200 or £300 aside or he would stake £350 to £300 and fight Tom Paddock. A meeting took place soon after, at which he and Paddock were matched on these terms but it all ended in smoke. Shortly after they were again matched for £150 aside, but this ended in a draw. Another engagement was entered into for £100, and this actually came off at Woking after several ineffectual attempts in other localities. *Bell's Life* denominated the encounter a mere scramble and not worthy of being called a fight. The result was apparent from the second round. Paddock displayed no points calculated to bring out the qualities of the Slasher. At the expiration of 42 minutes, Paddock after failing in his corner, jumped up and run after Perry, who was retiring to his own corner, dealt him a blow behind the ear and floored him close to his second's knee. The claim for a foul was allowed by the referee in favour of the Slasher. Perry then claimed the Belt, which Bendigo had received from Caunt. Bendigo refused to give it up, but offered to fight Perry for £500 aside. When the Slasher accepted, Bendigo backed out, but what became of the champion's belt, which now rightly belonged to the Slasher, is not known. Unwilling to remain idle, the Slasher declared his readiness to fight anyone who fancied him for £200. In May 1851, Harry Broome took up the challenge, and they met at Mildenhall. The science of Broome stood him in good stead, but it was evident that strength and weight would prove too much for him in the end, unless some accident turned in his favour. And so it happened in the fifteenth round that Broome fell on his knees, and the Slasher letting go his right at the same moment, caught him a severe blow just as he reached the ground. An appeal was made to Peter Crawley, the referee, who ruled it a decided foul, and declared Broome the winner. Crawley came in for a large share of abuse, and was even threatened by the Slasher, whereupon the burly veteran began "to peel" in order to have a round with Perry to justify his decision. Hostilities were only prevented by Perry being forced away by his friends. Perry talked of legal proceedings, but Broome received the stakes, and enjoyed the honour of championship until 1852.

He fought a great fight with Harry Orme in 1853 and beat him; the only championship contest worthy of the name and that had not ended unsatisfactorily for many years. After receiving the money for this affair Harry Broome was again matched with the Tipton Slasher for £200 a side, but after two deposits had been made Broome forfeited and publicly intimated his retirement from the prize ring. The Slasher was again dubbed champion, and desired a fresh match with Paddock. But as the latter backed out the Slasher held undisputed sway till his encounter with Tom Sayers.

This last great fight of the Slasher found him at 12 stone 10lbs., when he was seconded by Tass Parker and Jack Macdonold. After this defeat by Sayers his sun set for ever. Not only was he thinner, but his age began to tell on him. He was no longer "the Slasher." All his quickness and activity had left him and apparently his eye-sight failed him. Then he allowed bad judgment for a heavy lumbering man like him to force the fighting and pursue a little active fellow like Sayers. Early in the fight he injured his right hip by a sudden twist.

After his loss of the championship he slowly but gradually reverted to his former position in the social scale. On one occasion he entered the smoke-room of a favourite public-house in Tipton, dressed in smock frock and slouch hat, and on a certain gentleman present—a prominent member of the Local Board of Health—offering to treat him, he produced a roll of bank notes, and replied that he could pay for what he had himself. But this state of things did not last with him to the end. When he saw that pugilism would avail him no longer as a means of livelihood he went back to his original occupation as a boatman. In this connection he became a small night-soil contractor, and a dealer in stable manure. Making his purchases in the urban districts of the Black Country he boated it away to a considerable distance in the country, re-selling to the farmers at a fair profit. As to his places of residence, it is said that he kept a public-house at 67, Union Street, Tipton, that he lived at Spon Lane, and afterwards occupied the old toll-house at Catchem's Corner, Monmore Green. Misfortune overtaking him, this hero of the P.R. entered Wolverhampton Workhouse, where he ended his days ten or twelve years ago.

* * * * * *

A coloured print of the great fight between Sayers and Heenan was published by Geo Newbold, 303 Strand, W.C., which contained, among some hundreds of authentic portraits, those of several local celebrities connected with the Prize Ring.

The same firm also published, among other photographs, taken from life in 1860, that of George Rowley, of Wednesbury, who fought Cox, Palmer, and Ben Terry.

CHAPTER LX.—ONE OF THE SLASHER'S FIGHTS: TIPTON V. WEST BROMWICH.

According to another compilation of English Champions, this national honour may be claimed for a second representative of the Black Country. One Tass Parker, a West Bromwich man, having beaten Con Parker in 1849, is sometimes ranked as champion. No doubt, to local readers the encounter between this West Bromwich man and the redoubtable Tipton Slasher will prove more than ordinarily interesting especially as reported in the old style. To witness this the patrons of the prize ring journeyed down by steamer to the drear and inhospitable marshes of Dartford. There, on Tuesday, December 19, 1843, in weather as unpleasant as ever British sportsmen had to endure, the ring was pitched, and, with Peter Crawley as referee, the men set to. The attendance both of amateurs and professionals, was immense, and if ever men had an incentive to do their best it was Tass

Parker and the Slasher that day. But a more disappointing show was never afforded to ring-goers—that is, the good old class of ring-goers who expected value for their money. In the opening rounds Parker displayed his superior skill both in getting on to his man and getting away, but the Tipton Slasher had certainly greatly improved under the skilful mentorship of the Broomes, and was no longer the mere "hardy rough" which many up to that time considered him to be. He every now and then waited for, timed, and neatly stopped his clever and crafty assailant, inflicting severe punishment with his right upon Tass, who, finding he could not get near enough to deliver without exposing himself to heavy returns soon began to fight shy. Indeed, round after round, after getting in a blow, the West Bromwich gentleman resorted to that system of dropping which we have always held to be unmanly and un-English like, and in Tass's case it was peculiarly reprehensible, because he went down not only to avoid being hit, but also to provoke and irritate his less skilful adversary, and thus tempt him to deliver a foul blow or at the worst to bring the fight to a tie or wrangle. In this way sixty-seven rounds were fought with no prospect of an approach to a satisfactory decision. At this juncture—an hour and twenty-five minutes having been consumed—the Kentish Constabulary made their appearance and stopped the tedious exhibition. Of course, there was nothing left for the spectators but to re-embark and return disgusted and disappointed to the Metropolis. Then came the inevitable wrangling and ink-slinging. Johnny Broome, on behalf of the S1asher, requested a postponement for three months, and produced the following medical certificate.

"194, Blackfriars Road, December 25, 1843

"This certifies that we reduced a fracture of the fore-arm of William Perry on the 7th of November, and a fracture of the lower jaw on the evening of December the 19th. These serious injuries will require a period of at least three months before he can be in a situation to fight again.

"CHARLES AND JOHN BRADY, Surgeons."

With regard to that certificate we may say that it was not difficult in those days, nor would it be now, to obtain a similar document "for a consideration." It is true that the Slasher, during his period of training, injured his right arm while sparing with Harry Broome at Bristol. But the injury was at the time thought to be slight, and there were no symptoms of serious damage viable after the occurrence. Had there been a real fracture, it is difficult to suppose that Johnny Broome, who declared he had himself to find most of the battle-money, would not have cried off.

Johnny Broome was at Owen's that night, and had brought the Slasher with him—his right arm in a sling and a bandage under his jaw. A pretty bit of "fake" which elicited no end of chaff from Harry Hill and others, who twigged Johnny's game. Owen Swift kept a public-house near the Haymarket. Well, Johnny Broome opened the ball with his proposal for a three months' adjournment, and pointing to the poor bandaged Slasher, asked whether it was fair to ask a man in that state to fight under three months. The storm of chaff which assailed Johnny and the Tipton we shall never forget. Jem Burn wanted to know how it was that Mr William Perry ate three pounds of rump steak at Ben Caunt's on the previous Wednesday, if his jaw was so bad as Broome tried to make out? Owen Swift would like to know how it was that the Slasher, with a fractured right arm, gave Tass that slap on the cheek, of which the marks had not died away yet? And so on. Well, Johnny, finding that his three months' dodge wouldn't pay, proposed ten weeks. It was consequently agreed that the fight should take place on Tuesday, February 27, 1844. Then up rose the mighty form of Peter Crawley, who begged to inform the backers of both men that he must decline to act as referee after what had happened in the first fight.

Johnny Broome packed the Slasher off to the little Buckinghamshire market town of Ivinghoe, three and thirty miles from London, and about half way between Aylesbury and Tring. Here, later on, the Tipton was joined by Jemmy from Town.

In that fertile vale—the richest, we suppose, in all broad England—the Slasher took his breathings. On the whole, he was a steady man at his work whilst in training, but bad liberal ideas on the subject of old ale. Some trainers, notably the famous Captain Barclay, had great faith in this beverage, and considered it the best that a man could possibly take whilst in training. But then the Captain limited Tom Cribb to three pints per diem, whilst the Slasher thought as many quarts but a poor allowance. However, in a man of his gaunt frame it made less difference than it would have done in the case of one who was inclined to run to flesh, and as the Tipton went in conscientiously for hard exercise, his condition at the close of his period of preparation was as good as anyone could wish for. At any rate, it satisfied Johnny Broome who ran down several times to see him, and as Johnny had a pot of money on him, we may take it for granted that he would not have been easily satisfied.

Tass, in company with his brother Jem, who since his victories over Rowley and Harry Chapman had become something of a "pot" himself, went to the Five Bells at Finchley.

Many thought that Tass would be inclined to make more use of his heels than fists inside the twenty four foot ring. Johnny engaged an "excursion train," the price for tickets being half-a-guinea a head! The office was given for London Bridge, which in those days was the terminus for no less than four different railways, and they proceeded to Horley Common, where Tom Oliver had pitched the ring, in a spot high and dry and screened by a dense belt of firs from the view of travellers by rail or road. The weather was delightful, but although there kind been a sharp frost during the night, the genial influence of the sun had produced an unwelcome change in the paths and roads leading to the scene of action, and as "Shanks's mare‘' was the only mode of locomotion the quagmire through which the voyagers had to tramp, however agreeable it may be to their corns was anything but favourable to the polish on their boots. But these little drawbacks provoked nothing but fun and chaff; every one was in the best of spirits for overhead was blue sky and bright sunshine, and there was every prospect of a capital day's sport. Johnny Broome, with a foresight which did him credit, had provided a quantity of sawdust, which was liberally sprinkled in the twenty-four foot ring, and particularly in the men's corners. For the accommodation of the occupants of the inner circle, among whom were Lord Drumlanrig, Lord Longford, Lord Chetwynd, Lord Waldegrave, Alfred Harbord, Squire Osbaldstone, Captain Ross, Sir St. Vincent Cotton, Major Ouseley Higgins, Captain "Billy" Peel, "The Facer," &c, &c., there was an ample supply of stools, benches, and trusses of straw; whilst a few waggons, after the fashion of times gone by, afforded comfortable standing places for those who preferred the outer circle.

It was about half-past twelve when at last the ring and its *et cetaras* were ready, and the men were fetched from the King's Arms, where they had been resting—Tass Parker attended by Bob Fuller and "Colonel" Tom Reidie, the Slasher by Bob Castles. Tass sported a blue fogle with white spots, the Tipton a stone-coloured flag with pink spots, a great many of which were sold on the usual terms of a guinea or nothing.

On entering the ring the men shook hands good humouredly, and everything seemed in train for business as they retired to their corners. But these bright prospects were soon darkened when the question of selecting a referee came on. The umpires were quickly chosen—Johnny Hannan for Parker, and Tom Heywood, of Finchley, a well-known turfite, for the Slasher. But the choice of a referee was not so easily settled, and nearly an hour was wasted over the job. This was mainly Parker's fault; he objected to every one proposed by the Slasher's party. All this while the men were sitting, wrapped in blankets, in their respective corners. The Slasher, who had taken no part in the discussion, at last rose from his bottle-holder's knee and walking up to Tass, offered to fight without a referee, the battle to go on until one or other gave in; but Tass's friends were still obstinate.

Finally, after an hour had been wasted, and the spectators were expressing their impatience in the noisiest fashion, the stakeholder, Mr. Vincent Dowling, came forward and said that unless within five minutes Parker's backers agreed to fight without a referee or to toss for one, he should feel it his duty to give up the stakes to that man who was willing to abide by one or other of these propositions. Mr. Simeon Jacobs, who had all along been the principal obstruction, finding that he had no alternative, reluctantly agreed that the men should fight without a referee. This decision was hailed with shouts of approbation; the ring was speedily cleared; the umpires, provided with a "patent chronometer," took their seats together, and the crowd settled down to witness the fight. No one was allowed to come within ten feet of the twenty-four foot ring, with the exception of one person to take charge of the water and other refreshments of each combatant—Johnny Broome for the Slasher, and Jem Parker for his brother, and then at last the men stepped from their corners to fight.

Round 1.—Both men were in splendid condition. Tass, in particular, was the picture of vigorous health. His eye was clear and bright, his face ruddy, his skin transparent, his muscles finely developed, his flesh firm and hard. It was a pleasure to look upon his straight lissom figure, with the broad flat shoulders, the well-arched chest, and the muscular, finely-formed legs and arms. In ease and grace of attitude, Tass was far superior to his antagonist. But the Slasher had the pull in height, weight, and strength. He stood 6ft 0½in., and soared 12st. 10lb, whilst Parker's height was 5ft. 10in, and his weight 11st. 41b. The Tipton's great powerful form was, from the waist upwards, as fine a model for an Hercules as any sculptor could desire. His enormous shoulder-blades indicated the possession of tremendous hitting power and though his curiously bent, misformed knock-kneed, and "K"-shaped legs destroyed the simmetry of his appearance, yet they were very capable pedestals in their way, and the Slasher could move about pretty nimbly on them. Tass looked as bold as brass, and no one would have gathered from the expression upon his face that he had not a heart as big as a lion's. After a short spar Tass let fly with his left straight as a dart, but the Slasher stopped it easily and well. Evidently Johnny Broome's coaching kind improved the Tipton's science. As Parker showed a disposition to stand to his guns, the Slasher would not baulk him but went in straight for a rally, but Tass backed away, and of the blows exchanged hardly one got home. Tass just managed to land one on Perry's right cheek, which raised a slight mark, but that was all the mischief done, till Tass, in getting away from the Slasher's rush, slipped, fell on his knees, and so the round ended.

2 to 10.—Tass came up smiling and confident, to all appearance every whit as eager for fight as his opponent. After dodging, advancing, retreating, Parker popped in his left again in the Slasher's cheek, a stinger this time. The Tipton seemed to lose his temper, fought wildly right and left, missing most of his hits, but planting one tremendous right-hander under Tass's left arm, which made the West Bromwicher squirm. Then followed some catch exchanges till, as Parker was falling on his knees, the Slasher caught his head under his arm, held it as if in the vice, and hung on him till he fell tumbling over him. Tass appeared to be not a bit afraid, faced his man as bold as a lion, and shot in his left, which the Slasher threw aside cleverly with a jerk of his arm. Then the Tipton went in as though to demolish his foe, but his hitting was shockingly wild, and Tass stepping back quickly, had no difficulty in avoiding the ill-aimed, swinging blows levelled at him. The Tipton chased his man furiously round the ring, but never a blow did he get home—Tass all the while steady and cool on the look-out for an opening to pop in his left. At last the desired opportunity came. The Slasher with a furious lunge over-reached himself, and instantly Tass had him on the mouth—a hot one. "Look out for the claret," shouted Owen Swift, and the next moment a shout from Jem Parker announced that the first event was won by Tass. The roar of applause that came from Parker's pals seemed to make the Slasher fairly mad; he charged like an infuriated bull at his opponent, lashing out frantically right and left, without the slightest judgment or precision. Tass had no difficulty in evading the blows but for all that he didn't seem to like coming within range of them; he kept away as long as he could, and then went down on his knees amid hoots and yells from the Slasher's pals. "He's at his old game," shouted Johnny Broome. "Now, Tass, old chap, stand up and fight like a man." But the West Bromwicher's courage, like that of Bob Acres', was beginning to ooze through the palm of his hands. Those terrific slogs of the Slasher's seemed to have frightened him, and from that moment the battle resolved itself into a burlesque. At the opening of a round, indeed, Tass would come up looking as if he meant to do wonders, but he took precious good care not to get too near the long powerful arms of the Slasher, and the moment the latter let out, away the West Bromwich hero went, with wonderful celerity, Tipton after him, hitting away with no more judgment and precision than the commonest of country roughs. The connoisseurs in the inner ring were disgusted, as well they might be, and old stagers shrugged their shoulders. To detail the rounds would simply bore our readers out of all patience. With two exceptions, hardly a blow worth speaking of went home. Once Tass landed heavily on the jaw, and once the Slasher, with a back-hander, caught his man on the right eye,

which was a trifle puffed in consequence. For the rest it was all ducking, dodging, and dropping on one side, and wild, random, misdirected hitting on the other; some of the crowd were cheering, the rest chaffing and cursing, while confusion and the wildest excitement was rampant all round the ringside.

11 to 24.—What little pluck Parker had possessed was all gone by this time. He never attempted to face the Slasher, and the air rang with shouts of "Coward," "Cur," "Hound," and similar uncomplimentary epithet. Now and then, despite all Parker's caution and craftiness, the Slasher would get in one of his right-handed lunges under the left arm, and then, of course, Tass would drop instanter. Occasionally, indeed, he had a turn, popped in his left on the cheek and dropped as the Slasher's huge fist came whistling through the air. But to call such a performance as this a *fight* is simply a misuse of words. It is only fair to the Tipton, however, to say that, although he showed himself anxious to come to close quarters, and if he had had a man before him who would have stood up and fought him, he might, and probably would, have done better. The interest in the fight gradually died away. There was, however, some little excitement in the twentieth round, when Tass after popping in his left, and breaking away as usual, was followed quickly by the Slasher, who caught him a heavy whack on the jaw with his right, from the effects of which Tass staggered and fell. First knock-down for Tipton, and, needless to say, thereafter Parker was shyer than ever of coming within range of his adversary's fists Perry was now the favourite at 5 to 4, and all round the ring there was nothing to be heard but exclamations of disgust at Parker's disgraceful and unmanly behaviour.

25 to 133, and last.—Tass's cowardice was now more conspicicious than even in his former fight with Perry. The moment the Slasher went for him down fell the West Bromwicher. without the slightest pretence of standing up to fight. Blood was now coming from Parker's left hand, the knuckles of which had been severely cut against the Slasher's teeth but otherwise he had sustained very little damage, as was only to be expected from his cowardly mode of fighting. The Tipton was greatly irritated by the abominable behaviour of his adversary, and two or three times turned round to the umpires as if appealing whether such conduct were not foul. Over and over again the Slasher's umpire, Mr. Charles Yates, called foul, but Johnny Hannan would not respond but it was easy to see he was disgusted with Parker's performance as any one else. In the thirtieth round Tass, after retreating to his corner, endeavoured to get down to avoid one of the Slasher's furious rushes. The Tipton tried to hold him up, but in

vain, down he went, and the Slasher dropped on him with his knees. Parker's backer, Mr. Simeon Jacobs, immediately claimed the battle, on the ground that Perry's conduct was foul, but his appeal was drowned in hoots and yells of derision, In every other round at least Tass went down without waiting for the Slasher's fist to reach him, and tried to tempt his adversary into hitting him when he was on the ground. But the Tipton, though angry, was not to be betrayed into any act that could be construed into a foul. More than once Tass threw up his feet, so as almost to kick at his man as he rolled or scrambled over him after missing his one, two, In vain the Slasher tried to nail him right and left Tass ducked and tumbled whenever there was the slightest danger of being hit, and from all parts of the crowd there came a continuous storm of hoots, hisses, and indignation. Had there been a referee the fight must long ago have been decided against Tass, but for a long while Hannan declined to support his fellow umpire in his opinion of Tass's foul conduct. At last however, even Johnny Hannan's patience and forbearance were worn out, and he told Tass that if he went down again in the same cowardly fashion he should decide against him. A few rounds later (No. 126) Tass was guilty of such palable breach of the laws of the P.R., that Hannon agreed with Mr. Yates that a "foul" had been committed, which entitled Perry to the stakes. But in an instant Johnny was surrounded by a lot of Parker's pals, who swore they would brain him if he did not rescind his decision. Hannan, pale as ashes, was silent, and amid a fearful uproar the fight was renewed. But in the 133rd round the same thing happened, and this was too much even for Hannan; pale and trembling, but still resolute, Johnny backed up his brother-umpire in declaring that Parker had been guilty of an outrageous "foul," and in awarding the battle to the Slasher. Whereupon both umpires precipitately left the ring. The roughs were taken by surprise, and were incapable of stemming the torrent of general indignation which burst forth against them. But Tass endeavoured to justify his conduct on the ground that he was weak and exhausted, jumped to his feet and, rushing to the corner where Johnny Broome stood with the colours, which he had just entwined from the stake, in his hands, tore his own colours away with an energy which showed that it was not strength at any rate, in which he was lacking. And so ended disgracefully this most miserable and contemptible parody of a prize fight.

The stakes were given up to the Slasher, but he had not yet done with Master Tass, for two years later the pair of them again entered the ring to decide which was the better man.

SUPPLEMENTARY CHAPTER.—LLOYD'S PROVING HOUSE.

There is one establishment situate at the Factory, Tipton, likely to escape the notice of the passer by; and even the inhabitants of the surrounding district scarcely know the far-reaching character of the business carried on at the Public Proving House owned by Lloyd's Public Proving House Company, Limited. The machines are licensed by the Board of Trade, and the work carried on there is directly under the practical control of Lloyd's Committee, London. The certificates issued are signed by Mr. E. R. Isitt, Lloyd's superintendent, and they are recognised by every insurance concern throughout the world.

Under the same auspices, another testing house is established at Netherton, belonging to the same company; and together these testing houses are looked upon by the shipbuilders and shipowners as the most perfect testing agencies in existence, a preference being always given to their certificates before those issued from other machines.

The primary object of these machines is to test chain cables and anchors for seagoing vessels. The legislature has thought fit to enact that all such vessels shall be furnished with cables and anchors which have been subjected to certain tests which the Acts of Parliament specify; and it is rendered a serious matter for a manufacturer of cables or anchors to supply to a seagoing vessel such articles without first submitting them to such tests.

In former years cables were put on ships without testing, or perhaps their makers had testing machines at their own works; but the time came when these were discarded by the authorities, and the present stringent law came into force.

Besides testing cables and anchors these machines also test crane and other chains, iron and steel in all their varied sections, and in actual practice everything in connection with the engineering enterprise of these modern times. Every engineering requirement in steel or iron can now be tested by perfectly independent officials, from whom absolutely true results can be secured.

To anyone not conversant with the chain, cable, and anchor trade, it appears strange that two establishments like those at Tipton and Netherton should be placed at these places, seeing their main business is to test ground tackle for ships, and the nearest port is practically 100 miles distant, whilst the districts taking most of the articles tested are even 200 and 300 miles away; but the explanation is that the manufacture of chain, cables, and anchors is in a state of transition, and by one of those singular operations brought about by industrial energy and the fitness of the productions of the district, namely iron and fuel, it is settling down in South Staffordshire, the very centre of inland England.

It is said the oldest chain-making districts were on the banks of the Wear and the Tyne. South Wales, too, has a long-dated history. To-day South Staffordshire is competing severely with all these districts, and is doing so very successfully, for on the Tyne and the Wear more than one old-established business has had to be given up.

A few years ago the Admiralty authorities rarely sent an order for the cables and anchors for Government ships into South Staffordshire; but, to-day, Messrs. Henry P. Parkes and Co, of Tipton Green Chain and Anchor Works, Tipton, are employed on a five-years' contract for cables for the Admiralty. Resident Admiralty officers superintend the making of these cables, and then see them tested at the public machines alluded to. It is creditable, alike to the makers and to the material used, that the Admiralty are receiving into their stores cables that are given higher breaking strains than have ever before been attained.

The prospect, therefore, for the continued employment of these machines and the prosperity of this district is likely to be good for some time.

"Lloyds" is a name for ever on the tongue of the shipbuilder and ship-owner: it is mentioned in every specification for every part of a ship and its outfit, It may be little known to the inhabitants of the Black Country, even though it is represented in their midst by the two testing establishments described. It is a company established very many years ago, and about which a volume might be written. Suffice it for the present to say that besides its vast insurance business it controls the rules for the construction and classification of all ships, keeps a register of every ship built, and is the biggest authority known with respect to ship-building. For a ship to be classed A1 at Lloyds is to be unassailable in the British mercantile marine.

INDEX

Advowson 62, 64.
Agricola 115
Aldridge 25
All Saints 107
Alrewas 160
Ampletts Hall 153
Antinomians 115
Aris's Gazette 148
Aston Hall 55

Bagnall's Hall 153
Bagnall Street 156
Baptists 108, 110, 113
Bilston 15, 47, 50, 93, 136, 161
Bilston Causeway 156
Birch 35, 36
Birmingham 5, 42, 49, 55, 71, 72, 75, 113, 161, 175
Birmingham Canal Company 82
Birmingham Canal [Navigation] 94, 157, 165, 185, 186, 201
Birmingham & Staffs Gas Co. 145
Bishop of Lichfield 6, 7, 8
Black Cock Inn 41
Black Country 38, 107, 191, 204, 211
Blakeley Wood Colliery 156
Bloomfield 151, 155
Blue Fly Pit 166
Booker, Luke 5
Brindley, James 184
Broadwater's Fire Engine 157
Brooks Meadow 157
Butchers Forge Pool 157

Cannock 18, 185
Cannock Forest 7, 15
Carucate 3
Charlemont Hall 66
Cholera 141
Christchurch 165
Comberford 32, 61
Congregationalists 109, 110
Conygre, Cunnigres, Conigrie 155
Coppice, The 39
Cotterils Farm 154
Coventry, Bishop of 10
Cradley 114
'Crownings - in' 38
Crown Iron & Galvanizing Works 195
Curia Regis 8, 9

Darlaston 1, 17, 24, 25, 33, 65, 69, 136, 137
Dartmouth, Lord 45
Delves 11
Denbigh Colliery 166
Denbigh Hall 153
Dixon's Hall 153
Doe Bank Cottage 39
Domesday Book/Survey 1085-6 2-4, 6, 7
Dudley (Castle) 4-6, 28, 29, 39, 46, 52, 55-57, 82, 91, 92, 136, 139, 160, 161, 186, 196
Dudley Canal 157
Dudley, John 5
Dudley Poor Law Union 138
Dudley Port 135, 151, 160, 161
Dudley Priory 137
Dudley, Sir Richard 28
Dudley Volunteer Cavalry 169
Dudley Woodside 157
Dugdale, Sir William 11

Eadward 3
Eagle Coal & Iron Co, The 195
Edingale 10
Edwin, Earl 5
Ellowes, The 153
Erdeswick, Sampson 8, 33, 47
Ethelfleda 3

Finspoth 151
Fitz Ansculf, [William] 4, 5, 7
Fitzwarren, [Sir Jeffrey] 8, 12, 33
Flaxfield 155
Flax Leasur 39
Frankpledge 18
Free Libraries Act 145
Freeman, Sir Josiah 11

Galton Bridge 183
Gold's Green, Gold's Ground 155, 156
Gornal 5
Gorstie Croft 155
Gospel Oak 24, 39, 121 122
Gospel Oak Iron (Works) 99 196
Grand Junction Canal Co 199, 201
Great Barr 25
Greet, Great Bridge 91, 151, 152, 161
Great Bridge Iron & Steel 195
Great Civil War 54, 148
Great Exhibition 166
Great Western Railway 161
Greets Green 152
Grit Green 151

Haines 39
Halesowen (Abbey) 52, 136, 137
Hamstead 10, 27, 29, 42
Handsworth 10, 11, 27-29, 62
Harborne 18, 30, 136
Harvell's Oak (Hawthorn) 152
Hill, Sir Rowland 71
Hintes 7, 10
Himley 28, 48
'History of Staffordshire' 4
Hope Iron, Steel & Tinplate Co 196
Horseley, Horsley 24, 151, 155, 183, 184
Horseley Hall 153
Horseley Heath 64, 70, 92, 151

Independents 108

Jacobite Riots 109

Keir, James 163
Kidderminster 71
Kings Norton 55
Kingswinford 52

Lapley 22, 62
Lea Brook 39, 103, 151, 175
Lichfield 6, 7, 11, 18, 25, 45, 49, 55, 93, 107
Lichfield Cathedral 7
Littlehay 10
Lloyd's Public Proving House 219
London & North Western Railway 160, 161, 185
Longdon 7, 18, 34, 35, 37
Lower Wood 39

Methodism 111, 112, 114
Midland Railway Company 161
Mill Close 152
Mill, The 152
Moat Colliery 39
Moat Farm 38, 39
Moat House 153

Neptune Chain & Anchor Works 191
Nightingale 33
Nine Locks 169

Oakswell Hall 151
Ocker Hill 39, 92, 93, 103, 122, 136, 151, 160, 185
Offlow Hundred 6
Okell's Farm 154
Old Birmingham Canal 157
Oldbury 8, 185
Old Leathern Bottle, The 84
Oldswinford 52, 67
Oscott 10, 29
Ottery St Mary 1

Paget 34, 35, 44
Parkes 6
Parkfields 155
Park Lane Chapel 115
Pattshull 55
Peel, Sir Robert 135
Pensnett Chase 5, 15
Perry Barr 10, 29
Perry, William (The Tipton Slasher) 206-210, 212-218
Persehouse's Bridge 156
Plea Rolls 8
Poor Laws 137-139
Portway 152
Pound 42
Presbyterians (Presbyterianism) 108
Primitive Methodists 128
Princes End 16, 69, 71, 75, 94, 99, 136, 140, 151, 160
Pudding Lands 155

Queen Anne's Bounty 22
Queen Henrietta Maria 55

Roman Catholicism 108
Rotton Park Reservior 185
Round Oak Steel Works 194
Rounds Colliery 166
Rowley Hills 4, 185
Rowley Rag 185
Rowley Regis 7, 11,30, 52, 136, 139
Rugeley 18
Rushall Hall 54, 56, 57
Ryders Green 152

Salop 21
Sandwell 18, 45
Sandwell Monastery 64
Sandwell, Prior of 18
Sandwell Priory 137
Scott Arms Hotel 41
Sedgley 6, 8, 22, 24, 28, 47, 48, 50, 52, 135, 136, 138, 139
Sling, The 155
Smethwick 30, 184, 185
Soho 161
South Staffs Coalfield 186
South Staffs Railway 160, 161
St. Chads 101,
St. Edmunds 105
St. James 107
St. Johns 100, 105
St. Marks 103
St. Martins 72, 101, 102
St. Matthews 102, 104
St. Pauls 101, 105
St. Philips Church 71
Stafford 1, 3, 6, 15, 19, 21, 23, 29, 50, 55, 62, 94, 136
Staffordshire 1, 5, 6, 8, 9, 11, 25, 27, 32, 33, 54, 57, 114, 136, 151
Stourbridge 67, 161
Stourton Castle 55
Stour Valley Line 160
'Swags' 38
Swan Village 161

Tame 151
Tamworth 3, 10, 22, 25

Taylors Foundry 190
Telford, Thomas 184
Tibbington, Tibintone, Tybeton, Typpynton 2, 6-13, 15-19, 26-29, 31, 46, 48, 81, 116, 151
Tibbington Colliery 140
Tibbington Hall 16, 153
Tinker Fox, Colonel 55
Tipton Green 4, 113, 116, 135, 151, 155, 157
Tipton Green Chain & Anchor Works 193, 220
Tipton Parish Church 84
Tipton Slasher see William Perry
Tividale 106
Todd's End 151
Toll End 33, 103, 128, 135, 151, 175
Trysull 22, 62

Vasta 14
Venice of the Black Country 157

Wake, The 72
Walkers Hall 153
Walker, James 185
Walsall 15, 25, 31, 94, 161
Walsall Grammar School 94
Warwick 3
Waterloo St. Refuge Chapel 130
Water Orton 161
Watt, James 185
Wedgebury 33
Wednesbury 1, 3, 5, 7, 15-17, 19, 21, 22, 24-26, 29, 30, 32, 39, 40, 46, 47, 50, 52, 54, 55, 65, 69, 84, 91, 92, 104, 113, 135-137, 146
Wednesbury Church 6, 16, 30, 84, 93
Wednesbury Manor 6, 17, 26, 32
Wednesbury Oak 6, 24, 179
Wednesbury Old, Open Field 156
Wednesfield 57
Wesleyanism 110
Wesley, John, Charles, 110, 112-116, 118
West Bromwich 1, 7, 18, 20, 24, 25, 28, 30, 46, 52, 66, 91-93, 135, 136, 151
West Bromwich Heath 56, 114
Whorwood 45, 46, 54, 64
Willenhall 136
William Millington & Co 192
Willingsworth (Hall) 6, 151
Willingsworth Pool 157
Wirley, Robert 8, 28, 34
Wodensbury 19
Wolverhampton 7, 21, 39, 42, 136, 160
Wood's Engine Forge 157
Worcester 21, 50, 138
Workhouse 138, 140
Wyrley 8-12, 27, 33, 34, 44, 45